Colorado Backroads & 4-Wheel-Drive Trails

Charles A.Wells & Matt Peterson

FunTreks

G u i d e b o o k s

Adventure Responsibly

Published by FunTreks, Inc.
P.O. Box 3127, Monument, CO 80132-3127
Phone: Toll free 877-222-7623
Fax: 719-277-7411
Email: books@funtreks.com
Website: www.funtreks.com

Writing, design, photography and production by Charles A. Wells & Matt Peterson.

Edited by Susan Hindman

Fourth Edition

Designed and produced in the United States of America. Printed in China

Library of Congress
Control Number: 2018960569
ISBN: 978-1-934838-26-6

FREE trail updates and GPS downloads and Email newsletter available at www.funtreks.com.

To order additional books, call toll-free 1-877-222-7623 or order online at www.funtreks.com.

ACKNOWLEDGMENTS
    Thanks to everyone with whom we traveled or met on the trails for allowing us to use pictures of you and/or your vehicles. If we published pictures that you took, we gave you credit at the bottom of the picture.
    We would also like to thank staffers and rangers at the U.S. Forest Service, BLM and other government land agencies for their time and patience answering our many questions.

GUARANTEE OF SATISFACTION
We guarantee you will enjoy the trails in this book. If not, or if you are dissatisfied with the book in any other way, return it to us for a full refund. Or, call our toll-free number during business hours at 1-877-222-7623. We promise to do whatever it takes to make you happy.

DISCLAIMER
    Travel in Colorado's backcountry is, by its very nature, potentially dangerous and could result in property damage, injury or even death. The scope of this book cannot predict every possible hazard you may encounter. If you drive any of the trails in this book, you acknowledge these risks and assume full responsibility. You are the final judge as to whether a trail is safe to drive on any given day, whether your vehicle is capable of the journey and what supplies you should carry. The information contained herein cannot replace good judgment and proper preparation on your part. The publisher and authors of this book disclaim any and all liability for bodily injury, death or property damage that could occur to you or any of your passengers.
    We have made every effort to update trails to match U.S. Forest Service Motor Vehicle Use Maps (MVUMs) that were available at the time of this writing. We cannot match maps that have not yet been issued or keep up with annual changes to existing maps. We will attempt to report changes on our website, but make no guarantee of accuracy. You are ultimately responsible for following the latest and correct MVUM.

Note: Telephone numbers and website URLs that appear in this book were verified December 2018.

CONTENTS

TRAIL LIST

Green = Easy,   Blue = Moderate,   Red = Difficult

* New Trails

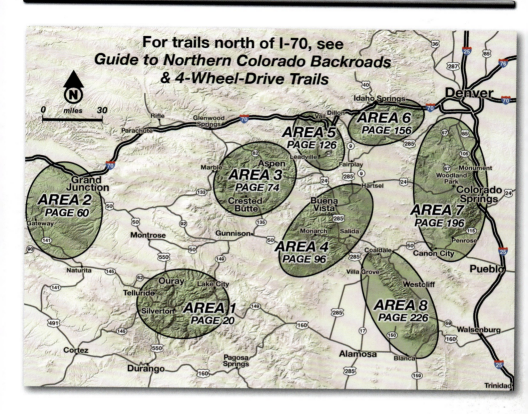

For trails north of I-70, see
Guide to Northern Colorado Backroads
& 4-Wheel-Drive Trails

AREA 2 PAGE 60
AREA 3 PAGE 74
AREA 4 PAGE 96
AREA 5 PAGE 126
AREA 6 PAGE 156
AREA 7 PAGE 196
AREA 1 PAGE 20
AREA 8 PAGE 226

Key for Trail Maps

Interstate	🚻 Public Toilet	📷 Scenic Point
Paved Road	⛽ Gas, Service	🏕 Picnic Table
Unpaved Road	🅿 Parking	🎣 Fishing
Easy Trail	🅂 Staging	🏠 Cabin
Moderate Trail	⛺ Camping	💨 Windmill
Difficult Trail	Mine	🦌 Ghost Town
Other Trails	🥾 Hiking Trail	∩ Arch
Described in Log	🚴 Mountain Biking	Ruins
Hiking Trail	Waterfall	Obstacle
Boundaries	Water Crossing	Unlicensed OK
	Bridge	No Unlicensed

TRAILS LISTED ALPHABETICALLY

6

TRAILS RATED BY DIFFICULTY

* Author's Favorites

Trails are more difficult as you scroll down the list.

#	Name	Pg.
	EASIER	
80.	Boreas Pass*	190
95.	Shelf Road, Phantom Canyon	222
69.	Peru Creek*	168
61.	Weston Pass	150
91.	Mount Herman Rd., Rampart Range	214
83.	Rampart Crossover	198
13.	California Gulch*	46
1.	Last Dollar Road	22
28.	Paradise Divide*	80
89.	La Salle Pass	210
50.	Shrine Pass	128
45.	Fourmile Area*	116
60.	Mount Bross	148
93.	Mount Baldy	218
86.	Phantom Creek, Signal Butte	204
17.	Eureka Gulch	54
3.	Governor Basin*	26
16.	Picayune & Placer Gulches*	52
48.	Marshall Pass via Poncha Creek	122
47.	Billings Lake	120
77.	Webster Pass, Handcart Gulch	184
12.	Red Mountain Mining Area*	44
25.	Rim Rocker*	72
8.	Clear Lake, Bandora Mine	36
23.	Little Dolores Canyon	68
98.	Hermit Pass	230
7.	Ophir Pass, Alta Lakes	34
97.	Hayden Pass	228
63.	Lost Canyon	154
85.	Rule Ridge	202

#	Name	Pg.
90.	Balanced Rock Rd.	212
92.	Schubarth Loop*	216
62.	Halfmoon Gulch	152
21.	Windmill Loop	64
79.	Peak 10 Breckenridge	188
99.	Medano Pass	232
81.	Geneva Creek	192
11.	Corkscrew Gulch, Hurricane Pass*	42
44.	Mount Princeton	114
54.	Hagerman Pass	136
14.	Engineer Pass*	48
58.	Mosquito Pass	144
29.	Aspen Mountain, Richmond Hill	82
73.	Deer Creek	176
55.	Mount Zion	138
56.	Chalk Mountain	140
52.	Slide Lake, Wurtz Ditch	132
49.	Rawley Mine, Bonanza	124
67.	Devil's Canyon	164
84.	Rainbow Falls	200
15.	Cinnamon Pass, Wager Gulch*	50
30.	Lincoln Creek Rd.	84
18.	Kendall Mountain	56
6.	Porphyry Gulch	32
71.	Santa Fe Peak	172
78.	Georgia Pass	186
68.	Argentine Pass, McClellan Mtn.*	166
19.	Stony Pass, Kite Lake	58
82.	Slaughterhouse Gulch	194
31.	Montezuma Basin	86
70.	Chihuahua Gulch*	170
65.	Cascade Creek	160
88.	China Wall	208
41.	Pomeroy Lakes	108

#	Name	Pg.
87.	The Gulches*	206
42.	Mount Antero	110
43.	Baldwin Lakes, Boulder Mountain	112
37.	Tincup Pass	100
2.	Yankee Boy Basin*	24
26.	Lead King Basin	76
38.	Hancock Pass	102
57.	Birdseye Gulch	142
51.	McAllister Gulch	130
4.	Imogene Pass*	28
72.	Saints John*	174
66.	Saxon Mountain	162
74.	North & Middle Fork of the Swan River	178
36.	Napoleon Pass	98
32.	Pearl Pass*	88
9.	Mineral Creek	38
35.	Tellurium Creek	94
34.	Italian Creek, Reno Divide	92
27.	Devil's Punchbowl*	78
5.	Black Bear Pass	30
33.	Taylor Pass	90
10.	Poughkeepsie Gulch	40
75.	Radical Hill	180
76.	Red Cone*	182
59.	Wheeler Lake	146
22.	The Tabequache	66
39.	Grizzly Lake	104
94.	Eagle Rock, Saran Wrap	220
24.	Calamity Mesa Loop	70
40.	Iron Chest Mine*	106
53.	Holy Cross*	134
64.	Spring Creek	158
46.	Chinaman Gulch, Carnage Canyon*	118
100.	Blanca Peak*	234
20.	Billings Canyon	62
96.	Independence	224
	HARDER	

NOTE: Order of trails is approximate. There may be little or no difference between trails close together on the list. Trails are constantly changing and so the order will change from day to day. Also, judgment of difficulty varies from person to person.

Trail ratings are very subjective. Conditions change for many reasons, including weather and time of year. An easy trail can quickly become difficult when washed out by a rainstorm or blocked by a fallen rock. You must be the final judge of a trail's condition on the day you drive it. If any part of a trail is difficult, the entire trail is rated difficult. You may be able to drive a significant portion of a trail before reaching the difficult spot. Read each trail description carefully for specific information.

● Easy

Gravel, dirt, clay, sand, or mildly rocky road. Gentle grades. Water levels low except during periods of heavy runoff. Full-width single lane or wider with adequate room to pass most of the time. Where shelf conditions exist, road is wide with minor sideways tilt. Clay roads, when wet, can significantly increase difficulty. Some trails can be driven in 2WD under ideal conditions. Others will need 4WD and, in some cases, low-range gearing.

Authors' Vehicles: (See photos)
A. 2017 Jeep Wrangler Sport: STOCK, 6-cyl. engine 4WD, stock highway tires and aftermarket "Sunrider" soft top.

B. 2017 Toyota Tacoma: STOCK, TRD Offroad package, CBI rock sliders, stock tow hooks, A/T tires and CB radio.

C. 2012 Jeep Wrangler Rubicon: Equipped with JKS 2.5" lift with stock control arms, 9.5TI Warn winch, Dana 44 rear axle; 4.88 gears, stock rubicon 4/1 transfer case, stock lockers front and rear, TERA FLEX skid plates, Notch Custom extended fenders, JCR Offroad bumpers, stock 6-cyl engine, 37 x 12.50 Cooper Discovery STT tires and CB radio.

® "Jeep" and "Toyota" are registered trademarks of manufacturers.

■ Moderate

Rutted dirt or rocky road. Careful tire placement may be necessary. Some grades fairly steep but manageable if dry. Soft sand possible. Sideways tilt will require caution. Narrow shelf roads possible. Backing may be necessary to pass. Water depths passable for stock high-clearance vehicles except during periods of heavy runoff. Mud holes may be present especially in the spring. Undercarriage may scrape occasionally depending on ground clearance. Rock-stacking may be necessary in some cases. Brush may touch vehicle. Four-wheel drive, low range, and higher ground clearance required in most cases. Standard factory skid plates and tow hooks recommended on many trails.

◆ Difficult

Grades can be very steep with severe ground undulation and large boulders. Sideways tilt can be extreme. Sand hills very steep with soft downslopes. Deep water crossings possible. Shelf roads extremely narrow; use caution in oversize vehicle. Passing may be difficult with backing required for long distances. Brush may scratch sides of vehicle. Body damage possible. Some trails suitable for more aggressive stock vehicles, but most trails require vehicle modification. Lifts, differential lockers, aggressive articulation, and/or winches recommended in many cases. Skid plates and tow hooks required.

Introduction

9

Got a 4x4 SUV, pickup or Jeep? Missing out on fun because you're afraid to go off road? Want to try it, but don't know how or where to start? Well, we're here to help.

FunTreks has been showing novice and experienced offroaders what to do and where to go for more than 20 years. That includes riders of ATVs, UTVs and dirt bikes. As a result, this book has been the top-selling off-road guidebook since 1998 when we went into business.

Other reasons our books are popular: First, we live in Colorado and our business is here. We are out driving trails all the time and just drove every trail in this book yet again. Second, we are dedicated to accurate and complete reporting of trail directions and conditions. Every map is created from scratch to show what's important to the off-road driver. Third, we show lots of photos—not just scenery, but trail conditions. And fourth, we guarantee satisfaction. Return the book for any reason if you're not happy.

What's New in This 4th Edition

We added a new area on the Western Slope with six new trails south of Grand Junction. (New trails north of Grand Junction are included in our Northern Colorado book.)

The number of "difficult" trails jumped by 12, making 42 in all. This occurred simply because the trails got harder. The remaining 58 trails are still easy and moderate trails.

Back by popular demand, the master trail list is shown three ways: numerically, alphabetically, and by difficulty.

And finally, we've switched to a new style of spiral binding that's easier to fold back. We've made the text pages thicker and more durable. The back cover tucks in and serves as a placeholder.

Get Free Trail Updates & GPS Downloads at www.funtreks.com

We have redone our website to include a separate information page for each and every trail in our 4-wheel-drive guidebooks. Now you can search for a trail and, if it's been updated, learn what has changed since the book was first published. Updates come from our own knowledge and from customer submissions. If you know of a change to a trail, please go to our website and submit an update. Sign up for our email newsletter and we'll send you updates free.

In addition, on each trail page of our website, you'll find a free GPS download of that trail that includes waypoints and a tracklog that match the book. Files are in universal .gpx format for use in many common mapping applications.

FunTreks—A Different Kind of App

There are lots of great all-purpose backcountry apps out there. We know because we use many of them ourselves. What makes our app different is that it specifically matches the trails in our books. The waypoints match the book, and the tracklog follows the route in the book. And you don't need an internet connection to see your position as you move along the trail. When you buy the app, it includes every trail we have. There is no need to buy each book.

If you hate the complexity of most apps, try ours. Our customers tell us it's the easiest app they've ever used.

GPS Settings

All GPS coordinates in this book are displayed using datum WGS84. Lat./Long. format is: hh/mm.mmm (not hours/minutes/seconds). Make sure your GPS unit is set the same way or you'll get different readings.

Explanation of Vehicle Symbols

Please read carefully before attempting any trail in this book.

SUV or Pickup Truck.

This symbol represents a street-licensed stock sport utility vehicle or pickup truck with 4-wheel drive. Minimum ground clearance should be 7" to 8" at low point of vehicle and about a foot at rocker panel. Low range is recommended for rocky, steep and high elevation trails. More aggressive models will have higher clearance and factory off-road enhancements such as skid plates, tow points and differential lockers. Longer and wider vehicles require more ground clearance.

In addition to vehicle capability and size, other factors such as driver's skill, tires and tolerance for damage greatly affect which trails can be driven. Every vehicle is different and every trail is different. Judgment as to whether a vehicle is capable of traversing a specific trail lies solely with the owner of the vehicle. Read each trail description carefully.

Hard-core Modified.

This symbol represents street-licensed vehicles that have been significantly modified for difficult hard-core situations. Most modifications are custom, but there are specific factory models that meet hard-core standards. Minimal tire size starts at 32", but 33" to 37" is more typical. Lifts of 3" or more, heavy-duty skid plates and accessories, increased articulation and differential lockers are the norm. Many additional modifications are possible.

These vehicles should be able to handle all trails in this book, with the possible exception of Trails 20, 46 and 96. These extreme trails require maximum modifications or a high tolerance for vehicle damage.

60"-Wide Side-by-Sides.

This symbol represents what are commonly called UTVs, or Utility Terrain Vehicles. They are generally considered unlicensed vehicles; however, some states allow licensing if modified for street use. Out-of-state street licensing is not yet recognized in Colorado, but a few local areas—e.g., Silverton, Lake City and Meeker—allow limited use on some roads. For the purposes of this book, UTV side-by-sides are considered unlicensed vehicles.

Capability of these vehicles ranges from simple utility uses on ranches and farms to extreme modifications for hard-core trail use. Their width prohibits use on 50" ATV trails. For this book, 4-wheel-drive capability is assumed.

When you see this symbol at the top of the page, it primarily indicates the trail allows unlicensed vehicles. The ratings of easy, moderate and difficult are open to far greater interpretation. Only the operator can determine the appropriateness of the trail.

50"-Wide ATVs and Side-by-Sides.

This symbol represents ATVs, All Terrain Vehicles, not wider than 50". It also represents 50"-wide side-by-sides. Both are generally considered unlicensed vehicles; however, some states allow licensing if modified for street use. Out-of-state street licensing is not yet recognized in Colorado, but a few local areas—e.g., Silverton, Lake City and Meeker—allow limited use on some streets. For the purposes of this book they are considered unlicensed vehicles.

These vehicles range in size from tiny 2WD machines for kids to large 4WD machines for adults. Generally, trails in this book are for 4-wheel-drive ATVs, but we know some 2-wheel-drive units can be quite capable.

When you see this symbol at the top of the page, it primarily indicates the trail allows unlicensed vehicles. The ratings of easy, moderate and difficult are open to far greater interpretation. Only the operator can determine the appropriateness of the trail.

 Dirt Bikes (Unlicensed). This symbol represents unlicensed dirt bikes only. Licensed, dual-purpose bikes can ride any trail in this book.

The symbol does not mean the trail is a single-track trail; it only means unlicensed dirt bikes are allowed. All trails in this book are wide enough for SUVs and Jeeps, but most are still great rides for dirt bikes. Some trails in this book connect to 50"-wide and single-track trails. These narrower trails are specified on Motor Vehicle Use Maps. (See page 13.)

Easy, moderate and difficult ratings do not apply to dirt bikes, but they do provide general information of what to expect. In addition, driving-time estimates will be less for dirt bikes.

All About Colorado

When to go. Each trail description includes our best guess as to the ideal time to drive that trail.

Conditions largely depend on the elevation of the trail and the amount of snow received over the winter. Some trails at low elevations open in late May. More trails open in June. High mountain passes typically can be crossed the first or second week in July; however, extremely high passes may open much later. Some years, the highest passes may not open at all. Some trails may open earlier because the roads are plowed. Generally in Colorado, the safest bet is to go in late July, August and September. September is also the peak time to enjoy fall color. You may squeeze in some very late season exploring in early October if no early winter snow has fallen. Start as early as possible in the day. Mornings are usually clear while afternoons are often cloudy with a greater chance of thunderstorms.

The weather. Colorado weather is often very pleasant and more moderate than people expect. Low humidity at high elevations keeps temperatures cool in the summer. There are few flies and mosquitoes except around wetlands. The downside to Colorado weather is that it is very unpredictable and can be extreme at times. It can snow anytime during the summer, especially at higher elevations and at night when temperatures drop. Colorado can also be very windy. Pack plenty of warm clothing regardless of how hot it might be when you depart. Also, make sure you drink plenty of fluids to help you adapt to the dry thin air and use plenty of sunscreen.

Lightning. Thunderstorms, hail and lightning are very common in Colorado, especially in the late afternoon. If possible, get below timberline if you see a storm approaching.

Fires and floods. Be aware of the possibility of forest fires and flash floods. Fires can move quickly, so watch for smoke when you are at higher points. At certain times of year, fire danger can be extremely high and the Forest Service will post fire danger warnings. During these times, campfires may be prohibited. Heavy rainstorms can cause flash floods at any time during the spring and summer. The danger is particularly acute if you are in a narrow canyon. If you have reason to believe a flash flood is imminent, do not try to outrun it. Abandon your vehicle and climb to higher ground.

Altitude sickness. Some people experience nausea, dizziness, headaches or weakness the first time at high altitude. This condition usually improves over time. To minimize symptoms, give yourself time to acclimate, drink plenty of fluids, decrease salt intake, reduce alcohol and caffeine, eat foods high in carbohydrates, and try not to exert yourself. If symptoms become severe, the only sure remedy is to return to a lower altitude.

Hypothermia. Hypothermia is possible even in the summer. If you get caught in a sudden shower at high altitude, your body temperature can drop suddenly. Always take rain gear and warm clothing.

Don't drink from streams. No matter how cool, clear or refreshing a mountain stream may appear, never drink the water without boiling it, using a filter or iodine tablets. Best to carry your own water.

Laws, Rules, Etiquette

• Follow MVUMs or risk getting a ticket. Fines can go as high as $5,000 and/or 6 months in jail. Know the rules for BLM land and other special-use areas.

• Once on the right trail, stay on it. Don't shortcut switchbacks, widen existing routes or make new trails.

• Vehicles going uphill have the right-of-way by Colorado law.

• Carry proper paperwork for your vehicle. Items may include driver's license, proof of insurance, vehicle registration and/or OHV registration.

• Don't drive or ride while under the influence of alcohol or drugs.

• Never drive or ride in a wilderness area. Follow special rules for wilderness study areas.

• Drive cautiously at all times, especially around blind curves.

• Cross streams at designated crossings only.

• Pull over at existing wide spots when you are out of your vehicle, not moving, or when overtaken by a faster vehicle. Use extra caution around hikers, bikers, horses and pack animals.

• Leave gates the way you find them unless posted otherwise.

• Public roads often cross or parallel private land. Respect rights of private property owners.

• Don't blast your radio or gun your engine. Don't blow your horn unless it is absolutely necessary.

• Pack out your trash, except in fee areas that have approved receptacles.

• Don't pick wildflowers, walk on delicate tundra or remove anything from historical sites.

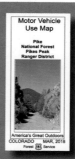

Motor Vehicle Use Maps (MVUMs)

Motor Vehicle Use Maps (MVUMs) are produced by the U.S. Forest Service and are free to the public. The maps identify legal OHV routes by vehicle type within ranger districts. You should reference a copy (paper or electronic) of each ranger district MVUM in which you travel to avoid being ticketed for driving on a closed or restricted road. The maps are legal documents used by law enforcement and replace the need for signage on the ground. The maps are updated frequently, ideally every year, so make sure you have the latest map. PDF files of the maps can also be downloaded for use on computers, tablets and smart phones. The maps are not user friendly, so spend a little time learning how to read them.

For a list of the latest published MVUMs, go to: www.fs.fed.us/recreation/programs/ohv/ohv_maps.shtml.

We also recommend an app called "Avenza." It allows you to download MVUMs free onto your tablet or phone. The app allows you to store many maps and the maps are geo-referenced, which allows you to see your location as you move along a route.

Disclaimer: FunTreks uses the latest MVUM at the time we drive the trail. However, we do not update our books every time a new MVUM is issued. When differences occur between our book and the latest MVUM, always follow the MVUM.

• Control your dogs. Don't let them bark or chase wildlife.

• Always camp close to the trail and use existing campsites whenever pos-

sible. Camp away from streams, lakes, hiking trails and historical sites. To avoid wildfires by catalytic converter, don't park in tall grass.

• Use existing fire rings for campfires when possible, or bring your own camp stove. Completely douse fires and leave campsite cleaner than you found it, which includes removing fire waste. Bring your own firewood if possible, even if it is not required.

• Bury human waste 6 to 8 inches deep at least 200 feet from any water source, campsite or trail. When possible, bring your own portable toilet.

• Avoid using soap around lakes or streams. Heat water to clean utensils.

• Finally, be courteous to everyone regardless of how they treat you. To save our trails, we must all be good ambassadors for motorized recreation.

Camping in U.S. Forests

Dispersed camping (a.k.a. dry camping or primitive camping). In many areas of the forest, you can camp along the road if you see a spot you like. Usually you can stay for 14 days. In some cases, the Forest Service limits camping to just certain designated spots. In this case, the spots are usually numbered or marked with a camping symbol. No services are provided and you must pack out your trash. MVUMs show where dispersed camping is allowed with small black dots on one or both sides of the road. Dispersed camping is usually first come, first served.

Fee campgrounds. Typically, fee campgrounds offer trash dumpsters and water stations with hand pumps. A few have electric plug-ins. You pay a posted fee at a self-pay station. Many campgrounds have a campground host who camps there in the summer. They can answer basic questions and often sell firewood.

In Colorado, it is usually very difficult to find a camp spot in a fee campground on the weekend (Friday and Saturday night). During the week, it is typically much easier. To make a reservation, go online to Recreation.gov. The process is a bit cumbersome, but it's fair. Popular campgrounds sometimes require reservations months in advance, especially for holiday weekends.

Backcountry Driving Tips

The basics. Practice on easy trails first to learn how to operate your off-road features. As your confidence builds, you'll want to try harder trails.

Low and slow. Shift into 4-wheel drive or low range before it is needed. Stay in low gear as much as possible for maximum power. With standard transmissions, minimize use of your clutch. As you encounter resistance on an obstacle or an uphill grade, apply a little gas. As you start downhill, allow the engine's resistance to act as a brake. If the engine alone will not slow you enough, help with light brake pressure. When you need more power but not more speed, press on the gas and feather the brake a little at the same time.

Rocks and other high points. Don't straddle rocks. Instead, drive over the highest point with your tire. This will help lift your undercarriage. If the point is too high, stack rocks on either side to create a ramp. Remove rocks when done. As you enter a rocky area, look ahead to identify the high points. Learn the low and vulnerable spots of your undercarriage. In difficult situations, it may be necessary to get out of your vehicle for a better look or use a "spotter" outside the vehicle to direct you.

If high centered. If you get lodged on an object, first have passengers get out to lighten the load. Try rocking the vehicle. If this doesn't work, jack up your vehicle and place something under the tires. Try going forwards and backwards. If you aired down your tires, reinflate them.

Scout ahead. When unsure of what's ahead, get out of your vehicle and walk the trail ahead of you. This gives you an opportunity to turn around at a wide spot of your choosing. Back up if necessary. Don't try to turn in a narrow confined area.

Blind curves. When approaching blind curves, assume that there is a speeding vehicle in your lane coming from the opposite direction. This will prepare you for the worst.

Driving uphill. Use extreme caution when attempting to climb a steep hill. Shift into low range first. Air down your tires to improve traction. Four factors determine difficulty:

Length of the hill. Momentum will help carry you over short hills, but not necessarily long hills.

Traction. A rock surface is usually easier to climb than soft dirt.

Bumpiness. Big bumps on steep grades may lift your tires off the ground and stop your progress, especially if your vehicle has poor articulation. Temporarily disconnecting your front sway bar will improve your articulation; however, this is difficult to do on some vehicles.

Steepness. This can be difficult to judge, so examine the hill carefully by walking up it first. Abort if you are not sure. If you proceed, approach it straight on and stay that way all the way to the top. Do not turn sideways or try to drive across the hill. Keep moving at a steady pace. Make sure no one is coming up the other side. Try not to spin your tires. If you lose traction, jiggle your steering wheel back and forth. This may give you additional grip in soft soil. If you stall, use your foot brake, and if necessary, your emergency brake, while you restart your engine. If you start to slide backwards even with your brake on, you may have to ease up on the brake enough to regain steering control. Don't allow your wheels to lock up. If you don't make it to the top of the hill, shift into reverse and back down slowly in a straight line. Try the hill again, but only if you think you learned enough to make a difference. Ease off the gas as you approach top of hill.

Driving downhill. Make sure you are in 4-wheel drive. Air down your tires to improve traction. Go straight down the hill; do not turn sideways. In low gear, allow the engine's compression to hold you back. Do not ride the clutch. Feather the brakes slightly if additional slowing is needed. Do not allow the wheels to lock up. If you start to slide sideways, ease up on the brake and accelerate slightly to maintain steering control. Turn in the direction of the slide as you would on ice or snow.

Parking on a steep hill. Put your vehicle in low-range reverse gear if pointing downhill or in low-range forward gear if pointing uphill. For automatic transmissions, shift to park. Set your emergency brake hard, but don't depend on it holding. Always block your wheels to avoid vehicle creep.

Side hills and tippy situations. Side hills can be very dangerous, so try to avoid them if possible. No one can tell you how far your vehicle can safely lean. Travel in a group and watch similar vehicles. Although SUVs have a high center of gravity, don't get paranoid; your vehicle will likely lean more than you think. Drive slowly to avoid bouncing. Use extreme caution if the road surface is slippery. Turn around if necessary.

Passing on narrow shelf roads. When possible, wait for road to clear. If surprised by an oncoming vehicle, don't panic. By law, the vehicle going uphill has the right-of-way, but in the real world common sense should apply. It might make more sense for the uphill vehicle to back up if a wide spot is closer. Often one vehicle can back up easier than a large group. Don't be forced too

close to the outer edge or to tip your vehicle excessively on a high inside bank. Both situations are dangerous. If necessary, talk to the other driver.

Crossing streams and water holes. You must know the depth of the water and what your vehicle can go through. Fast-flowing deep water can float you downstream. You don't want water in your air intake or to cover your engine computer module. If you don't know where these things are, consult your owner's manual or talk to your dealer. You can learn much by traveling with vehicles similar to yours. Low cooling fans can throw water on your engine and cause it to stall. I've seen people cover their grill with cardboard or canvas to push water to the side. This only works if you keep moving at a steady pace. Check differentials later for possible water contamination.

Always cross streams slowly at designated water crossings. Don't drive upstream or downstream except in areas where it is allowed.

Mud. Plan ahead, equip your vehicle with proper tires and carry tire chains. Install tow points and, if possible, differential lockers. Air down your tires to improve traction. Go around mud if it doesn't widen the trail. Make sure you are in 4-wheel drive. Low range may or may not help. If you enter mud, use momentum and keep moving at a steady pace. Try not to spin your tires. Follow existing ruts. If you get stuck, try backing out. If that doesn't work, dig around tires to break the suction. Borrow tire chains if you don't have any. If tire is spinning on one side only, try feathering your brakes while accelerating gently. If all else fails, ask a friend or passerby to strap you out.

Ruts or washouts. If a rut runs parallel to the road, you might be able to straddle it or drive in the bottom. The goal is to center your vehicle to remain level. Cross ruts at a 45-degree angle using momentum. However, without differential lockers or good articulation, one wheel may spin in the air while the other does nothing.

Sand. Dry sand is more difficult to cross than wet sand. Make sure you are in 4-wheel drive. Airing down will improve traction. Keep moving using momentum as much as possible. Stay in high gear and try to power through without spinning your tires.

Snow and ice. The best advice is to avoid snow and ice completely. Call ahead for trail conditions. Have proper tires and carry tire chains. Make sure you are in 4-wheel drive. Ice or snow on a shelf road is extremely dangerous especially when going uphill or downhill. If you are returning over the same route, remember that water can freeze later in the day. Abort if necessary.

Washboard roads. Washboard roads are annoying to everyone and can't be avoided in the Colorado backcountry. Air down your tires to improve traction and soften the ride. Experiment with different speeds to find the smoothest ride. Slowing down is usually best, but some conditions may be improved by speeding up a little. Be careful around curves where you could lose traction and slide. Check your tires to make sure they are not overinflated.

Airing down. A typical SUV can usually be aired down to 18 to 20 lbs. without noticeable handling difficulties at slow speeds. The tire should bulge slightly. Carry a small air pump that plugs into your cigarette lighter to reinflate. I've seen large tires on hard-core rigs aired down to as little as 3 to 5 lbs.

Winching

Winches are helpful but not always necessary unless you travel by yourself or drive hard-core trails on a regular basis. If you go with another vehicle, you can strap each other. Make sure you have tow points, however. If you get a

Checklist

Things to consider taking depending on vehicle and space available:

• Plenty of food and drinking water. Consider water purification tablets or a water filter.
• Rain gear plus warm clothing.
• Sleeping bags in case you get stuck overnight even if you are not planning to camp.
• A good first aid kit including sunscreen and insect repellent.
• Candle, matches, lighter, fire starter.
• An extra set of keys, glasses, watch.
• Toilet paper, paper towels, wet wipes and trash bags.
• A large plastic sheet or tarp.
• Detailed topographic maps, map atlas.
• GPS unit or compass.
• Sharp knife or Leatherman.
• If you plan to make a fire, carry your own firewood.
• Work gloves.
• A heavy-duty tow strap.
• Fire extinguisher.
• Jumper cables.
• Fuses and electrical tape.
• Flashlight and extra batteries.
• A full tank of gas. Extra gas for long trips.
• A good set of tools including specialized tools for UTVs, ATVs and dirt bikes.
• Baling wire and duct tape.
• An assortment of hose clamps, nuts, bolts and washers.
• A full-size spare tire.
• Tire repair kit.
• A tire pressure gauge, electric tire pump that will plug into your cigarette lighter and a can of nonflammable tire sealant.
• A jack that will lift your vehicle fairly high off the ground. Carry a high lift jack if possible, especially on more difficult trails. Test your jack before you leave.
• Shovel, tree saw, axe. Folding shovels work great.
• Tire chains.
• CB radio, cellular phone or satellite phone.
• Portable toilet.
• Tent.

Store items in tote bags or large plastic containers so they can be easily loaded when it is time to go.

winch, also carry work gloves, a tree strap, a snatch block and a shackle.

Winching tips:
• Your winch cable should be lined up straight with the pulling vehicle. If

you can't pull straight, attach a snatch block to a tree to form an angle.

• Attach your winch line to the largest tree possible using a tree strap and clevis. If no tree is large enough, wrap several smaller trees. The strap should be as low as possible.

• Keep your engine running while winching to maximize electrical power.

• Help the winch by driving the stuck vehicle slowly in low gear. Don't allow slack in the winch cable.

• To double your pulling power, attach a snatch block to the stuck vehicle and run the cable back to the starting point.

• Set the emergency brake on the anchor vehicle and block the wheels if necessary. You may have to strap to another vehicle or large tree.

• Stay well clear of the winch line at all times. If it breaks, it will likely snap back and could seriously injure or kill someone. Don't rely on a blanket draped over the line to make it safe.

• Make sure there are at least 5 wraps of the winch cable left on the spool. Ten wraps are recommended for synthetic winch rope.

• If tow points are not available on the stuck vehicle, attach the winch cable to the frame not the bumper. If you are helping a stranger, make sure he understands that you are not responsible for damage to his vehicle.

• When finished winching, don't let the end of the cable wind into the spool. Hook end to sturdy part nearby like a tow point or brush guard.

OHV Registration and Permits

Off-highway vehicle registrations and permits are administered by **Colorado Parks & Wildlife**. Go to cpw.state.co.us and look under "Things To Do" for the OHV registration page.

We also find it convenient to go to staythetrail.org. This site explains the process in more detail, plus it has links to the exact pages you need on the Parks & Wildlife website. Once in staythetrail.org, look for the section on "Registrations and Permits."

The site has other helpful information. Read on.

Stay the Trail Colorado

This organization is run by OHV people for OHV people. They're on your side. Their mission is to educate OHV enthusiasts and promote responsible use of public lands.

Besides having the registration and permit information mentioned above, staythetrail.org is helpful in other ways. It has one clickable list of all Colorado MVUMs and BLM Travel Management Maps. You can select from PDF, ZIP and KMZ formats. In addition, you can learn how to download the "Avenza" app to help you manage your maps.

Another section on the site has a list of special trails that require an OHV permit even on vehicles with license plates. These trails differ from other BLM and Forest Service roads because they exist primarily for recreation rather than transportation. The site refers to them as "Full-Size Trails." Eight trails in this book fall under this requirement: #20, #24, #34, #36, #37, #38, #46 and #96.

The site also has a handy interactive trail locator map. Use the free site often and support it with your donations.

COHVCO - Colorado Off Highway Vehicle Coalition

This organization was formed in 1987 to promote legislation to help OHV recreation in Colorado. They do an amazing job of fighting back against a growing number of heavily funded, anti-OHV forces. Please go to their website at www.cohvco.org and learn how you can help them keep trails open.

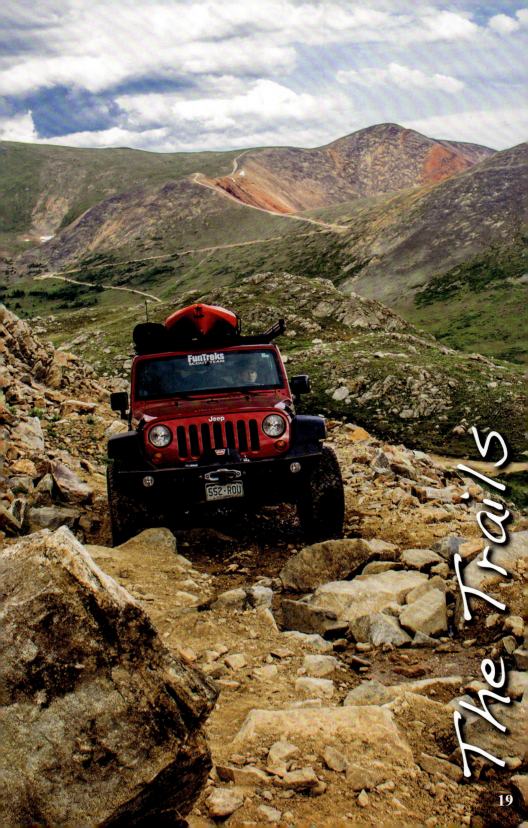

The Trails

Green = Easy, Blue = Moderate, Red = Difficult

Ouray, Silverton, Lake City, Telluride

The San Juan Mountains of southwest Colorado may be the most beautiful and accessible place in America to go off-highway exploring. Here, you are allowed to go deep into the backcountry, visit historic mine buildings, cross high passes and enjoy views reserved for an adventurous few.

The area has just the right balance of easy, moderate and difficult roads to satisfy all driving skill levels. All routes in Area 1 allow riding of unlicensed vehicles, which, in Colorado, include ATVs, UTVs and dirt bikes (regardless of whether they are licensed in another state). Many of the routes are county roads that require all riders to have a driver's license and carry proof of liability insurance.

At the end of the day, return to your choice of four remarkable mountain towns. You'll discover unique shopping, hotels, restaurants, museums and full-service RV parks.

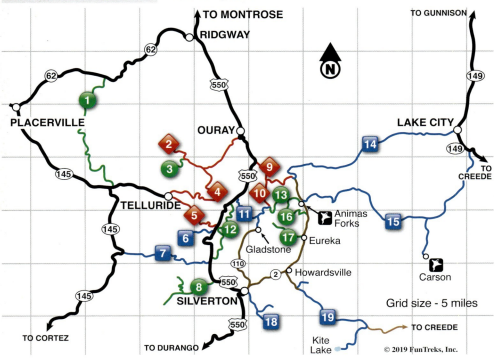

© 2019 FunTreks, Inc.

Grid size - 5 miles

Couple enjoys scenic views along Yankee Boy Basin, Trail #2, rated difficult.

Good camping spots with scenic views on south end of trail.

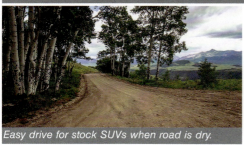
Easy drive for stock SUVs when road is dry.

Family relaxes above Telluride (Waypoint 03).

Overview: This scenic ranchland and forest backroad is a great alternative to the paved drive between Ridgway and Telluride. You'll see abundant wildflowers through early summer, great fall color and stunning mountain views. Enjoy camping, hiking and mountain biking. Plan plenty of time to visit Telluride, a great summer destination. Information can be found at the visitor center on the west end of town. Open to all vehicles between Waypoints 02 and 05 from May 16 to November 30.

Rating: Easy. Rutted dirt road suitable for high-clearance, 2-wheel-drive vehicles when dry. Slick clay can be impassable when wet even for 4-wheel-drive vehicles.

Stats: Length: About 20 miles. Time: About 2 hours. High point: 10,600 ft. Best time of year: Mid June-Sept.

Current Conditions: Uncompahgre N.F., Norwood Ranger District. Call (970) 327-4261.

Getting There: Head west on Highway 62 from Ridgway about 12 miles. Turn left on well-marked Last Dollar Road 0.8 mile west of mile marker 12. Follow signs to airport if starting in Telluride.

MILEAGE LOG:

START

0.0 Zero trip odometer [Rev. Miles]
Head south on well-maintained C.R. 58P. [20.4]
01 N38 05.994 W107 54.748

2.1 Bear left. [18.3]

2.5 Bear slightly right. [17.9]

5.0 Turn left where Last Dollar Road narrows and heads towards the forest. [15.4]
02 N38 03.041 W107 57.436

6.5 Bear right and cross small creek. [13.9]

10.5 Continue straight where Alder Creek Trail goes left. [9.9]

12.4 Cross broad talus slopes. [8.0]

12.9 Road twists downhill with beautiful mountain views and intersects with better road T60. Great camp spot to right (pictured left). Turn left and head downhill through residential area. [7.5]
03 N37 59.008 W107 56.997

16.4 Stay left where Deep Creek Road goes right. [4.0]
04 N37 58.414 W107 54.380

18.6 After passing Telluride Airport, intersect with paved road and turn left. [1.8]
05 N37 57.188 W107 53.684

20.4 End at Highway 145. Left goes to Telluride; right to Placerville. [0.0]
06 N37 57.060 W107 52.120

Get FREE trail updates & GPS downloads at www.FunTreks.com

Seasonal wildflowers on south end of trail.

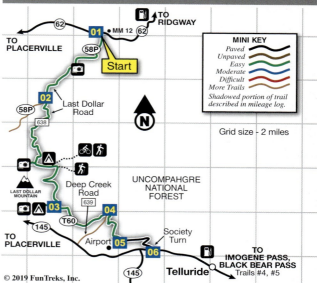

TO RIDGWAY

TO PLACERVILLE

Start

Last Dollar Road

MINI KEY
Paved
Unpaved
Easy
Moderate
Difficult
More Trails
Shadowed portion of trail described in mileage log.

N

Grid size - 2 miles

LAST DOLLAR MOUNTAIN

Deep Creek Road
639

UNCOMPAHGRE NATIONAL FOREST

TO PLACERVILLE

Airport

Society Turn

Telluride

TO IMOGENE PASS, BLACK BEAR PASS
Trails #4, #5

© 2019 FunTreks, Inc.

South side descends gradually.

Popular with bikes.

Yankee Boy Basin

Group gathers at end of trail where popular Mount Sneffels Trailhead begins.

Narrow spot under rock overhang.

Historical Highlight: *You'll pass tailings of Camp Bird Mine as you climb. In its heyday, this mine had advanced creature comforts, including hot running water, electric lights and steam heat. It was discovered in 1896 by Tom Walsh, who felt that the 400 miners who worked there should be treated to a decent lifestyle. He required only eight hours of work per day rather than the standard 12. He sold the mine in 1902 for $5.2 million. The mine continued to operate until 1911 and made over $26 million.*

Overview: One of the most popular destinations in the Ouray area due to its stunning natural beauty, rich history and colorful wildflowers. At the height of spring color, photographers flock to the area. Popular landmarks include the Drinking Cup, Twin Falls, Atlas Mill, Camp Bird Mine and the rock overhang. Because the area is used so heavily, camping is restricted to designated areas and a fee is charged to camp. Road open to all vehicles May 1 to Nov. 11.

Rating: Difficult. The lower portion of the trail is easy. Beyond the toilet, the trail gets rocky, narrow and steep, but is suitable for aggressive, high-clearance, stock SUVs. A gate for the upper portion of the trail is closed until the snow melts, usually in late June or early July.

Stats: Length: 9.3 miles. Time: 3 to 5 hours. High point: 12,400 ft. Best time of year: Mid July-Sept.

Current Conditions: Uncompahgre N.F., Ouray R.D. Call (970) 240-5300.

Getting There: Head south from Ouray on U.S. 550. Just 0.4 mile from the Beaumont Hotel on Main Street, turn right on Camp Bird Road 361.

MILEAGE LOG:

START

0.0 Zero trip odometer **[Rev. Miles]**
Follow wide gravel road uphill. Be cautious of high cliffs on left. **[9.3]**
01 N38 01.057 W107 40.481

3.6 Popular photo spot called the Drinking Cup. Look for natural spring nearby. **[5.7]**

4.6 Stay right as road becomes C.R. 26. (Camp Bird Mine is left.) **[4.7]**

5.4 Traverse narrow shelf road and pass under dramatic rock overhang. **[3.9]**

5.9 Continue straight. (Imogene Pass, Trail #4, is left.) Watch for remains of Sneffels Townsite as you continue. **[3.4]**
02 N37 58.523 W107 44.707

6.8 Stay right on F.S. 853.1B. (Governor Basin, Trail #3, is to left.) Road gets steeper. Watch for Twin Falls on left. **[2.5]**
03 N37 58.756 W107 45.533

7.7 Public toilet and parking to left. Stay right, ignore side trails on left. **[1.6]**

8.3 Seasonal gate and parking. You may proceed if open. Best and most adventurous part of trip remains. **[1.0]**
04 N37 59.344 W107 46.630

9.1 Stay right. (Road to lake on left is open to motorized vehicles.) **[0.2]**

9.3 Trail ends at small parking area for Mount Sneffels Trailhead. No motorized vehicles beyond this point. **[0.0]**
05 N37 59.696 W107 47.080

Drinking Cup photo spot.

Great views at Waypoint 04 before trail rating turns to difficult.

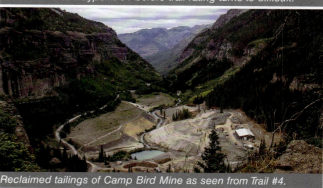

Reclaimed tailings of Camp Bird Mine as seen from Trail #4.

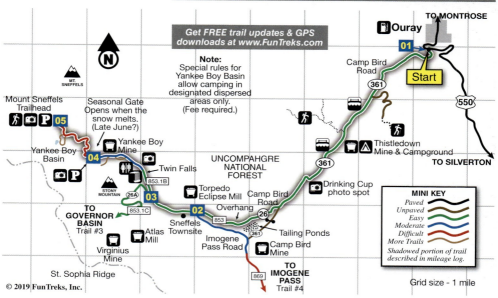

Get FREE trail updates & GPS downloads at www.FunTreks.com

Note:
Special rules for Yankee Boy Basin allow camping in designated dispersed areas only. (Fee required.)

TO MONTROSE

Ouray

Camp Bird Road

Start

550

TO SILVERTON

Thistledown Mine & Campground

Drinking Cup photo spot

361

361

26

MT. SNEFFELS

Mount Sneffels Trailhead

05

Seasonal Gate Opens when the snow melts. (Late June?)

Yankee Boy Mine

Yankee Boy Basin

04

Twin Falls

853.1B

STONY MOUNTAIN

26A

03

853.1C

TO GOVERNOR BASIN Trail #3

Virginius Mine

Atlas Mill

St. Sophia Ridge

Torpedo Eclipse Mill

Overhang

853

02

Sneffels Townsite

Imogene Pass Road

UNCOMPAHGRE NATIONAL FOREST

Camp Bird Road

Tailing Ponds

361

Camp Bird Mine

869

TO IMOGENE PASS Trail #4

MINI KEY
Paved
Unpaved
Easy
Moderate
Difficult
More Trails
Shadowed portion of trail described in mileage log.

Grid size - 1 mile

© 2019 FunTreks, Inc.

25

Climb narrow shelf road at start.

Camp spot near Waypoint 02.

Family enjoys view of Mountain Top Mine.

Historical Highlight: The boarding house, still standing at the Mountain Top Mine, is a relatively recent structure compared to other mines in the area. It was first constructed in 1912 to house 30 men and later expanded to three stories to accommodate 50 men. In 1922, this mine was the largest employer in Ouray County, but went bankrupt just two years later. The mine has been worked sporadically as late as 1996 and there is still a slight chance that it could be opened in the future. It has been designated a Ouray County Landmark. (Source: Nov. 7, 2008, story in The Hub by Don Paulson.)

Overview: Gorgeous high-elevation scenery and incredible wildflowers. Trail accesses historic mines including the massive Virginius Mine and the Mountain Top Mine. Mines are on private land, so you are not allowed to drive all the way to them. View from a distance and stay out of buildings. Popular trail for Jeep tours. Side trip to Sidney Basin is worth the trip. Roads open to all vehicles May 16 to Nov. 30.

Rating: Easy. Shelf road is narrow in spots, but the main trail is wide and flat. Sidney Basin has one steep choppy hill and large embedded rock near end.

Stats: Length: 2.6 miles one way. Time: 2 to 3 hours. High point: 12,020 ft. Best time of year: Mid July-Sept.

Current Conditions: Uncompahgre National Forest, Ouray Ranger District. Call (970) 240-5300.

Getting There: Head south from Ouray on U.S. 550. Just 0.4 mile from the Beaumont Hotel, turn right on Camp Bird Road, C.R. 361. Bear right after 4.6 miles past the Camp Bird Mine on C.R. 26. The turn for Governor Basin is a total of 7.0 miles from 550.

MILEAGE LOG:

0.0 Zero trip odometer [Rev. Miles]
Bear left off Yankee Boy Basin Road, Trail #2. After crossing small bridge, stay right. **[2.6]**
01 N37 58.756 W107 45.533

0.7 Stay left and go by a waterfall. Climb steeply on a narrow, rocky road. **[1.9]**

0.8 Stay left on shelf road. [1.8]

1.5 Stay right. **[1.1]**

1.8 Bear right at "T" intersection. Left is fun side trip to Sidney Basin and Atlas Mine ruins. **[0.8]**
02 N37 58.490 W107 45.927

2.3 Road levels out briefly. Great spot for lunch with large boulders to climb. Incredible views and seasonal wildflowers. (Closed road going steeply uphill behind boulders goes to Virginius Mine.) Main trail continues to right. **[0.3]**
03 N37 58.268 W107 46.338

2.6 End at Y intersection. Gate marks private property. View from a distance and stay out of buildings. **[0.0]**
04 N37 58.207 W107 46.618

Get FREE trail updates & GPS downloads at www.FunTreks.com

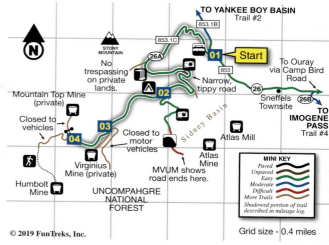

TO YANKEE BOY BASIN
Trail #2

853.1B

853.1C

26A

STONY MOUNTAIN

No trespassing on private lands.

01 Start

To Ouray via Camp Bird Road

853

26

Narrow, tippy road

Sneffels Townsite

26B

TO IMOGENE PASS
Trail #4

Mountain Top Mine (private)

02

Closed to vehicles

03

04

Closed to motor vehicles

Sidney Basin

Atlas Mill

Virginius Mine (private)

MVUM shows road ends here.

Atlas Mine

Humbolt Mine

UNCOMPAHGRE NATIONAL FOREST

MINI KEY
Paved
Unpaved
Easy
Moderate
Difficult
More Trails
Shadowed portion of trail described in mileage log.

© 2019 FunTreks, Inc.

Grid size - 0.4 miles

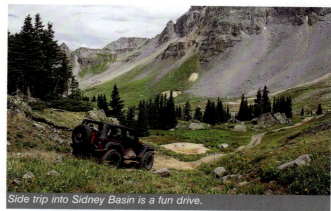
Side trip into Sidney Basin is a fun drive.

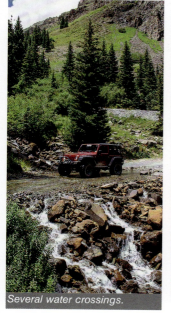
Several water crossings.

Abundant seasonal wildflowers at Waypoint 03.

Imogene Pass

Room to park and take in the views at the pass.

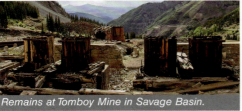

Remains at Tomboy Mine in Savage Basin.

Historical Highlight: Work at the Tomboy Mine began in the 1880s and continued until 1927. The mine was a rich producer of gold, and at one time 900 people lived in Savage Basin, the large glacial cirque below the mine. Many people lived there all year long, and snow tunnels were the only way to get around during the long, cold winters. A fascinating book, Tomboy Bride by Harriet Fish Backus, wife of an assayer, tells what it was like to live in the camp.

Overview: Imogene Pass is the second-highest drivable pass in Colorado. The drive is one of the most thrilling in the state. At Savage Basin, you'll pass through Tomboy Townsite, once one of the most active mining towns in Colorado. A great deal of mining debris is still scattered about. Most is on private property and is dangerous to explore. Unlicensed vehicles are not permitted on lower half of south side and must start trail from Camp Bird Road. Road is open May 16 to Nov. 30, but is usually blocked by snow until early July. Can close in early October.

Rating: Difficult. Do not take this trip lightly. The road is rocky, steep and narrow in places and passing can be dangerous. Stock SUVs should have low-range gearing, 4-wheel drive, high clearance and skid plates. Experienced drivers only.

Stats: Length: 11.9 miles. Time: 3 to 4 hours. High point: 13,114 ft. Best time of year: Mid July-Sept.

Current Conditions: Uncompahgre N.F., Norwood and Ouray Ranger Districts. Call (970) 327-4261.

Getting There: Although this trip can be driven in either direction, we find it easier starting in Telluride. This allows you to drive downhill on the steeper, rockier north side. Take the first part of the day to reach Telluride via Ophir Pass, Trail #7, or difficult Black Bear Pass, Trail #5.

In Telluride, find Oak Street on the north side of town. It does not intersect with Colorado (Main Street) so it must be accessed from Aspen or Fir Streets (see map detail). Tomboy Road goes to the right at the very end of Oak after Gregory.

MILEAGE LOG:

0.0 Zero trip odometer **[Rev. Miles]** Narrow road crosses above a residential area, then begins climb up switchbacks. **[11.9]**
01 N37 56.410 W107 48.700

1.6 First spot wide enough to pull over where people can pass. As you climb, each switchback becomes more dramatic. Look for Black Bear, Trail #5, across valley. **[10.3]**

3.7 Pass through the Social Tunnel. **[8.2]**

4.5 Arrive at Savage Basin and Tomboy Townsite. The road passes north of the townsite with various driver's choices. All roads come back together before begining steep climb to pass. **[7.4]**

6.7 Imogene Pass. Take time to enjoy the incredible views, then continue down other side. **[5.2]**
02 N37 55.892 W107 44.114

7.0 Driver's choice at roughest part of trail. Road gets steeper and rockier. Choose the best route for your vehicle. **[4.9]**

8.0 Narrow ledge road where passing is dangerous. Wait for road to clear before proceeding. Watch for dramatic overlook on left where you can pull over.

Dangerous cliffs. Continue downhill through scenic Imogene Basin. **[3.9]**

9.1 Cross creek and stay right downhill. Private roads on left go to mines. **[2.8]**

9.6 Cross creek and stay left downhill. Richmond Basin is uphill to right. **[2.3]**
03 N37 57.230 W107 43.500

9.8 Stay right. Lesser roads go left to building. **[2.1]**

10.6 Bear left uphill, then wind through woods on rocky terrain. Views of Camp Bird Mine on right. **[1.3]**
04 N37 57.970 W107 43.744

11.9 Cross creek last time next to bridge and connect to Trail #2. (Left are Yankee Boy and Governor Basins.) Turn right to reach Highway 550. **[0.0]**
05 N37 58.520 W107 44.720

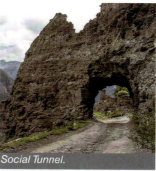
Social Tunnel.

Bridge at Waypoint 03.

Dramatic overlook above Imogene Basin on north side.

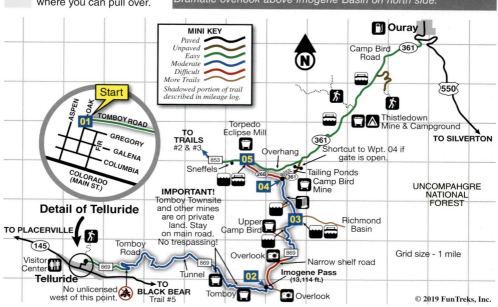

MINI KEY
Paved
Unpaved
Easy
Moderate
Difficult
More Trails
Shadowed portion of trail described in mileage log.

N

Ouray

Camp Bird Road
361
550

Start
ASPEN
OAK
01 TOMBOY ROAD
GREGORY
FIR
GALENA
COLUMBIA
COLORADO (MAIN ST.)

Detail of Telluride

TO TRAILS #2 & #3
Torpedo Eclipse Mill
853
Sneffels
Overhang
05
26B
361 Shortcut to Wpt. 04 if gate is open.
Tailing Ponds
Camp Bird Mine
04

IMPORTANT!
Tomboy Townsite and other mines are on private land. Stay on main road. No trespassing!

Upper Camp Bird
03
Richmond Basin

TO PLACERVILLE

145
Visitor Center
Telluride
869
Tomboy Road
Tunnel
869
Overlook
02
Imogene Pass (13,114 ft.)
Narrow shelf road
Overlook

No unlicensed west of this point.
TO BLACK BEAR Trail #5
Tomboy
Overlook

Thistledown Mine & Campground

TO SILVERTON

UNCOMPAHGRE NATIONAL FOREST

Grid size - 1 mile

© 2019 FunTreks, Inc.

29

Black Bear Pass

Descending ledges toward switchbacks. Loose shale and tippy spots are not for faint of heart.

Most vehicles must back up to make tight turns.

Wildflowers are abundant in the spring.

Overview: Incredible views from high above Red Mountain Pass and Telluride. Close-up views of historic mines and dramatic waterfalls. Feel the mist from spectacular Bridal Veil Falls. Road is closed October through May 15. Switchbacks are one-way downhill; no return to start. Unlicensed vehicles should turn around before going down one-way switchbacks or have pick-up vehicle waiting at the bottom.

Rating: Difficult. Most of the trail is easy to moderate. The difficult rating is based on a mile-long stretch of dangerous switchbacks above Bridal Veil Falls. Your vehicle should have low-range

4WD, good tires, good brakes, excellent articulation and a fully functional emergency brake.

Stats: Length: About 10 miles. Time: 2 to 3 hours. High point: 12,800 ft. Best time of year: July-Sept.

Current Conditions: San Juan and Uncompahgre N.F. Call Norwood Ranger District at (970) 327-4261.

Getting There: Head south from Ouray on U.S. 550 about 13 miles. Turn right on well-marked Black Bear Road just after the summit of Red Mountain Pass, near mile marker 80.

MILEAGE LOG:

START

0.0 Zero trip odometer **[Rev. Miles]** Follow County Road 16 west. **[6.5]**
01 N37 53.808 W107 42.802

1.0 Bear right, climb switchbacks (left is Porphyry Gulch, Trail #6). **[5.5]**
02 N37 53.720 W107 43.560

2.3 Begin to level out across barren terrain. **[4.2]**

2.9 Stay left. Ignore roads to right. **[3.6]**

3.2 Black Bear Pass. Stay left and continue down other side. **[3.3]**
03 N37 53.970 W107 44.597

4.9 Stay right (left is closed road to Ingram Lake). **[1.6]**

5.2 Stay left (right is closed road to Black Bear Mine). **[1.3]**

6.2 One-way portion of trip begins. Descend over several large ledges with no bypasses. **[0.3]**

6.5 Steep, narrow spot with loose shale. Tight switchbacks follow as you descend. **[0.0]**
04 N37 55.358 W107 45.681

7.3 Turn right where 2-way traffic begins near the powerhouse for Bridal Veil Falls. Road splits several times, but all roads lead to the bottom.

9.8 Pandora Mine. Licensed vehicles can continue from here into Telluride.
05 N37 55.930 W107 46.874

Note: Reverse mileage is not included to Waypoint 05 because this part is one way.

Get FREE trail updates & GPS downloads at www.FunTreks.com

Bridal Veil Falls.

Descending north side of pass.

Cross under waterfall after Waypoint 04.

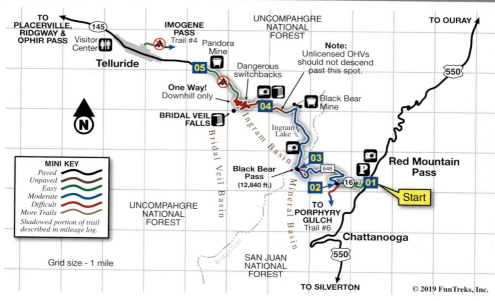

© 2019 FunTreks, Inc.

Porphyry Gulch

High shelf road entering Porphyry Gulch is very narrow and will intimidate some drivers.

Wildflowers near the lakes.

Hike to Bullion King Lake.

Overview: Although short, this trail is fun to drive and very scenic with lakes and waterfalls at the end. There is very little room to park hauling trailers for unlicensed vehicles at the start of F.S. 822 along Highway 550. Many people go in the entrance to Black Bear, Trail #5, and cut over on the unmarked road shown on map. Jurisdiction of this road is unclear, since it crosses private property. Although this side road is wide and well traveled, it could close without notice.

Rating: Moderate. Mostly easy except for one section of high, narrow shelf road that may intimidate novice drivers. Hike if you don't feel comfortable.

Stats: Length: 2.5 miles one way. Time: 1 to 2 hours. High point: 12,500 ft. Best time of year: Early July-Sept.

Current Conditions: San Juan Mountains Center in Silverton. Call (970) 387-5530 (closed in winter).

Getting There: Head south from Ouray on U.S. 550 about 13.5 miles. Turn right on F.S. 822 about a half mile after milepost 80. From Silverton, drive north on 550 about 9 miles.

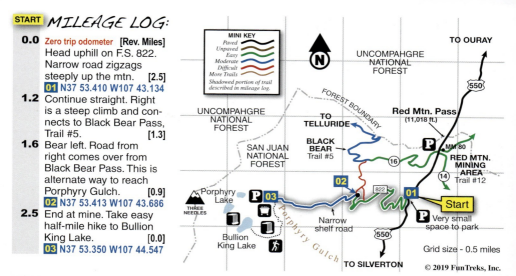

START **MILEAGE LOG:**

0.0 Zero trip odometer [Rev. Miles] Head uphill on F.S. 822. Narrow road zigzags steeply up the mtn. [2.5]
01 N37 53.410 W107 43.134

1.2 Continue straight. Right is a steep climb and connects to Black Bear Pass, Trail #5. [1.3]

1.6 Bear left. Road from right comes over from Black Bear Pass. This is alternate way to reach Porphyry Gulch. [0.9]
02 N37 53.413 W107 43.686

2.5 End at mine. Take easy half-mile hike to Bullion King Lake. [0.0]
03 N37 53.350 W107 44.547

MINI KEY
Paved
Unpaved
Easy
Moderate
Difficult
More Trails
Shadowed portion of trail described in mileage log.

TO OURAY

UNCOMPAHGRE NATIONAL FOREST

FOREST BOUNDARY

Red Mtn. Pass (11,018 ft.)

UNCOMPAHGRE NATIONAL FOREST

TO TELLURIDE

BLACK BEAR Trail #5

SAN JUAN NATIONAL FOREST

16

822

550

MM 80

RED MTN. MINING AREA Trail #12

14

01 Start

Very small space to park

Porphyry Lake

03

Porphyry Gulch

Narrow shelf road

Bullion King Lake

THREE NEEDLES

02

TO SILVERTON

Grid size - 0.5 miles

© 2019 FunTreks, Inc.

Not much room to pass on shelf road.

Lots of parking at end of trail at Waypoint 03.

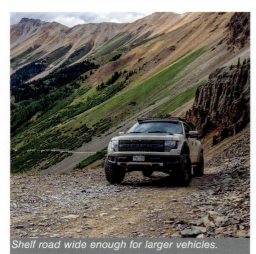
Shelf road wide enough for larger vehicles.

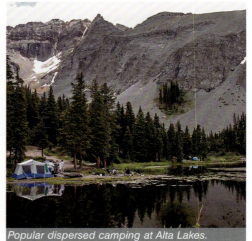
Popular dispersed camping at Alta Lakes.

Great shortcut between Highways 550 and 145.

Historical Highlight: Built in 1891, Ophir Pass was originally a toll road between Silverton and Telluride. The town of Ophir was a supply town for hundreds of mines in the area. Today it is a quaint residential community.
Alta was once a bustling mining town serving the Alta-Gold King area from 1877 to 1948 when the mill was destroyed by fire. This was one of the first towns in Colorado where alternating electrical current was used for power.

Overview: Ophir Pass is a convenient and scenic way to get from Silverton to Telluride. Seasonal wildflowers grow thick at higher elevations. Alta Lakes has great camping and picnicking in a beautiful mountain setting. Camp in designated spots. Unlicensed vehicles are allowed on Ophir Pass Road east of the town of Ophir; however, you cannot ride through town. Watch for signs. Snowplows usually clear Ophir Pass in June. Road to Alta Lakes is closed October through May 15.

Rating: Moderate. Applies to narrow, rocky shelf road on the west side of Ophir Pass. Passing an oncoming vehicle can be a little scary for a novice driver. Wait for traffic to clear before starting across. The last tenth of a mile

to Alta Lakes is rocky and requires high clearance to reach camping.

Stats: Length: Ophir is 10 miles, Alta Lakes 4.4. Time: About 3 hours for both trails combined. High point: 11,789 ft. Best time of year: Late June-September.

Current Conditions: San Juan and Uncompahgre N.F., Norwood R.D. Call (970) 327-4261.

Getting There: **Ophir Pass:** Head north from Silverton on U.S. 550 about 4.8 miles. Turn left on C.R. 8 near mile marker 75. **Alta Lakes:** After completing Ophir Pass going east to west, head north on Highway 145 about 2 miles and turn right at sign for Alta Lakes Road.

MILEAGE LOG:

0.0 Zero trip odometer [Rev. Miles]
OPHIR PASS:
Head west on C.R. 8, a wide gravel road. [9.9]
01 N37 50.856 W107 43.494

0.4 After bridge, continue straight where C.R. 100 joins on right. This road connects to south end of Trail #12. [9.5]

1.0 Continue straight. Not much to see on C.R. 8C to left. [8.9]

2.9 Stay right on main road. Left is bypass with dispersed camping. [7.0]

4.2 Ophir Pass. Continue straight down other side. When road narrows, wait for uphill traffic. [5.7]
02 N37 51.050 W107 46.767

6.6 Unlicensed vehicles must turn around here. Licensed can continue through Ophir. [3.3]

9.9 Highway 145. Turn right for Alta Lakes. [0.0]
03 N37 51.719 W107 52.194

0.0 Zero trip odometer
ALTA LAKES:
Follow well-marked C.R. 64F uphill. [4.4]
04 N37 53.038 W107 53.311

3.6 Road swings right uphill and winds through remains of Alta. [0.8]

4.2 Stay left at sign for Gold King Basin. [0.2]

4.4 Arrive at toilet next to lake. Explore roads that circle around lake. Lots of great camp spots and two smaller lakes. [0.0]
05 N3753.077 W107 50.801

Columbines near the pass.

East side legal for unlicensed.

Pass can open as early as July.
Photo by Brian Powell

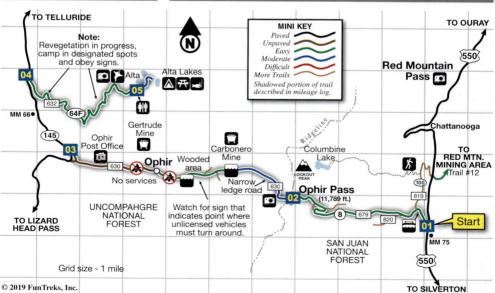

TO TELLURIDE

Note:
Revegetation in progress, camp in designated spots and obey signs.

N

TO OURAY

MINI KEY
Paved
Unpaved
Easy
Moderate
Difficult
More Trails
Shadowed portion of trail described in mileage log.

04
632
64F
MM 66
145
03
630
Ophir Post Office
Gertrude Mine
Ophir
No services
Wooded area
Alta
05
Alta Lakes

Carbonero Mine

Columbine Lake

LOOKOUT PEAK
Ridgeline

Red Mountain Pass

Chattanooga

TO RED MTN. MINING AREA
Trail #12

550

Narrow ledge road
630
Ophir Pass
(11,789 ft.)
8
679
820
100
819
02

UNCOMPAHGRE NATIONAL FOREST

Watch for sign that indicates point where unlicensed vehicles must turn around.

TO LIZARD HEAD PASS

SAN JUAN NATIONAL FOREST

01 **Start**
MM 75
550

TO SILVERTON

Grid size - 1 mile

Upper section of trail is narrow and steep.

Clear Lake near 12,000 ft. elevation.

No significant structures at Bandora Mine.

Historical Highlight: *South Mineral Creek, like so many other areas around Silverton, was the site of silver strikes in the early 1880s. The Bandora Mine, however, was mined much later during World War II. It shut down in 1950. A 1945 article in the* Silverton Standard *tells the story of Wilbur Tharp Maxwell, a soldier who returned safely from World War II only to be killed in the mine in 1945.*

Overview: Beautiful valley close to Silverton offers great hiking, biking and fishing. Spectacular climb to high mountain lake with beautiful seasonal wildflowers. Several large campgrounds along South Mineral Creek suitable for motorhomes and large campers. This area is very popular for fishing and camping. Minimal structures remain at Bandora Mine, but the drive is fun.

Rating: Easy. Mostly wide graded road. Climb to Clear Lake is the hardest part with steep, rutted and narrow switchbacks. Suitable for any high-clearance stock SUVs with low range and a confident driver.

Stats: Length: 8.1 miles to lake. Add 3.3 miles to the end of F.S. 585. Time: 2 to 3 hours. High point: 11,950 ft. Best time of year: Late June-September.

Current Conditions: San Juan Mountains Center in Silverton. Call (970) 387-5530 (closed in winter).

Getting There: Head north from Silverton on U.S. 550 about 2 miles. Turn left on well marked C.R. 7.

MILEAGE LOG:

0.0 Zero trip odometer **[Rev. Miles]**
Head west on C.R. 7 past many camping areas located along Mineral Creek. **[8.1]**
01 N37 49.094 W107 42.150

3.7 Turn right uphill on C.R.12 (F.S. 815). The first 3 miles do not require 4WD, but when the road narrows, you'll want low range for power. The road may intimidate novice drivers. **[4.4]**
02 N37 48.330 W107 45.778

7.8 Flattens out at top. Bear right and go around smaller first lake. **[0.3]**

8.1 Arrive at small parking area at Clear Lake. To see Bandora Mine, return to Waypoint 02. **[0.0]**
03 N37 49.570 W107 46.920

0.0 Zero trip odometer
At Waypoint 02, turn right and continue west on main road, F.S. 585, towards South Mineral Campground. **[3.3]**

0.6 Continue straight. Campground on left. Popular Ice Lake hiking trail starts from parking lot on right. **[2.7]**

0.8 Continue straight. Waterfall on right. **[2.5]**

2.9 Continue straight. Bandora Mine on right. **[0.4]**

3.0 Continue straight. Road on left has camping and fishing. **[0.3]**

3.2 Cross shallow water crossing. **[0.1]**

3.3 Road forks and ends at dispersed camp spots along edge of forest. **[0.0]**
04 N37 46.828 W107 48.235

Road narrows as you climb.

Seasonal wildflowers at lake.

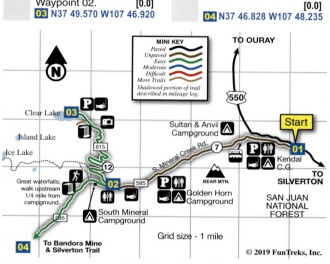

MINI KEY
Paved
Unpaved
Easy
Moderate
Difficult
More Trails
Shadowed portion of trail described in mileage log.

TO OURAY

550

Start

Clear Lake **03**

Island Lake

Ice Lake

815

12

585

Great waterfalls; walk upstream 1/4 mile from campground.

02

585

04 To Bandora Mine & Silverton Trail

South Mineral Campground

Golden Horn Campground

BEAR MTN.

Sultan & Anvil Campground

S. Mineral Creek Rd.

7

Kendal C.G.

TO SILVERTON

SAN JUAN NATIONAL FOREST

Grid size - 1 mile

© 2019 FunTreks, Inc.

Springtime brings many colors.

Several small water crossings between Waypoint 02 and 04.

Hidden waterfall below Waypoint 02.

Passing can be challenging in some spots.

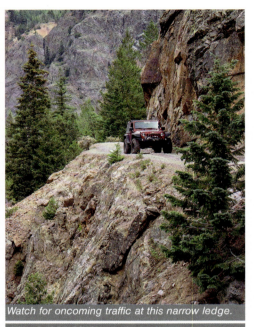
Watch for oncoming traffic at this narrow ledge.

Historical Highlight: *The town of Mineral Point (a.k.a. Mineral City), located near the San Juan Chief Mill, existed during a period from 1873 to the 1890s. It served as a mid point stop for prospectors heading for what would soon become the town of Ouray. Stagecoaches and wagons used this road before Highway 550 existed. Side roads, south of Waypoints 03 and 04, once ran through Mineral Point. As you drive through the area, please respect what remains.*

Overview: From Ouray, this is the quickest and most direct way to the Alpine Loop and Engineer Pass, but it is also the most difficult. Road climbs up scenic narrow canyon and accesses Poughkeepsie Gulch and Mineral Point. Hidden waterfalls at Poughkeepsie entrance. This popular trail has limited parking at start and can get quite congested on busy weekends.

Rating: Difficult. Starts out quickly with difficult spot that has optional easier lines. Rocky and steep in places, especially after Waypoint 02. Stock 4x4 SUVs can do it with careful tire placement and patience. No room to pass along several sections of narrow ledge roads. High clearance, low range and skid plates recommended.

Stats: Length: 7 miles. Time: 1 to 2 hours. High point: 12,080 ft. Best time of year: June-Sept.

Current Conditions: Uncompahgre N.F., Ouray R.D. Call (970) 240-5300. In summer call San Juan Mountain Center in Silverton at (970) 387-5530.

Getting There: From Beaumont Hotel in Ouray, head south 3.8 miles on Highway 550 and turn left at sign for Alpine Loop (C.R. 18).

MILEAGE LOG:

START

0.0 Zero trip odometer [Rev. Miles]
Follow a wide, rocky road
uphill. [7.0]
01 N37 59.310 W107 38.956

0.8 Cross narrow shelf road
along cliff. Watch for
oncoming traffic because
there is no room to pass.
[6.2]

1.6 Continue straight past
Mickey Breene Mine. [5.4]

2.4 Stay left uphill over large
rock outcrop. Poughkeep-
sie Gulch is to right. Look
for hidden waterfall below
and to the right. [4.6]
02 N37 58.017 W107 37.640

4.1 Small shed on left marks
location of Des Ouray
Mine. [2.9]

4.3 Bear left uphill. Camping
to right. [2.7]

5.2 Bear left uphill. Straight
goes to San Juan Chief
Mill and Mineral Point
(more difficult). [1.8]
03 N37 57.715 W107 35.738

5.8 Vault toilet on right and
view of San Juan Chief
Mill below. [1.2]

6.1 Continue straight. Road
to right goes to Mineral
Point. [0.9]

7.0 After trail flattens out, you
intersect with C.R. 2. Left
goes to Engineer Pass,
Trail #14; right goes to
Cinnamon Pass, Trail #15,
and Silverton. [0.0]
04 N37 57.437 W107 34.529

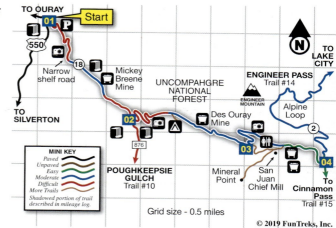

MINI KEY
Paved
Unpaved
Easy
Moderate
Difficult
More Trails
Shadowed portion of trail
described in mileage log.

Grid size - 0.5 miles

© 2019 FunTreks, Inc.

ATV explores Mineral Point area.

Switchbacks after Wpt. 02.

Trail follows Mineral Creek.

Poughkeepsie Gulch

Group waits their turn to try obstacle at Waypoint 03.

Photo by Roger Marquez

Trail climbs valley towards the pass.

Upper part of trail winds along the edge of Lake Como. This photo was taken from Hurricane Pass.

Overview: Scenic, remote valley offers variety of challenges for hard-core enthusiast. Most come to try their luck at the main obstacle at Waypoint 03 or just to watch others. Snow is usually not plowed, so trail opens later in the season. Stay off trail during wet periods. Connects to Trails #11 and #13.

Rating: Difficult. Uphill direction described here. Easier going downhill. Can be muddy at the bottom during wet periods. One long, steep climb of loose rock is challenging without lockers. Winch points available at obstacle. ATVs should use alternate route to avoid obstacle.

Stats: Length: 4.1 miles. Time: About 1 hour in a properly equipped vehicle. High point: 12,500 ft. Best time of year: Late July-September.

Current Conditions: Uncompahgre N.F., Ouray R.D. Call (970) 240-5300.

Getting There: From Beaumont Hotel in Ouray, head south 3.8 miles on Highway 550 and turn left at sign for Alpine Loop and Engineer Pass (County Road 18). Follow Mineral Creek, Trail #9, located on page 38, uphill 2.4 miles and turn right at sign for Poughkeepsie Gulch. To drive trail downhill, access via Trails #11 or #13.

0.0 Zero trip odometer **[Rev. Miles]** Head south from Mineral Creek, Trail #9. Stay out of muddy spots along side of trail. **[4.1]** **01** N37 58.027 W107 37.632

0.2 Driver's choice. Left goes up to waterfall. **[3.9]**

1.5 Driver's choice. We stayed left. **[2.6]**

1.8 Camp spots on right. **[2.3]**

2.1 Continue straight. Lesser road on left goes to mine. **[2.0]**

2.2 Continue straight up steep hill with loose rock. Ignore lesser trail to right. **[1.9]**

2.6 At top of hill, stay right. Left is alternate route to Lake Como. **[1.5]** **02** N37 56.000 W107 37.320

2.8 Steep rock has no bypass, turn around and use alternate route if you can't make it. Winch if necessary. Trail turns south after obstacle. **[1.3]** **03** N37 55.920 W107 37.550

2.9 Select from various challenging driver's choices. All trails eventually come back together. **[1.2]**

3.5 Alternate route joins on left. **[0.6]**

4.1 Intersect with major road. Left goes over California Pass to Animas Forks. Right goes over Hurricane Pass to Corkscrew Gulch, Trail #11. Right also goes to Gladstone and Silverton. **[0.0]** **04** N37 55.224 W107 37.192

Get FREE trail updates & GPS downloads at www.FunTreks.com

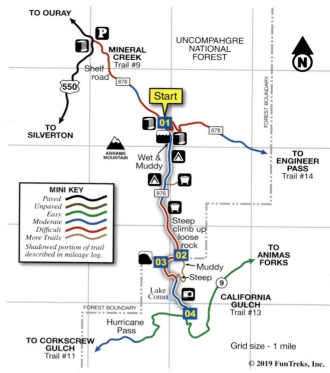

TO OURAY

P

MINERAL CREEK
Trail #9

Shelf road

550

878

UNCOMPAHGRE NATIONAL FOREST

N

FOREST BOUNDARY

Start

01

878

878

TO SILVERTON

ABRAMS MOUNTAIN

Wet & Muddy

TO ENGINEER PASS
Trail #14

MINI KEY
Paved
Unpaved
Easy
Moderate
Difficult
More Trails
Shadowed portion of trail described in mileage log.

876

Steep climb up loose rock

02
03
←Muddy
←Steep

9

TO ANIMAS FORKS

CALIFORNIA GULCH
Trail #13

Lake Como

04

FOREST BOUNDARY

Hurricane Pass

TO CORKSCREW GULCH
Trail #11

Grid size - 1 mile

© 2019 FunTreks, Inc.

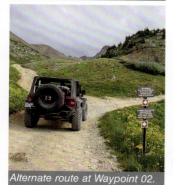

Alternate route at Waypoint 02.

This section of loose rock is usually very wet.

ATVs near the top after climbing steep switchbacks. Amazing views in every direction.

Large staging area at start of trail on Hwy. 550.

Historical Highlight: Just south of where Corkscrew Gulch leaves U.S. 550, several roads wind around in the trees. Here and there, a building can be found. This is all that remains of the once important mining town of Ironton. In 1890, the town provided supplies for many rich mines in the area and had a population of over 300. The town had its own water system, an electric plant, fire department and post office. The town managed to survive long after the silver market collapsed around the turn of the century. People actually lived in Ironton until the 1960s. The lumber from the buildings was carted off over the years, so not much remains.

Overview: This scenic trail cuts through the heart of old mining country as it winds between Red Mountain #1 and #2. Watch for logging trucks on lower part of trail. You can park and camp at bottom end of trail off Highway 550. From the bottom, you can also explore Gray Copper Gulch, which is left at the first major fork, marked as Brown Mountain. Trails become impassable in the winter season.

Rating: Easy when dry. The road is wide and graded most of the way; however, one section of narrow switchbacks at the top may be intimidating to novice drivers. If wet, the trail becomes more difficult due to slippery clay soil.

Stats: Length: Corkscrew is 4.8 miles. Add 2.3 for Hurricane Pass. Time: 1 to 2 hours in good weather. High point: 12,407 ft. Best time: Late June-Sept.

Current Conditions: Uncompahgre N.F., Ouray R.D. (970) 240-5300. BLM Gunnison Field Office (970) 642-4940.

Getting There: From south end of Ouray, head south 7.8 miles on U.S. 550 and turn left at what appears to be a dam. There's a wood bridge and large parking area on the left. If you are coming from Silverton through Gladstone, Poughkeepsie Gulch or California Gulch, you will drive the trail from top to bottom starting at C.R. 10.

START MILEAGE LOG:

0.0 Zero trip odometer [Rev. Miles]
Head south from Highway 550 through parking and camping areas. [4.8]
01 N37 56.343 W107 40.295

0.1 Stay right following signs for Corkscrew Gulch. [4.7]

1.0 Continue straight. [3.8]

1.2 Road plowed through mining area. [3.6]

1.5 Continue straight. Ignore lesser road on left. [3.3]
02 N37 55.377 W107 40.516

2.8 Pass toilet. Begin climbing switchbacks. [2.0]

3.7 Continue straight at high point. Great views. [1.1]
03 N37 54.392 W107 39.658

4.7 After passing another toilet, bear right. [0.1]

4.8 Reach C.R. 10. [0.0]
04 N37 54.620 W107 38.719

0.0 Zero trip odometer
Bear left for Hurricane Pass. Right goes downhill to Gladstone. [2.3]

1.1 Bear left. Right is easy side trip that eventually dead-ends. [1.2]
05 N37 54.834 W107 37.723

1.6 Bear right. [0.7]

1.7 Continue straight across Hurricane Pass. [0.6]

2.3 Intersect with top of Poughkeepsie Gulch, Trail #10, on left. Right goes over California Gulch, Trail #13, to Animas Forks. [0.0]
06 N37 55.224 W107 37.192

Looking down on Como Lake from Hurricane Pass.

First vault toilet is a popular stopping place.

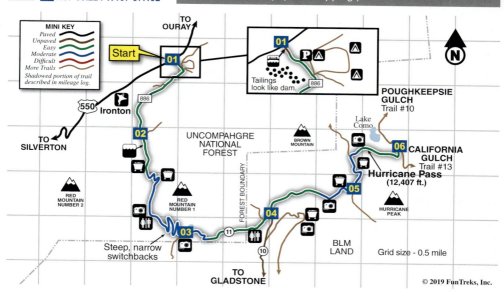

© 2019 FunTreks, Inc.

43

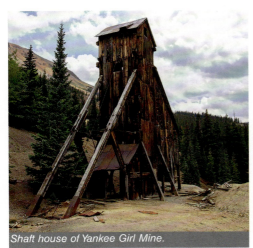

Shaft house of Yankee Girl Mine.

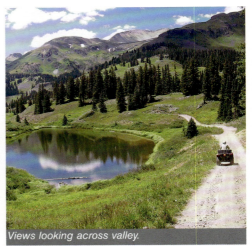

Views looking across valley.

Easy high route with 360-degree views.

Historical Highlight: Don't miss an opportunity to see the Red Mountain Peaks at sunset. Their fluorescent red and yellow glow is unlike anything you've ever seen. To prospectors back in 1879, that glow was the promise of vast riches. Indeed, over the next two decades, fortunes were extracted from these mountains in the form of gold, silver, lead and copper. No less than six towns—Chattanooga, Red Mountain City, Guston, Hudson Town, Rogerville and Ironton—grew out of this promising valley. Fortunately, many important mine buildings from that golden era are still standing.

Overview: The northern portion of this route takes you on a historic tour of the Red Mountain mining district and a townsite once known as Guston. Route features the often photographed shaft house of the Yankee Girl Mine. Some of the road follows an old grade of the Silverton Railroad. The southern portion continues south on U.S. Basin Road and provides high views of U.S. 550 and all surrounding mountains.

Rating: Easy. A fun, meandering road covering a variety of terrain from graded gravel to narrow two-track. Suitable for all stock 4x4 SUVs with moderate ground clearance. Do not drive this route during wet periods. Northern half has many side roads and can be a bit

confusing without a good map. Stay on designated trails, no open riding areas.

Stats: Length: 9.1 miles. Time: 2 to 3 hours. High point: 12,100 ft. Best time of year: Late June-Sept.

Current Conditions: San Juan Mountains Center in Silverton. Call (970) 387-5530 (closed in winter).

Getting There: From the Beaumont Hotel in Ouray, head south 10.0 miles on U.S. 550. Turn left 0.8 mile south of milepost 84 on marked C.R. 31 at the end of a tight switchback. The southern exit point is 5.5 miles north of Silverton and 0.7 mile north of the turn for Ophir Pass, Trail #7.

START MILEAGE LOG:

0.0 Zero trip odometer [Rev. Miles]
Exit Highway 550 east on C.R. 31. Road winds downhill and crosses 2 bridges. Swing left uphill after the 2nd bridge. [3.2]
01 N37 55.306 W107 41.920

0.9 Bear right. Left goes to mines. [2.3]

1.1 Continue straight past Yankee Girl Mine. Road swings left then right up rough switchback. [2.1]

2.1 National Bell Mine on right. Turn left and climb short distance, then turn right. If you miss this little jog, you'll exit to Highway 550. [1.1]
02 N37 54.240 W107 42.191

2.3 Stay right. You'll soon exit the woods and go past a pond and Longfellow Mine. [0.9]

3.0 Follow most traveled road to Highway 550. [0.2]

3.2 To continue on southern part of this trail, stay left follow C.R. 14 east. [0.0]
03 N37 53.765 W107 42.812
Zero trip odometer

0.0 From Wpt. 03, head east on C.R. 14 a few hundred feet. [5.9]

0.1 Turn right following F.S. 825. Continue south. [5.8]
04 N37 53.740 W107 42.740

0.6 After the road swings east, turn right. [5.3]
05 N37 53.450 W107 42.440

1.0 Jog left then right around a cabin. [4.9]

1.3 Road drops downhill and crosses small creek. After steep climb, road levels out across a high scenic ridge. [4.6]

3.0 Road turns right and drops downhill. [2.9]

3.8 After road turns south, avoid lesser roads to left. Drop downhill and swing left through Brooklyn Mine. [2.1]
06 N37 51.730 W107 42.960

5.9 After a long descent on wide road, you reach Highway 550 south of mile marker 76. [0.0]
07 N37 51.491 W107 43.441

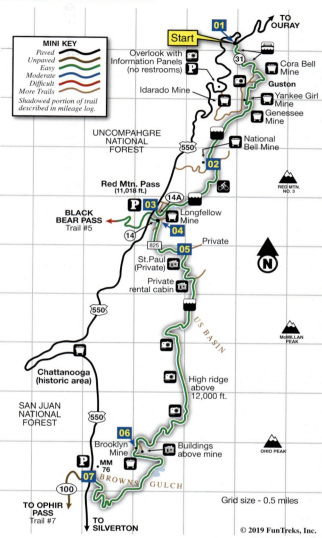

MINI KEY
Paved
Unpaved
Easy
Moderate
Difficult
More Trails
Shadowed portion of trail described in mileage log.

TO OURAY

Start

Overlook with Information Panels (no restrooms)

Cora Bell Mine

Guston

Idarado Mine

Yankee Girl Mine

Genessee Mine

UNCOMPAHGRE NATIONAL FOREST

National Bell Mine

RED MTN. NO. 3

Red Mtn. Pass (11,018 ft.)

14A

BLACK BEAR PASS
Trail #5

Longfellow Mine

14

825

Private

St. Paul (Private)

Private rental cabin

McMILLAN PEAK

N

US BASIN

Chattanooga (historic area)

SAN JUAN NATIONAL FOREST

High ridge above 12,000 ft.

OHIO PEAK

Brooklyn Mine

Buildings above mine

MM 76

BROWNS GULCH

Grid size - 0.5 miles

100

TO OPHIR PASS
Trail #7

TO SILVERTON

© 2019 FunTreks, Inc.

Northern half passes through one of the most historic mining areas in Colorado.

California Gulch

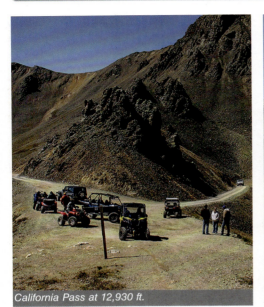
California Pass at 12,930 ft.

Old truck on right at 1.0 mile point.

Lower part of California Gulch.

Historical Highlight: *Animas Forks was active between 1875 and the early 1920s. In 1885, its summer population reached a high of 450 people. The Silverton Northern Railroad reached the town in 1904 when the giant Gold Prince Mill was built. The mill lasted only six years before it was closed.*

Overview: East end of trail starts at historic Animas Forks Ghost Town, gateway to the Alpine Loop. A remote, memorable drive with many well-preserved mine buildings. Awesome views. Trails not passable in winter.

Rating: Easy. Road is in good condition most of the summer. Heavy snow on east side of California Pass is usually plowed by late June. Low range recommended for upper portion of trail.

Stats: Length: 4.6 miles. Time: About an hour one way. High point: 12,930 ft. Best time of year: Late June-Sept.

Current Conditions: Contact the San Juan Mountains Center in Silverton at (970) 387-5530 (closed in winter).

Getting There: From northeast end of Silverton, bear right on C.R. 2. Follow signs to Alpine Loop. After 11.4 miles, reach fork at Waypoint 01.

MILEAGE LOG:

0.0 Zero trip odometer [Rev. Miles]
Turn left and go past vault toilets and Animas Forks parking area. Continue north and follow trail as it turns west past the large Columbus Mill. **[4.6]**
01 N37 55.600 W107 33.794

1.0 Road on right goes to flat area with old truck. **[3.6]**

1.3 Go past massive Frisco Mill at entrance to Bagley Tunnel. **[3.3]**

1.8 Continue straight. Road to Picayune and Placer Gulches, Trail #16, goes left. The road swings south and climbs through a broad valley. **[2.8]**
02 N37 55.905 W107 35.400

1.9 Continue straight past lesser road on left. **[2.7]**

3.9 Road turns uphill to west and starts earnest climb towards California Pass. In early season, you will not be able to proceed if road is not plowed. **[0.7]**

4.6 California Pass. Looking west, you can see a wide road to the left climbing to Hurricane Pass, Trail #11. To the right is Pough-keepsie Gulch, Trail #10, descending past Lake Como. **[0.0]**
03 N37 55.064 W107 37.048

Frisco Mill. Please leave everything as you find it.

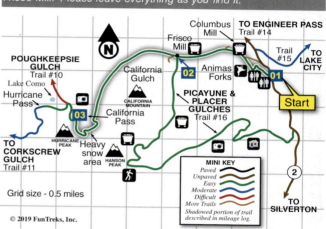

© 2019 FunTreks, Inc.

Grid size - 0.5 miles

MINI KEY
Paved
Unpaved
Easy
Moderate
Difficult
More Trails
Shadowed portion of trail described in mileage log.

Large parking area at the base of Animas Forks ghost town. Popular gathering point on weekends.

Watch for large flocks of sheep grazing in valley.

Forest Service on patrol in Jeep Rubicon.

Our stock Wrangler Sport and this Toyota 4Runner had no problems reaching 12,800-ft. Engineer Pass.

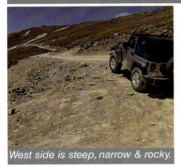

West side is steep, narrow & rocky.

Cabin at 4.4 miles open to public.

Historical Highlight: *Engineer Pass Road was a major stagecoach and freight route when it opened in the late 1870s. Like so many other roads in the area, it was built by Otto Mears as a toll road. Watch for kiosks along the route that describe key features. Take some time to see the town of Henson and the Ute-Ulay Mine. The mine was discovered in 1871 and sparked the development of Lake City.*

Overview: This trail, combined with Cinnamon Pass, Trail #15, constitutes most of the famous Alpine Loop. It is an exhilarating trip for drivers of all experience levels. There are many mines and points of historical interest along the route. The east side of the trail follows Henson Creek where you'll find excellent places to camp and fish.

Rating: Moderate. The majority of the drive, coming down the east side of the pass, is easy. However, the west side, between Wpts. 01 and 02, is very steep, narrow and rocky in spots. Caution should be used at all times especially in wet weather. Novice backcountry drivers may be intimidated. Don't drive if snow covered. You'll want 4-wheel drive with low range gearing and high ground clearance. No seasonal closures except by weather.

Stats: Length: Almost 21 miles. Time: 3 hours one way. High point: 12,800 ft. Best time of year: Mid June-Sept.

Current Conditions: Contact the San Juan Mountains Center in Silverton at (970) 387-5530 (closed in winter).

Getting There: From Ouray: Follow directions for difficult Mineral Creek, Trail #9. **From Silverton:** From the northeast end of town, take C.R. 2 a total of 14 miles northeast following signs for the Alpine Loop. The road gets rockier and steeper north of Animas Forks. **From Lake City:** Drive over Cinnamon Pass, Trail #15, from east to west, or just drive Engineer in reverse direction. To reach Engineer from Lake City, take 2nd Street west from Highway 149, then turn left on Bluff Street and follow signs to Alpine Loop.

MILEAGE LOG:

START

0.0 Zero trip odometer [Rev. Miles]
Head north on C.R. 2 where Mineral Creek, Trail #9, ends. Road is very steep and rocky. [20.6]
01 N37 57.446 W107 34.526

0.8 Hard left at rocky switchback. [19.8]

1.5 Narrow and steep. [19.1]

1.9 Stay right and follow shelf road around other side of mountain. Oh Point Overlook to left. [18.7]

2.3 Engineer Pass marked with kiosk. Road easy from here down. [18.3]
02 N37 58.458 W107 35.118

4.4 Swing left downhill. Photogenic cabin on right. [16.2]

4.7 Private "Thoreau's Cabin" on left. [15.9]

5.5 Continue straight. Hard right is entrance to Schafer Gulch 4x4 trail. [15.1]
03 N37 58.705 W107 33.203

6.2 Continue straight. Hard right is another way into Schafer Gulch. [14.4]

6.3 Vault toilet on right. [14.3]

7.1 Bonanza Empire Chief Mill on left. [13.5]

8.6 Rose Lime Kiln right. [12.0]

9.6 Whitmore Falls on right. Hike down to falls. [11.0]

11.4 Cabins on left are remains of historic Capitol City.[9.2]

11.5 Turn right where lesser road continues straight. [9.1]
04 N38 00.449 W107 27.994

13.5 Pass through steep-walled canyon. Henderson Creek on right. [7.1]

15.4 Toilet on left, followed by C.R. 23, Nellie Creek 4x4 road & hiking trail. [5.2]
05 N38 01.226 W107 24.043

16.7 Historic town of Henson and Ute-Ulay Mine. Picnic area, dam. [3.9]

19.8 Large OHV staging area on left. [0.8]
06 N38 01.302 W107 19.765

20.4 Come into town of Lake City. Turn right on 2nd St. at 3-way stop. [0.2]

20.6 State Hwy. 149, Gunnison Ave. Right goes to Cinnamon Pass, Trail #15. [0.0]
07 N38 01.643 W107 19.002

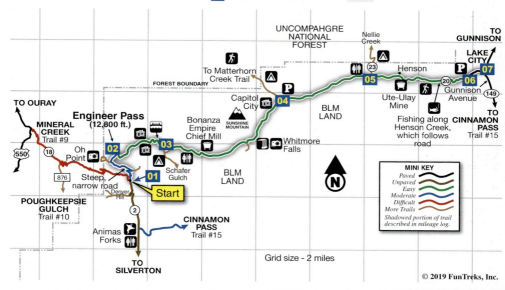

The town of Henson and the Ute-Ulay Mine. Brochures are available for a self-guided walking tour.

49

As you crest the hill at 4.1 miles you see this great view of American Basin below.

Restored buildings at Carson Ghost Town.

Historical Highlight: The town of Carson, on Wager Gulch Trail, was established in 1882 with an operating post office between 1889 and 1903. The town served the St. Jacobs Mine and others in the area, which produced gold, silver, lead, copper and zinc. The few buildings that remain are only a tiny part of the town that, at one time, was large enough to straddle the Continental Divide.

Overview: This trail, combined with Engineer Pass (Trail #14), constitutes most of the famous Alpine Loop. The western half of the trip passes many historic points and climbs to outstanding views. Side trip up Wager Gulch takes you to Carson Ghost Town. Cinnamon Pass Road also accesses beautiful American Basin, one of the best places in the area for wildflowers. On the west side, staging is available across from Eureka Campground (see map); on the east side, at Waypoint 06. No seasonal closures except by weather.

Rating: Moderate. Most of this trail is easy; however, the western end is steep and rocky in a few places. The side trip up Wager Gulch is more difficult. All roads, when dry, are suitable for any stock 4x4 SUV with moderate ground

clearance. The side trip up American Basin is borderline difficult.

Stats: Length: 27 miles plus 3.7 miles for Wager Gulch (one way). Time: 3 to 4 hours. High point: 12,640 ft. Best time of year: Early June-Sept.

Current Conditions: Contact the San Juan Mountains Center in Silverton at (970) 387-5530 (closed in winter).

Getting There: **From Ouray:** Follow directions for Mineral Creek, Trail #9, then head south 1.4 miles on C.R. 2 to Cinnamon Pass on left. **From Silverton:** Head north on C.R. 2 about 12 miles and turn right uphill after Animas Forks. **From Lake City:** Head south on Highway 149 and turn right on C.R. 30 after 2.3 miles.

MILEAGE LOG:

0.0 Zero trip odometer [Rev. Miles]
CINNAMON PASS:
From C.R. 2, northeast of Animas Forks, head east uphill following signs to Cinnamon Pass. [27.0]
01 N37 56.034 W107 34.117

2.2 Cinnamon Pass. Continue east downhill. [24.8]

4.1 Great view of American Basin straight ahead.[22.9]

4.5 Stay Left. Road that joins on right goes to American Basin, a great side trip that offers more challenge. [22.5]
02 N37 55.873 W107 30.859

6.0 Pass through Burrows Park/White Cross/Tellurium. [21.0]

7.4 Copper Creek hiking trail on left. Small roofless cabin on right. [19.6]

8.1 Continue straight past parking area with toilet. Hiking trails on both sides of road. [18.9]
03 N37 56.216 W107 27.645

11.1 Continue straight. Walk to overlook of Sherman Townsite on right. [15.9]

12.2 Continue straight. Road on right goes to Sherman Townsite. [14.8]
04 N37 54.224 W107 24.710

13.3 Continue straight. Mill Creek F.S. Campground on right. [13.7]

13.9 Vault toilet on right. [13.1]

15.1 Wager Gulch on right. (See separate description at right.) [11.9]
05 N37 54.356 W107 21.630

17.4 Go past Williams Creek F.S. Campground. [9.6]

19.1 Staging area on left. [7.9]
06 N37 56.344 W107 18.892

23.1 Stay left on paved road where C.R. 33 goes right across bridge. [3.9]

25.9 Beautiful Lake San Cristobal on right. [1.1]

27.0 State Highway 149. [0.0]
07 N37 59.986 W107 17.837
Left 2.3 miles goes into Lake City, where you can connect to Engineer Pass, Trail #14.

0.0 Zero trip odometer at Wpt. 05
WAGER GULCH:
Head south on C.R. 36 following sign to Carson townsite. [3.7]

0.1 Continue straight. Avoid private drives. [3.6]

1.7 Stay right uphill. Now on Gunnison F.S. 568. [2.0]

3.5 Stay left and cross creek. [0.2]

3.7 Carson Ghost Town. [0.0] Many miles of roads to explore beyond this point.
08 N37 52.130 W107 21.740

MINI KEY
Paved
Unpaved
Easy
Moderate
Difficult
More Trails
Shadowed portion of trail described in mileage log.

© 2019 FunTreks, Inc.

Grid size - 2 miles

The east side descent from Cinnamon Pass is rocky in spots but fairly gradual.

We recommend optional 0.7-mile side trip to Sound Democrat Mill (rated moderate).

Stamps are amazingly well preserved inside.

Historical Highlight: The Treasure Mountain Gold Mining Company was active during the early 1900s, which explains why buildings here are still in relatively good condition. The Sound Democrat Mill is one of the best preserved examples of an amalgamation stamp mill on public lands in the western United States. It was built in 1906 with one stamp mill and later expanded to four. Inside you'll find much of the original equipment preserved. Please, once inside, just look and take pictures. Absolutely, do not climb around on things or remove anything.

Overview: Beautiful high views with historic mines and buildings directly along the route. Two major mine structures featured on this trail include the Treasure Mountain Gold Mining Company and the well-preserved Sound Democrat Mill. Interesting side roads to explore left at Waypoint 02. No seasonal closures except by weather.

Rating: Easy. The trail is a bit steep and narrow at the beginning, but the road is relatively smooth. Side roads are mostly moderate. Suitable for stock, high clearance 4x4 SUVs and pickup trucks.

Stats: Length: 6.5 miles plus 0.7 for side trip to Sound Democrat Mill. Time: 2 hours. High point:12,680 ft. Best time to go: Mid June-Sept.

Current Conditions: Contact the San Juan Mountains Center in Silverton at (970) 387-5530 (closed in winter).

Getting There: From the northeast end of Silverton, bear right on C.R. 2 and follow signs to Alpine Loop. After 10.5 miles, make a hard left uphill, almost reversing direction, on C.R. 9. This spot is about a mile before Animas Forks.

START

MILEAGE LOG:

0.0 Zero trip odometer **[Rev. Miles]**
Steep and narrow at the start. Try to avoid vehicles coming down. **[6.5]**
01 N37 54.980 W107 33.485

0.4 Bear right uphill. Left is network of fun roads to explore. **[6.1]**
02 N37 54.724 W107 33.585

1.1 On left is cluster of building of the Treasure Mtn. Gold Mining Co. **[5.4]**

1.4 Follow road hard right uphill. Straight goes back downhill to Wpt. 02. **[5.1]**
03 N37 54.715 W107 34.457

3.6 After traversing side of mountain on narrow shelf, you reach high flat area. Stay right. Left ends just over the hill. This begins your descent into Placer Gulch. **[2.9]**

4.0 Turn hard right and follow switchbacks downhill. **[2.5]**

4.6 Stay left to continue down Placer Gulch. **[1.9]**
04 N37 54.610 W107 36.000
(Right at Wpt. 04 is short recommended side trip to Sound Democrat Mill, pictured at left. This side road is rated moderate at the bottom.)

4.8 Stay left. Loop on right has distant view of Sound Democrat Mill below. **[1.7]**

6.5 Placer Gulch runs into California Gulch. **[0.0]**
05 N37 55.896 W107 35.392
Right goes to Animas Fork Ghost Town and back to Silverton. Left goes to California Pass and beyond.

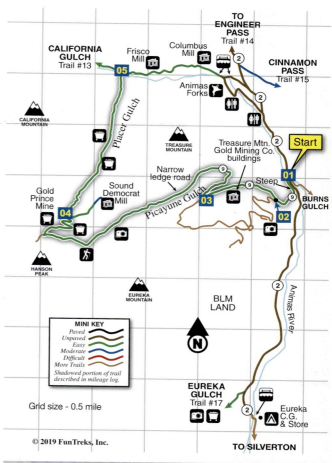

TO ENGINEER PASS Trail #14

CALIFORNIA GULCH Trail #13

Frisco Mill

Columbus Mill

CINNAMON PASS Trail #15

05

Animas Forks

CALIFORNIA MOUNTAIN

Placer Gulch

Treasure Mtn. Gold Mining Co. buildings

Start

TREASURE MOUNTAIN

Narrow ledge road

9

Steep

9

01

BURNS GULCH

Gold Prince Mine

Sound Democrat Mill

Picayune Gulch

03

02

04

HANSON PEAK

EUREKA MOUNTAIN

BLM LAND

2

Animas River

MINI KEY
Paved
Unpaved
Easy
Moderate
Difficult
More Trails
Shadowed portion of trail described in mileage log.

Grid size - 0.5 mile

N

© 2019 FunTreks, Inc.

EUREKA GULCH Trail #17

2

Eureka C.G. & Store

TO SILVERTON

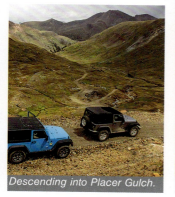
Descending into Placer Gulch.

Buildings at the Treasure Mountain Gold Mining Company.

Eureka Gulch

Eureka Campground is built on the original Eureka Townsite just south of the start of trail.

Eureka Campground Store.

Tram station still standing on this visit.

Historical Highlight: *Eureka was established in 1875 with an active post office until 1942. Sunnyside Mine produced over $50 million. Mines under Lake Emma collapsed in 1978 and the lake drained. No one was hurt, but it took 2 years to clean up the damage. Judge Terry's Midway Mill was the final destination for ore in the early tramway system. The Angle Tram Station was part of a second tram system to carry ore to the newer Sunnyside Mill. The foundations of this mill can be seen on left as you start up the trail.*

Overview: View remains of giant Sunnyside Mill at bottom, then follow road to Sunnyside Mine site at the top. Take side trip to see remains of Judge Terry's Midway Mill. Photograph unique Angle Tram Station and waterfalls in the spring. Large parking lot with toilet along C.R. 2 at base of trail. No seasonal closures except by weather. Eureka Campground recommends you make reservations by email as follows: terri@eurekacampground.com.

Rating: Easy. Road is mildly rocky but fairly wide even at the top. Side trip on lower portion of trail is somewhat overgrown with one rocky water crossing just before Midway Mill. Main road is suitable for stock 4x4 SUVs. High clearance needed on side trip.

Stats: Length: 3.6 miles one way. Add 0.7 mile one way for side trip. Time: Allow 1 to 2 hours. High point: 12,600 ft. Best time of year: Late June-Sept.

Current Conditions: Contact the San Juan Mountains Center in Silverton at (970) 387-5530 (closed in winter).

Getting There: From the northeast end of Silverton, bear right on County Road 2 and follow signs to Alpine Loop. After 7.7 miles, road curves around campground at Eureka Townsite and crosses a bridge. Watch for wide road that joins on left 0.3 mile after major parking and staging area.

MILEAGE LOG:

0.0 *Zero trip odometer* [Rev. Miles]
EUREKA GULCH:
Follow wide gravel road
uphill. [3.6]
01 N37 53.120 W107 33.850
0.4 Road on left dead-ends in
short distance. [3.2]
1.1 Continue straight. Road
on left is side trip to Judge
Terry's Midway Mill, de-
scribed below. [2.5]
02 N37 52.977 W107 34.858
2.5 Short road goes left to flat
area below Angle Tram
Station. Great spot for
photos. Hiking to tram station is extremely difficult.
[1.1]
3.1 Stay right. [0.5]
3.6 Right goes to remains
of Sunnyside Mine. Left
goes to empty bowl that
was once Lake Emma.
[0.0]
03 N37 54.050 W107 36.872
0.0 *Zero trip odometer*
**SIDE TRIP TO JUDGE
TERRY'S MIDWAY MILL**
Head downhill from Way-
point 02. [0.7]
0.6 Water crossing. [0.1]
Ruins of Judge Terry's
Midway Mill on right.
0.7 Road continues short
distance to secluded
camp spot. Turn around
anytime. [0.0]

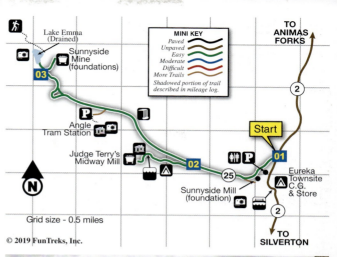

MINI KEY
Paved
Unpaved
Easy
Moderate
Difficult
More Trails
Shadowed portion of trail
described in mileage log.

Grid size - 0.5 miles

© 2019 FunTreks, Inc.

Roads now cross the dry lake bed of Lake Emma.

Midway Mill had collapsed.

Looking down on remains of Sunnyside Mill from edge of trail.

A light rain covers Silverton, view from Waypoint 04.

Sealed-off mine adit.

High roads are narrow in places.

Old train car near begining of trail.

Overview: Fun drive close to town of Silverton. Incredible high views of town from end of trail at Waypoint 04. Lots of mines and mine tailings. It's fun to watch the trains enter and leave town. At peak season, three trains come and go in the afternoon. Lots to do in town.

Rating: Moderate. Much is easy, but several places are bumpy and slow-going. No major obstacles. Use caution if you go out to Waypoint 04 where there is little room to turn around. Most high-clearance SUVs with an experienced driver can do it.

Stats: Length: Round trip returning to start is about 15 miles. Time: 3 to 4 hours. High point: 12,700 ft. Best time of year: Late June-Sept.

Current Conditions: Contact the San Juan Mountains Center in Silverton at (970) 387-5530 (closed in winter).

Getting There: Trail departs from east side of Silverton. Head northeast through center of town on Green Street and turn right on 14th Street. Go about 0.3 mile and cross bridge over Animas River. Trail goes right on C.R. 33.

MILEAGE LOG:

0.0 Zero trip odometer **[Rev. Miles]**
Head south on wide, graded C.R. 33. **[7.3]**
01 N37 48.664 W107 39.520

1.2 Continue straight. Lesser road joins on left. **[6.1]**

2.2 Old wooden train car on left. **[5.1]**

2.9 Bear left uphill. Right is side trip on C.R. 33A, an easy drive out to a large campspot. **[4.4]**
02 N37 46.984 W107 39.049

4.5 Hard left at large, sealed-off mine adit. **[2.8]**
03 N37 47.321 W107 37.818

5.4 Stop here at wide spot to turn around if you are uncomfortable continuing. To continue, follow shelf road around cell towers. Be cautious of traffic returning from overlook. **[1.9]**

5.6 Bear left. DO NOT attempt to go uphill to the right, very dangerous side trail. **[1.7]**

5.7 Overlook of Silverton with small turn around. **[1.6]**
04 N37 47.611 W107 38.645

6.9 Return to Wpt. 03 and continue straight. **[0.4]**

7.3 Driver's choice. Both short forks lead to mines. Explore and return to start of trail. **[0.0]**
05 N37 47.158 W107 37.422

Get FREE trail updates & GPS downloads at www.FunTreks.com

© 2019 FunTreks, Inc.

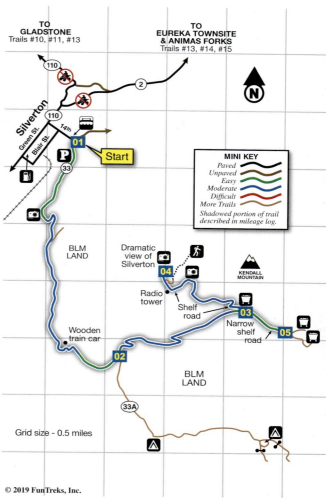

TO GLADSTONE
Trails #10, #11, #13

TO EUREKA TOWNSITE & ANIMAS FORKS
Trails #13, #14, #15

N

Silverton
Green St.
Blair St.
14th
110
2
33
01
Start

MINI KEY
Paved
Unpaved
Easy
Moderate
Difficult
More Trails
Shadowed portion of trail described in mileage log.

BLM LAND

Dramatic view of Silverton
04

KENDALL MOUNTAIN

Radio tower
Shelf road
03
Narrow shelf road
05

Wooden train car
02

BLM LAND

33A

Grid size - 0.5 miles

Mine adit at Waypoint 03.

Silverton is an authentic western town with lots to see and do.

Starting down south side of Stony Pass. Do not approach sheep, guard dogs will protect them.

Buffalo Boy Tram House.

Historical Highlight: Howardsville Townsite is located just north of the start; however, an active mining company now occupies this area. At its peak in the 1870s, Howardsville had about 30 buildings and 150 people. It had its own post office until 1939 and was Silverton's major rival for many years. The ore bucket that hangs over the road as you climb towards Stony Pass is part of a cable and tram system that starts at the Buffalo Boy Tram House.

Stony Pass was once a major supply route between Del Norte and Silverton. In 1882, the Denver and Rio Grande narrow gauge railroad was completed into Silverton and Stony Pass was abandoned.

Overview: This trail crosses the Continental Divide through an area rich in mining history. There are kiosks all along the route that explain points of interest. Buffalo Boy Tram House and Kite Lake are the highlights of the trip. Consider taking the Old Hundred Gold Mine Tour to learn about the history of the area. Road is open all year except during springtime if muddy.

Rating: Moderate. Mildly rocky and steep in a few places but suitable for aggressive high-clearance SUVs with low range. Pole Creek can get quite deep in the spring. The side trip up to Buffalo Boy Tram House is steep and narrow. The road to Kite Lake can get muddy, narrow, steep and rocky.

Stats: Length: 5.8 miles to Stony Pass. Another 12.1 miles to Kite Lake. Side trip to Buffalo Boy Tram House adds 1.5 miles one way. Time: Allow a full day for everything. High point: 12,650 ft. Best time of year: July-Sept.

Current Conditions: Contact the San Juan Mountains Center in Silverton at (970) 387-5530 or Rio Divide Ranger District (719) 657-3321 (call for road closure status).

Getting There: From Silverton, head northeast 4 miles on County Road 2. Turn right on C.R. 4 at Howardsville.

MILEAGE LOG:

0.0 Zero trip odometer [Rev. Miles]
Head southeast follow-
ing signs to Old Hundred
Gold Mine Tour. [5.8]
01 N37 50.140 W107 35.700

0.2 Stay left. Right bypasses
entrance to mine tour. [5.6]

1.0 Pass entrance to mine
tour. [4.8]

1.7 County Roads 3 and 4
join. Bear left uphill on
C.R. 3. [4.1]
02 N37 48.917 W107 34.700

3.3 Continue on main road.
Left is side trip to Buf-
falo Boy Tram House
described below. [2.5]
03 N37 49.007 W107 34.175

5.8 Stony Pass. [0.0]
04 N37 47.749 W107 32.966

0.0 Zero trip odometer
From Wpt. 04, continue
south over pass. [12.1]

0.4 Colorado Hiking Trail
crosses. [11.7]

5.4 Cattle guard. [6.7]

5.9 Cross Pole Creek if not
too deep. [6.2]

6.2 Turn right on C.R. 3A at
sign to Beartown. [5.9]
05 N37 45.729 W107 28.016

6.6 Head west and cross Pole
Creek again. [5.5]

10.4 Pass through site of
Beartown. Not much
remains. [1.7]
06 N37 43.230 W107 30.400

11.2 Continue straight. F.R.
787 goes left to camp
spots. [0.9]

11.7 Parking area for hiking
trail. [0.4]

12.1 Arrive at small cabin at
Kite Lake. Road continues
to other end of lake. Turn
around. [0.0]
07 N37 42.718 W107 31.510

0.0 Zero trip odometer

SIDE TRIP TO BUFFALO BOY TRAM HOUSE:
Head uphill on C.R. 3B. [1.5]

0.1 Bear right. Road narrows
in places with tight switchbacks. (Left is interesting
mine.) [1.4]

1.5 Buffalo Boy Tram House.
Turn around here. [0.0]
08 N37 48.573 W107 33.313

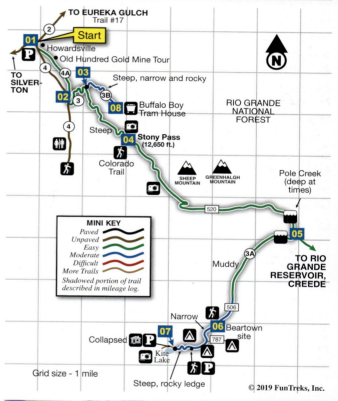

Wildflowers bloom along the edge of Kite Lake.

TO EUREKA GULCH
Trail #17

Start

01 P
Howardsville
Old Hundred Gold Mine Tour

TO SILVER-TON

03 Steep, narrow and rocky

3B

02

3

4A

4

08 Buffalo Boy Tram House

Steep

04 Stony Pass (12,650 ft.)

Colorado Trail

SHEEP MOUNTAIN
GREENHALGH MOUNTAIN

RIO GRANDE NATIONAL FOREST

Pole Creek (deep at times)

520

05 TO RIO GRANDE RESERVOIR, CREEDE

3A
Muddy

506

Narrow

07
Collapsed
Kite Lake

06 Beartown site
787

Steep, rocky ledge

MINI KEY
Paved
Unpaved
Easy
Moderate
Difficult
More Trails
*Shadowed portion of trail
described in mileage log.*

Grid size - 1 mile

© 2019 FunTreks, Inc.

Pole Creek was very shallow when we drove through it.

Green = Easy,   Blue = Moderate,   Red = Difficult, *= New

Grand Junction, Fruita, Gateway, Naturita

Area 2 is all new. Trails are on the Western Slope, south of I-70 around Grand Junction. For trails north of I-70 in this area, see our other Colorado book, *Guide to Northern Colorado Backroads & 4-Wheel-Drive Trails*.

Western Slope terrain is quite different than that east of the Continental Divide. The area is mostly sparsely populated rangeland and foothills with less pine forest, more junipers and more sagebrush. The soil typically contains more clay, which makes it slippery when wet.

Trail #25 is part of the larger Rim Rocker Trail, which is a popular backcountry route between Colorado and Moab, Utah. We've selected what we think is the most scenic and interesting portion of the route.

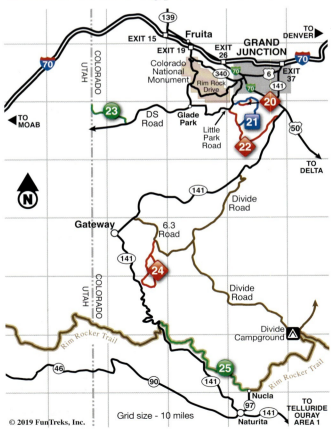

© 2019 FunTreks, Inc. Grid size - 10 miles

Unique red rock sandstone on *The Tabequache, Trail #22, rated difficult.*

Billings Canyon

"Table Rock" obstacle is very challenging. Pick a line that is best for your vehicle.

Photo by Jeff Bates

Photo by Jeff Bates

Taking the hard line on Gatekeeper.

Photo by Jeff Bates

Lunch break at the half-way point.

Overview: Officially opened in 2004, this trail was built to test the most capable vehicle. Offroaders travel long distances to be able to say they've driven Billings Canyon. Credit goes to Grand Junction Four Wheelers who keep this trail open, fun and challenging. Don't forget to try the Cut Off on your way out.

Rating: Difficult. This trail is extreme. Several obstacles have no easy lines and rock-stacking is frowned upon. A very skilled driver can do it with 35-inch tires, lockers, a winch and good articulation, but only if the easiest lines are taken. Do not attempt alone.

Stats: Length: Billings Canyon Jeep Trail by itself is 1.4 miles. Time: 2 to 3 hours. High point: 5,659 ft. Best time of year: spring and fall.

Current Conditions: BLM Grand Junction Office. Call (970) 244-3000.

Getting There: From Grand Junction, head west on Highway 340 about 1 mile. Turn left on Monument Road and then turn left again on D Road. D Road eventually turns south and becomes Rosevale Road. Turn right on Little Park Road and then drive another 4.2 miles to Third Flats Trailhead on your left.

START

MILEAGE LOG:

0.0 Zero trip odometer **[Rev. Miles]**
Head northeast on Third Flats Road, a 4WD road. Stay on main road ignoring lesser side roads. **[2.2]**
01 N39 00.077 W108 36.249

0.4 Continue straight where start of the Cut Off trail goes right downhill. **[1.8]**
02 N39 00.209 W108 35.858

0.6 Continue straight. Right is Billings Canyon Road and the exit of Billings Canyon Jeep Trail. **[1.6]**
03 N39 00.215 W108 35.686

2.2 Turn right downhill and look for Billings Canyon Jeep Trail sign on right at bottom of hill. This begins the extreme part. **[0.0]**
04 N39 00.472 W108 34.489

0.0 Zero trip odometer
Billings Cyn. Jeep Trail
From Wpt. 04 head up ravine. Note "Out of Bounds" signs.

0.2 Gatekeeper. Left is hardest line.

0.7 Poser Rock on right.

0.9 Roger's Wreck followed by Table Rock.

1.1 Crick's Rock, then Wicki Up.

1.2 Last obstacle Waterfall. Do not drive around.

1.4 Trail ends at "T" intersection. Turn right to return to Wpt. 03 and exit via Third Flats Road. Don't forget to try the Cut Off on the way out.

Get FREE trail updates & GPS downloads at www.FunTreks.com

Watch for rattlesnakes!

GRAND VALLEY JEEP CLUB
Please **DO NOT STACK ROCKS IN THIS AREA**
Follow posted signage.

DETAIL OF GRAND JUNCTION

70 Grand Ave.
Riverside Pkwy.
340
D Rd.
Monument Rd.
Little Park Road
Rosevale Rd.
S. 5th St.

TO GRAND JUNCTION (See detail at right.)

Little Park Road

Third Flats Road

Cut Off
02
03

P

01
Start

Waterfall

Third Flats Trailhead

TO BANGS CANYON STAGING AREA

ATV trails

Billings Canyon Road

To Bangs Canyon

BLM LAND

Third Flats Road

Third Flats Road

Gatekeeper
04

Billings Canyon Jeep Trail

Table Rock

Poser Rock

ONE WAY

Crick's Rock

The Fin

Roger's Wreck

Billings Canyon Road

BLM LAND

WINDMILL LOOP Trail #21

Grid size - 0.3 miles

MINI KEY
Paved
Unpaved
Easy
Moderate
Difficult
More Trails
Shadowed portion of trail described in mileage log.

© 2019 FunTreks, Inc.

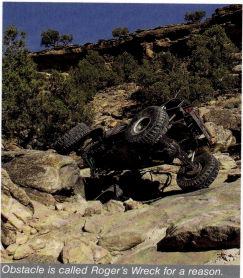
Obstacle is called Roger's Wreck for a reason.

There is no bypass to the Waterfall.

63

Scenic descent to Gunnison River at 4.5 miles.

The namesake windmill.

Most people just drive to river and turn around.

Narrowest part of shelf road—go slow.

Overview: Fun drive close to Grand Junction with views looking back at the town. Attractions include a stop on the shoreline of the river and the windmill, after which the trail is named. After visiting the windmill, you can return the way you came or go out difficult Trail #22, The Tabequache.

Rating: Moderate. Much is easy, but several places are bumpy and slow. No major obstacles. One narrow rocky shelf road. Read trail description for The Tabequache, Trail #22, before proceeding past Wpt. 05. SUVs with high-clearance, skid plates, low gears and a skilled driver can do the entire loop.

Stats: Length: Only 9 miles to reach Wpt. 05. Allow an hour. The entire loop to Bangs Canyon Trailhead is 17.6 miles. Time: 3 to 4 hours. High point: 6,160 ft. Best time: spring and fall.

Current Conditions: BLM Grand Junction Office. Call (970) 244-3000.

Getting There: From Grand Junction, head west on Hwy. 340 about 1 mile. Turn left on Monument Rd. and then turn left again on D Road. D Road eventually turns south and becomes Rosevale Road. Turn right on Little Park Road and drive another 4.2 miles to Third Flats Trailhead on left.

MILEAGE LOG:

0.0 Zero trip odometer **[Rev. Miles]**
Head east on Third Flats
Road. Follow more trav-
eled road ignoring side
trails.   **[6.3]**
01 N39 00.132 W108 36.438

0.4 Continue straight.   **[5.9]**

0.6 Continue straight. Right is
Billings Canyon Rd. and
the exit of Billings Canyon
Jeep Trail.   **[5.7]**
02 N39 00.215 W108 35.686

2.2 Continue straight where
Billings Road takes you to
the start of Billings Jeep
Trail.   **[4.1]**
03 N39 00.550 W108 34.419

3.8 Stay right.   **[2.5]**

4.3 Stay right again then
carefully cross narrow
shelf road. Do not pro-
ceed if wet.   **[2.0]**

4.6 Stay right where lesser
road goes left to dead
end.   **[1.7]**

6.1 Join wash then exit the
wash on the left.   **[0.2]**

6.3 Reach bottom of steep
rocky climb. Trail gets
rougher from here.   **[0.0]**
04 N39 00.580 W108 31.399

0.0 Zero trip odometer
From Wpt. 04 turn sharp
right up rocky hill. Trail
wanders along plateau
with occasional rocky
sections.   **[6.8]**

2.7 Turn left to visit Windmill
then return and continue
heading west.   **[4.1]**
05 N38 58.659 W108 32.523

6.7 Pass through fence line
then descend steep rocky
hill. (Point of no return. If
hill looks too difficult, do
not proceed.)   **[0.1]**

6.8 Reach "T" intersection
with The Tabequache,
Trail #22.   **[0.0]**
06 N38 56.923 W108 35.594
Turn right to exit using
directions on page 67
starting at Wpt. 03. Reach
Bangs Canyon Trailhead
at 4.4 miles. Do not at-
tempt unless you have a
capable vehicle and are a
skilled driver!

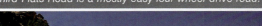
Third Flats Road is a mostly easy four-wheel-drive road.

Steep rocky climb at Waypoint 03.

65

Entrance from Hwy. 141 begins very rough.

Shelf road after the natural spring.

Bentonite soil should be avoided when wet.

Overview: The best of the Bangs Canyon Recreation Area can be found in this recently opened trail. It has a mix of everything, from high plateaus to narrow canyon shelf roads to a playground where you can test your vehicle's limits. The scenery gets more beautiful the further you drive on this trail. Trail was opened with the help of Grand Junction Four-Wheelers.

Rating: Difficult. Most of the southern part is easy to marginally moderate terrain. After Wpt. 02, trail gets more difficult with loose rock climbs and small challenging ledges. Hardest part between Wpt. 03 and 04 has driver's choices, but they were all similarly difficult when we drove it. Very high ground clearance is needed. Playground is optional. Do not attempt the trail when wet.

Stats: Length: 17 miles. Time: 4 to 5 hours. High point: 7,270 ft. Best time of year: spring and fall.

Current Conditions: BLM Grand Junction Office. Call (970) 244-3000.

Getting There: Head south on Hwy. 50 from Grand Junction about 10 miles and turn right on Highway 141. Drive another 1.3 miles to small access road on right. Staging can be found on south side. To drive in reverse, use directions from Trail #21, but continue past Third Flats Road another mile to Bangs Canyon Trailhead on left.

66

MILEAGE LOG:

0.0 Zero trip odometer [Rev. Miles]
Start at kiosk and head west up narrow rocky trail. [12.6]
01 N38 58.443 W108 27.716

0.4 Stay left where private trail goes right. [12.2]

5.5 First of 3 driver's choices. [7.1]

7.8 Stay left, side trail goes to overlook. [4.8]

9.0 Stay right following signs for Tabequache. ATV trail goes left. [3.6]
02 N38 54.468 W108 34.535

9.8 After loose, rocky downhill section, there's a steep, rocky climb. [2.8]

10.7 Stay left, then there's a small obstacle. [1.9]

12.6 Continue straight where Windmill Loop, Trail #21, goes right. [0.0]
03 N38 56.918 W108 35.599

0.0 Zero trip odometer at Wpt 03
Head north on easy road. [4.4]

0.3 Driver's choice past natural spring on left. Trail gets progressively more difficult after this. [4.1]

1.5 Stay left. Hell's Hole ATV trail on right. [2.9]

2.0 Stay right downhill. Trails eventually come together at bottom of ravine. [2.4]

2.3 Turn sharp left and climb back up. Follow arrows painted on slickrock. [2.1]
04 N38 58.621 W108 35.788

3.1 Playground on left, stay right to bypass. [1.3]

3.9 Stay right crossing wide slickrock. Look for opening in fence with sign. [0.5]

4.3 Continue straight. [0.1]

4.4 Reach Bangs Canyon Trailhead and staging area. [0.0]
05 N38 59.322 W108 37.046
To exit, continue to Little Park Road and turn right for Grand Junction, about 7 miles.

Get FREE trail updates & GPS downloads at www.FunTreks.com

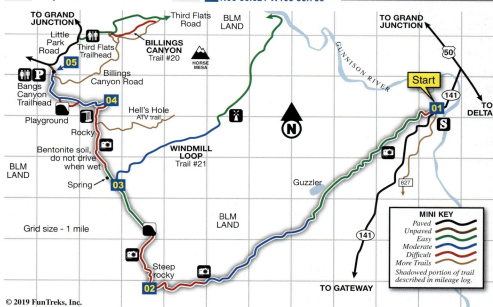

© 2019 FunTreks, Inc.

Grid size - 1 mile

MINI KEY
Paved
Unpaved
Easy
Moderate
Difficult
More Trails
Shadowed portion of trail described in mileage log.

Parts of trail look a lot like Moab.

Entrance to Playground is well marked.

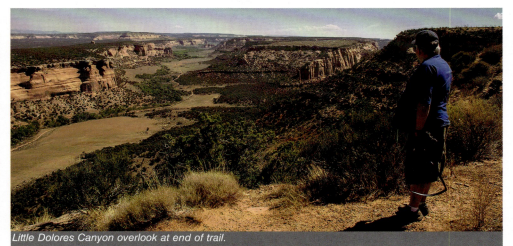
Little Dolores Canyon overlook at end of trail.

Keep an eye out for The Overhang on the right.

Most of the trail has trees blocking canyon view.

Overview: Remote in-and-out route with overlooks of Kings Canyon and Little Dolores Canyon. Add to that a trip through spectacular Colorado National Monument (fee area) and you are in for a full day of scenic views. Good dispersed camping along the trail. Unlicensed vehicles can stage at the intersection just before the start. To explore more, continue east on DS Road to the Dolores Triangle in Utah.

Rating: Easy. Variety of conditions from graded roads to narrow, rutted and sandy roads. Steep in a few places with small rocky ledges. Do not attempt if wet.

Stats: Length: 26 miles round trip. Time: 4 to 5 hours. High point: 7,270 ft. Best time of year: spring and fall.

Current Conditions: BLM Grand Junction Office. Call (970) 244-3000.

Getting There: Get off Interstate 70 at Exit 19. Head south on C.R. 340 and enter the Colorado National Monument (fee area) on your right. Continue through the park for 11 miles then turn right towards Glade Park. Go another 5 miles and turn right on DS Road. Start of trail is another 13.7 miles on the right just after private drive.

MILEAGE LOG:

START

0.0 Zero trip odometer **[Rev. Miles]**
Follow wide road north
past residence.   **[12.9]**
01 N38 57.134 W108 56.822

0.7 Stay left.   **[12.2]**

1.2 Turn left. Right goes to
Little Dolores Road. **[11.7]**
02 N38 58.099 W108 56.605

2.5 Stay left. Road on right
goes to a small window
arch.   **[10.4]**

3.2 Continue straight. Kings
Canyon on right.   **[9.7]**

3.9 Turn right downhill to
avoid private land.   **[9.0]**

6.7 Small undercut ledge with
a view on right named
The Overhang.   **[6.2]**

9.5 Drop down into valley
then continue east.   **[3.4]**

11.1 At triangle intersection
turn right. Left is private
ranch land.   **[1.8]**
03 N38 58.949 W109 02.918

12.5 Stay left at fork.   **[0.4]**

12.9 Reach Little Dolores
Canyon overlook. Road
continues to a camping
spot. When done, return
the way you came.   **[0.0]**
04 N39 00.464 W109 03.059

Small rocky ledge.

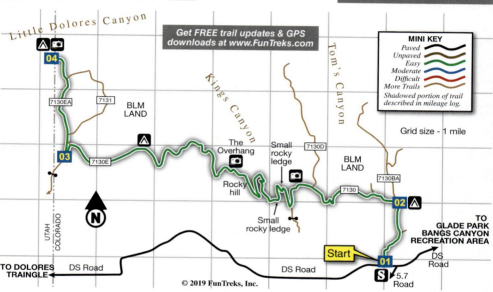

Get FREE trail updates & GPS
downloads at www.FunTreks.com

MINI KEY
Paved
Unpaved
Easy
Moderate
Difficult
More Trails
Shadowed portion of trail
described in mileage log.

Grid size - 1 mile

© 2019 FunTreks, Inc.

Our trip to the trailhead includes a scenic drive through Colorado National Monument (fee required).

Even dry bentonite is slippery on slopes like this.

Tricky narrow spot at Mike's Rock.

Photo by Jerry Smith

Lunchtime on winter snow run.

Overview: This trail is a popular route during "Rock Junction," Grand Junction's annual summertime 4x4 event. The trail is remote and seldom used the rest of the year, so trail conditions can worsen. The long loop is scenic with plenty of off-road challenges. Take a GPS and explore many other trails in the surrounding area. Be sure to fill up in Gateway before heading out.

Rating: Difficult. Several obstacles have no bypasses. The road is very rocky in spots due to excessive erosion of soft soils. Some sections of the trail have Bentonite clay which is slippery when wet or dry. One narrow spot along a shelf road forces you very close to the edge. Don't drive this trail by yourself.

Stats: Length: 16.6 miles. Time: About 4 hours. High point: 6,700 ft. Best time of year: spring and fall.

Current Conditions: BLM Grand Junction Office, Call (970) 244-3000.

Getting There: From Gateway: Head north on Hwy. 141 about 4 miles to 6.3 Road on right. **From Grand Junction:** Take Hwy. 50 south and turn right on Hwy. 141. Go about 39 miles to 6.3 Road on left.

From 6.3 Road: (Reference small map on pg. 71) Cross one-lane bridge and continue east. Pass through wash and eventually climb to high shelf road. At 5.8 miles stay left on 405. At 7.4 stay right on more-traveled 405. When you reach major intersection at 8.7 miles, continue straight on 405.3B to Waypoint 01 at 12.6 miles.

MILEAGE LOG:

START

0.0 Zero trip odometer [Rev. Miles]
Stay left following sign to
Calamity Camp.   [8.5]
01 N38 37.219 W108 51.692

0.7 Stay straight. Calamity
Camp on left.   [7.8]

1.3 Continue straight through
New Verde Mine. Lesser
road on left goes to more
buildings then loops back
to main road.   [7.2]

1.6 Stay straight.   [6.9]

2.2 Continue straight. Confusing network of roads on
right go up to unused
airstrip.   [6.3]
02 N38 35.721 W108 51.302

2.8 Stay right. Left goes to
cabin.   [5.7]

5.8 Continue straight where
road goes right.   [2.7]
03 N38 33.356 W108 51.049

7.4 Stay right. Left is private
ranch.   [1.1]

8.5 Reach small rest area
with good overlook of
La Sal Mountains.   [0.0]
04 N38 32.638 W108 51.900

0.0 Zero trip odometer
From Wpt. 04 continue
uphill to the right.   [8.2]

0.3 Twisted Drop.   [7.9]

1.6 Squeeze past Mike's
Rock on narrow shelf
road.   [6.6]

2.8 You reach Hog Back
washout, followed by
Drop-Off Corner.   [5.4]

4.0 Narrow spot called the
Squeeze.   [4.2]

4.8 Stay left uphill.   [3.4]

5.1 Turn right where left goes
to overlook.   [3.1]
05 N38 35.086 W108 52.207

6.1 Stay left, road gets easier.
Right goes to network of
trails that reach the airstrip and New Verde Mine
where you started.   [2.1]
06 N38 35.700 W108 52.004

8.2 Arrive back at Wpt. 01
where you started.   [0.0]

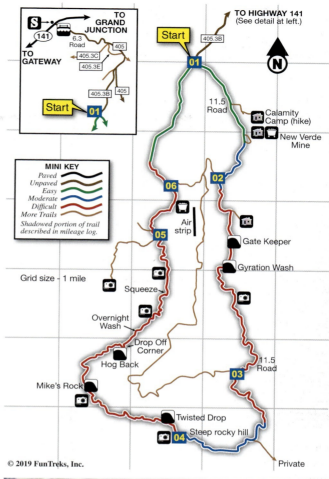

TO GRAND JUNCTION

TO HIGHWAY 141
(See detail at left.)

Start 01 405.3B

141 6.3 Road 405.3C 405

TO GATEWAY 405.3E

405.3B 405

Start 01

MINI KEY
Paved
Unpaved
Easy
Moderate
Difficult
More Trails
*Shadowed portion of trail
described in mileage log.*

Grid size - 1 mile

© 2019 FunTreks, Inc.

11.5 Road

Calamity Camp (hike)

New Verde Mine

02

06

Air strip

05

Gate Keeper

Gyration Wash

Squeeze

Overnight Wash

Drop Off Corner

Hog Back

Mike's Rock

11.5 Road

03

Twisted Drop

Steep rocky hill

04

Private

Twisted Drop.

Photo by Jerry Smith

The entire trip is quite scenic.

71

As you descend to Waypoint 03, you can see the La Sal Mountains in the distance near Moab, Utah.

A little break from the sun at Waypoint 04.

Historical Highlight: This trip takes you past the townsite of Uravan. The name is a combination of the words "uranium" and "vanadium." The town sprang up overnight back in the 1940s. It processed uranium oxide, also called yellowcake, which was used for the top-secret Manhattan Project in the development the atomic bomb during WWII. By the 1970s, as the demand for uranium decreased, the town began to die. Clean-up operations began immediately and by December 1986, the town was just a memory.

Overview: This route is the middle portion of the popular 160-mile-long Rim Rocker Trail. This section has beautiful views of the Uncompahgre Plateau to the east, red rock canyons to the west, and Utah's La Sal Mountains also to the west. Most people take two days to drive the entire trail, starting in Montrose, Colorado and ending in Moab, Utah. Detailed information about the entire route can be found at www. rimrockertrail.org. Naturita has a hotel, gas station and restaurants.

Rating: Easy. Mostly graded dirt with occasional rougher unmaintained sections. One water crossing can be too deep to cross during high-flow periods, like in the spring and after heavy rain-

storms. Trail ends with a steep descent down a rocky hill to Highway 141. Trail can be impassable when wet. Stock vehicles with high clearance, four-wheel drive and low-range gearing can do it.

Stats: Length: 34 miles. Time: About 4-5 hours. High point: 5,944 ft. Best time of year: fall, when water is low.

Current Conditions: BLM Montrose Field Office. Call (970) 240-5300.

Getting There: From Placerville, head west on Highway 145 towards Naturita for 36 miles. Once you reach Naturita, turn right on C.R. 97. Head north 3.5 miles to Nucla City Park. Trail starts here with information kiosks.

MILEAGE LOG:

START

0.0 Zero trip odometer **[Rev. Miles]**
From town park, head west on 10th Street which becomes CC Road. **[7.6]**
01 N38 15.621 W108 32.762

1.6 Turn right on 2700 Road heading north. **[6.0]**

3.8 Turn left on AA road. **[3.8]**

4.5 Turn right on 2600. **[3.1]**

6.0 At "T" intersection, turn left on Z26. **[1.6]**

7.6 Turn left on V19 Road. Divide Rd. continues north into National Forest. **[0.0]**
02 N38 19.241 W108 36.740

0.0 Zero trip odometer
From Wpt. 02, continue west on V19 Road. Cross public and private land following green signs with Rim Rocker stickers. **[17.0]**

3.2 Continue straight. **[13.8]**

7.5 Turn hard right towards a water crossing. Check to see how deep it is before driving through it. **[9.5]**

8.8 Turn hard left uphill. **[8.2]**

11.6 Turn right followed by left onto U17 Road. **[5.4]**
03 N38 22.415 W108 43.768

14.3 Stay left. **[2.7]**

15.5 Turn hard left and then join more traveled road S17 Road west into canyon. **[1.5]**

17.0 Hard right continues the Rim Rocker. Straight accesses Hwy. 141. **[0.0]**
04 N38 23.771 W108 45.147

0.0 Zero trip odometer
From Waypoint 04, continue uphill on T16 Road, which later chang-

es to unmarked Q12 Road as it follows along the edge of the mesa. **[9.3]**

3.5 Continue straight where road goes right. **[5.8]**

8.1 Start long rocky descent towards the highway. **[1.2]**

9.3 Reach Highway 141. **[0.0]**
05 N38 26.247 W108 50.286
To continue the Rim Rocker Trail, turn left on the highway. At 1.5 miles turn right off the highway and cross one-lane bridge. The next part of the trail starts here but does get tricky navigating. Go online www.rimrocker. org to get a good map and follow "Rim Rocker" stickers on signs.

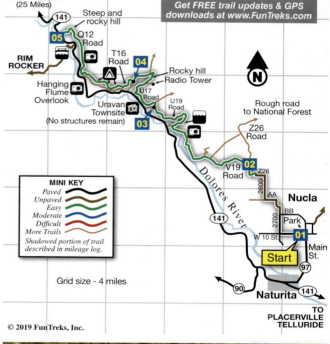

Dolores River.

TO GATEWAY (25 Miles)

Steep and rocky hill

RIM ROCKER

Q12 Road

T16 Road **04**

Rocky hill
Radio Tower

Hanging Flume Overlook

U17 Road

U19 Road

Uravan Townsite (No structures remain) **03**

Rough road to National Forest

Z26 Road

V19 Road **02**

Z26

2600

AA

Nucla

BB Park

2700

W 10 St.

01

Main St.

Start

97

Naturita

90

141

TO PLACERVILLE TELLURIDE

Dolores River

MINI KEY
Paved
Unpaved
Easy
Moderate
Difficult
More Trails
Shadowed portion of trail described in mileage log.

Grid size - 4 miles

© 2019 FunTreks, Inc.

Volunteers replace old sign.

Rocky hill before Waypoint 04 is the toughest section.

Crested Butte, Aspen, Marble, Gunnison

Four-wheeling is not the first thing you think about when someone says "Aspen" or "Crested Butte." These towns are so famous for skiing, other activities, especially motorized, are seldom mentioned. Nonetheless, this beautiful area has some of the most exciting and challenging off-road trails in Colorado.

Most people are surprised to learn they can actually drive down the face of Aspen Mountain Ski Area. Although the privilege has been recently limited to licensed vehicles only, the fact that you can do it at all is amazing. Owners of unlicensed vehicles need not lament, however. All other trails in the area, except two are open to them, including recognized names like Devil's Punchbowl, Pearl Pass, Italian Creek, and new for this book, Tellurium Creek.

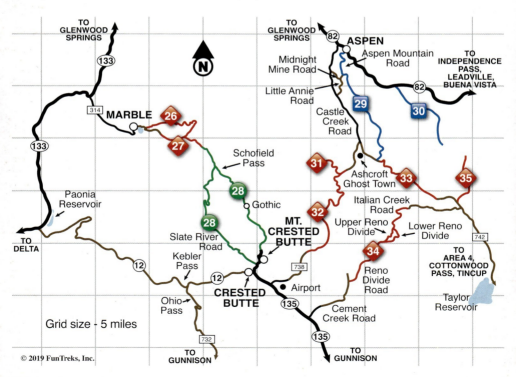

© 2019 FunTreks, Inc.

Grid size - 5 miles

74

Side-by-sides make their way up Tellurium Creek, Trail #35, rated difficult.

Heading south on F.S. 315 along the North Fork of Crystal River approaching Waypoint 04.

Overview: Stunning scenery bordering the Maroon Bells-Snowmass Wilderness. Abundant seasonal wildflowers, fall color, great hiking and mountain biking. Makes a convenient loop when combined with the west half of Devil's Punchbowl, Trail #27. Loop route goes past one of Colorado's most famous landmarks, the Crystal Mill. Open seasonally May 21-Nov. 22. Unlicensed vehicles can stage at the corner of Park St. and 3rd just south of the fire station.

Rating: Difficult. Rating based on a few rocky spots and stretches of narrow shelf road where it is difficult to pass. An experienced driver can get a stock, high-clearance, 4x4 SUV through when the trail is dry. West end is steep and

very slippery when wet.

Stats: Length: 7.8 miles. Time: About 2 hours plus return time. High point: 10,800 ft. Best time of year: July-Sept.

Current Conditions: White River N.F., Sopris R.D. Call (970) 963-2266.

Getting There: From Glenwood Springs: Take Highways 82 and 133 south past Redstone. Follow signs east to Marble on F.S. 314 before McClure Pass. Zigzag through Marble and climb rough road east beyond Beaver Lake to sign for Lead King Basin, F.S. 315, on left. **From Crested Butte:** First drive Paradise Divide, Trail #28, to Schofied Pass. Then follow reverse directions for difficult Devil's Punchbowl, Trail #27.

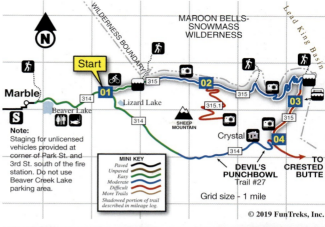

MILEAGE LOG:

0.0 **Zero trip odometer** [Rev. Miles]
Head east on 315 and climb through forest. [7.8]
01 N39 04.486 W107 09.545

0.7 Continue straight past small parking spot for hiking trailhead and cross rocky stream. Climb switchbacks up steep dusty road. This section is extremely slippery when wet. Narrow and difficult to pass. [7.1]

2.1 Bear left. Right is great side trip to top of Sheep Mountain. [5.7]
02 N39 04.680 W107 07.495

4.1 Tight turn in middle of long switchback that marks highest point of trail. Many wildflowers.[3.7]

6.3 After a long descent down narrow switchbacks, cross stream and head south. Ignore roads to left. [1.5]

6.6 Cross bridge and turn right. Trail weaves through trees, then follows high rocky shelf road above North Fork of the Crystal River. [1.2]
03 N39 04.403 W107 05.286

7.8 Trail descends rocky section and connects to Trail #27. Left goes uphill through the dangerous Devil's Punchbowl, then continues on to Schofield Pass and Crested Butte. Right loops back to Marble along the Crystal River, passes through tiny town of Crystal, featuring the famous Crystal Mill. [0.0]
04 N39 03.555 W107 05.780

Get FREE trail updates & GPS downloads at www.FunTreks.com

Note:
Staging for unlicensed vehicles provided at corner of Park St. and 3rd St. south of the fire station. Do not use Beaver Creek Lake parking area.

MINI KEY
Paved
Unpaved
Easy
Moderate
Difficult
More Trails
Shadowed portion of trail described in mileage log.

Grid size - 1 mile

© 2019 FunTreks, Inc.

End of trail is rocky.

Narrow in places.

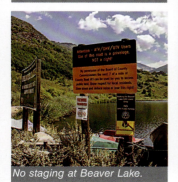

No staging at Beaver Lake.

Descending N.E. side of Sheep Mountain into Lead King Basin.

77

Devil's Punchbowl

Crystal Mill is privately owned—obey signs.

This spot is wide enough to pass.

Tight squeeze between rock wall and boulder.

Historical Highlight: Crystal, a silver mining camp in the 1880s, served many mines in the area and once had a population of more than 400. Silver was mined from crystalline quartz, after which the town was named. Several historic buildings still remain.

Several fatal accidents have occurred on this trail, including the worst in Colorado history. In July 1970, nine tourists died when their vehicle plummeted off the ledge above the Devil's Punchbowl.

Overview: This route runs from Marble to Crested Butte over Schofield Pass. The Crystal Mill, on the western side, draws tourists by the thousands. The mill is one of the most photographed structures in Colorado. The big draw for 4-wheelers, however, is the trip through Crystal Canyon, featuring spectacular Devil's Punchbowl, a deep pool of water below a dramatic waterfall. Scenery along the entire trip is unsurpassed. Many historical features. Open seasonally May 21-Nov. 22 after Wpt. 03.

Rating: Difficult. First portion of trail to the Crystal Mill is rocky. East of Crystal, the road becomes extremely narrow as it climbs steeply along the daunting vertical walls of Crystal Canyon. Dangerous backing required to pass. Rock slides and lingering snow can close the trail at any time. Novice drivers should avoid section between

Wpts. 03 and 04. Although not recommended for stock SUVs, experienced drivers can reach the town of Crystal but should not continue. Low-range, skid plates are a must.

Stats: Length: 10.6 miles. Time: 2 hours one way. High point: 10,707 ft. Best chance of being open: Mid July to Sept.

Current Conditions: White River N.F., Sopris R.D. Call (970) 963-2266.

Getting There: **From Glenwood Springs:** Take Highways 82 and 133 south past Redstone. Follow signs east to Marble on F.S. 314 before McClure Pass. Zigzag through Marble on 314 until you reach the parking area (not staging) next to Beaver Lake. **From Crested Butte:** Follow directions for Paradise Divide, Trail #28, and turn left on F.S. 317 at Schofield Pass.

MILEAGE LOG:

0.0 Zero trip odometer **[Rev. Miles]**
From Beaver Lake, head east uphill on 314. **[6.0]**
01 N39 04.357 W107 10.901

1.5 Stay right on 314 following signs to Crystal. Left is Trail #26. **[4.5]**
02 N39 04.486 W107 09.545

1.8 Stay right around tiny Lizard Lake. **[4.2]**

5.3 Crystal Mill on right. **[0.7]**

5.5 Pass through historic town of Crystal. **[0.5]**

5.7 Stay left. **[0.3]**

6.0 Arrive at wide intersection. Left returns to Marble via Lead King Basin, Trail #26. **[0.0]**
03 N39 03.555 W107 05.780
Zero trip odometer

0.0 Continue straight from Wpt. 03. Novice drivers

heed warning signs. **[4.6]**

1.4 Cross short bridge below Devil's Punchbowl and begin climbing dangerous rocky ledge. Wait for any vehicles coming down. **[3.2]**
04 N39 02.994 W107 04.663

1.8 Trail turns left and crosses river. Worst part of canyon is done. **[2.8]**

2.3 After rocky, muddy section through tight brush, cross creek with great waterfall to left. **[2.3]**

4.6 Pass through scenic valley on easy road and climb to Schofield Pass. Left takes you through Gothic to Crested Butte. Right takes you over Paradise Divide to Crested Butte. See Trail #28. **[0.0]**
05 N39 00.958 W107 02.844

Great trail for smaller OHVs.

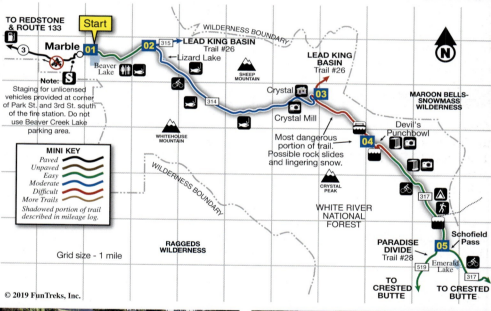

MINI KEY
Paved
Unpaved
Easy
Moderate
Difficult
More Trails
Shadowed portion of trail described in mileage log.

Grid size - 1 mile

Note:
Staging for unlicensed vehicles provided at corner of Park St. and 3rd St. south of the fire station. Do not use Beaver Creek Lake parking area.

© 2019 FunTreks, Inc.

Waterfall on left near end of trail.

Heed warnings. This trail is not for beginners.

Gothic Road below Emerald Lake is a beautiful, easy drive when dry.

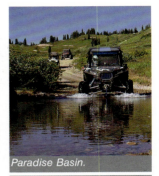
Paradise Basin.

Looking down steep switchbacks before Waypoint 02.

Historical Highlight: Along the eastern half of this loop, you'll go through the town of Gothic. Although a significant number of buildings remain today, at one time, the town consisted of over 200 buildings with a population around 3,000. Gothic was established in 1879 as a result of a large silver strike in what is now part of the Maroon Bells-Snowmass Wilderness. Many of the buildings have been restored, and today part of the town is occupied in the summer by students and scientists of the Rocky Mountain Biological Laboratory.

Overview: A beautiful, stressless drive. In season, wildflowers are everywhere. Limited designated camping along road in addition to fee F.S. campgrounds. Washington Gulch, F.S. 811, is a beautiful alternate way to reach Paradise Divide. Northern portion of Gothic Road is closed between March 1 and June 30 depending on snow and mud conditions. Unlicensed vehicles can ride to Marble but are only allowed on roads in the national forest.

Rating: Easy. Slate River Road is a wide graded road. As it climbs towards Paradise Divide, it becomes a narrower shelf road, but there is still plenty of room to pass. Any high-clearance vehicle can reach Schofield Pass via Gothic Road when everything has dried out. In early summer, however, Gothic Road can be blocked by snow below Emerald Lake. Call ahead to find out if road is passable.

Stats: Length: Main loop 27.2 miles. Time: 2 to 3 hours. High point: 11,250 ft. Best time of year: July-Sept.

Current Conditions: Gunnison N.F., Gunnison R.D. Call (970) 641-0471.

Getting There: Take Hwy. 135 north 0.8 mile from the visitor center in Crested Butte and turn left on Slate River Road 734. To drive the loop in the opposite direction, follow signs to the Mt. Crested Butte Ski Area and continue on to Gothic and Schofield Pass. Just after the pass, turn left on F.S. 519.

MILEAGE LOG:

0.0 Zero trip odometer [Rev. Miles]
Head northwest on wide, graded Slate River Road. **[14.4]**
01 N38 52.808 W106 58.584

2.5 Stay right after private Nicholson Lake. **[11.9]**

3.5 Continue straight. Gunsight Pass is left. **[10.9]**

4.6 Oh-Be-Joyful C.G. on left. **[9.8]**

5.0 Forest boundary. **[9.4]**

7.2 Continue straight. Poverty Gulch and Daisy Hiking Trail to left. Good parking here. **[7.2]**

9.0 Make hard right up tight switchback and begin steeper climb. **[5.4]**

10.8 Continue straight. Washington Gulch Road 811 joins on right. **[3.6]**
02 N38 58.462 W107 03.462

11.9 Crest Paradise Divide and stay right. Choice camp spots here. Descend into Paradise Basin. **[2.5]**
03 N38 59.306 W107 03.854

13.8 Bear right. **[0.6]**

14.4 Bear right at T with F.S. 317 to immediately reach Schofield Pass. (Left goes to Marble through Devil's Punchbowl, Trail #27.) **[0.0]**
04 N38 00.965 W107 02.841

0.0 Zero trip odometer
From Wpt. 04, head south past Emerald Lake. Below lake, road may be blocked by snow. **[12.8]**

3.2 Continue straight. Rustlers Gulch to left. **[9.6]**
05 N38 59.347 W107 00.661

3.8 Gothic C.G. on right. **[9.0]**

4.2 Seasonal closure gate 3/1 to 6/30. No unlicensed vehicles south of this point. **[8.6]**

5.8 Pass through historic town of Gothic. **[7.0]**
06 N38 57.479 W106 59.344

9.9 Pavement begins before Mt. Crested Butte Ski Area on left. **[2.9]**

11.9 Start of Washington Gulch Rd. on right. **[0.9]**

12.8 Complete loop back to start of Slate River Road. **[0.0]**

Get FREE trail updates & GPS downloads at www.FunTreks.com

Emerald Lake below pass.

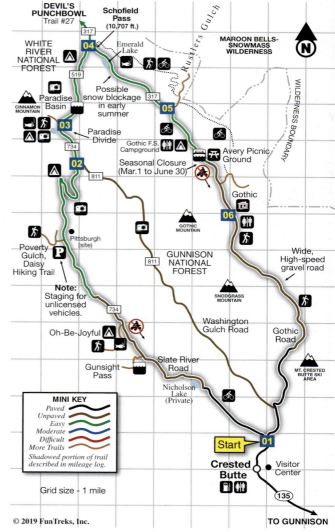

MINI KEY

Paved
Unpaved
Easy
Moderate
Difficult
More Trails
Shadowed portion of trail described in mileage log.

Grid size - 1 mile

© 2019 FunTreks, Inc.

TO GUNNISON

Easy winding trail to top of Aspen Mountain.

Road winds up Richmond Hill.

View from top of gondola.

Watch for hikers and bikers.

Historical Highlight: Like so many mountain towns in Colorado, Aspen started as a bustling silver-mining town in the 1880s. The first ski lift opened after World War II, and the ski area gradually developed into a three-mountain, world-class destination.

Overview: Climb through the heart of beautiful Aspen Ski Area. At the summit, have lunch with gondola-riding tourists or picnic at tables provided. After lunch, escape the crowds with a backcountry drive along remote Richmond Ridge. Visit historic Ashcroft Ghost Town at end of trip. At the time of this writing, unlicensed vehicles were not allowed on this trail. Check future MVUMs for possible changes.

Rating: Moderate. Aspen Summer Road and the first part of Richmond Hill Road are easy, but steepness requires 4-wheel drive. The southern end of Richmond Hill Road, as you near Taylor Pass, is rocky and steep with possible muddy sections.

Stats: Length: 21.2 miles. Time: 3 to 4 hours. High point: 12,300 ft. Best time of year: Late June-Sept.

Current Conditions: White River N.F., Aspen R.D. Call (970) 925-3445.

Getting There: Head east on Highway 82 (Main Street) all the way through Aspen to Original Street and turn right (south). Continue straight on Original Street at the 4-way stop where Highway 82 goes left (east). Keep going south past Durant and East Ute Street as the road narrows and enters what appears to be a driveway between condominiums. Bear right around back of building and make short climb to start of Aspen Summer Road. If gate is not open due to temporary maintenance, you can reach top of mountain via Midnight Mine Road, shown on map.

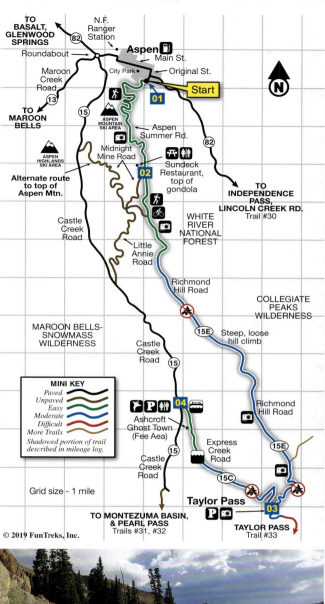

MILEAGE LOG:

One lane near top of Express Creek Road.

START

0.0 Zero trip odometer [Rev. Miles]
Follow sign for Aspen Summer Road and begin climb passing under gondola lift. **[4.6]**
01 N39 11.110 W106 49.060

0.3 Stay left. Right returns to bottom. **[4.3]**

1.8 Follow road as it curves around restaurant. **[2.8]**

3.3 Bear left downhill at "T" intersection. **[1.3]**

4.5 Bear left past end of gondola building. **[0.1]**

4.6 Parking area on left. Walk uphill behind building to Sundeck Restaurant and picnic tables. **[0.0]**
02 N39 09.068 W106 49.122

0.0 Zero trip odometer
Stay left to reach Richmond Hill. Right descends mountain via Midnight Mine Road. **[16.6]**

1.5 Stay left. Road joins on right. **[15.1]**

1.6 Continue straight. Avoid road that goes right uphill and one that curves downhill to left. **[15.0]**

4.3 Continue straight. Note signs that identify wilderness on left. **[12.3]**

5.0 Steep descent and tougher terrain through the woods. **[11.6]**

9.7 After exiting woods, trail goes up and down until it reaches a high point above 12,000 feet. Avoid this area when lightning is present. **[6.9]**

10.5 Drop downhill and bear right. **[6.1]**

11.9 Continue to descend to Taylor Pass. Bear right and follow Express Creek Road downhill. (Left goes to Taylor Park via Trail #33.) **[4.7]**
03 N39 01.217 W106 45.358

16.6 Intersect with paved Castle Creek Road. Aspen is 11 miles to the right. Left goes to Ashcroft Ghost Town and continues south to Montezuma Basin and Pearl Pass, Trails #31 and #32. **[0.0]**
04 N39 03.614 W106 48.052

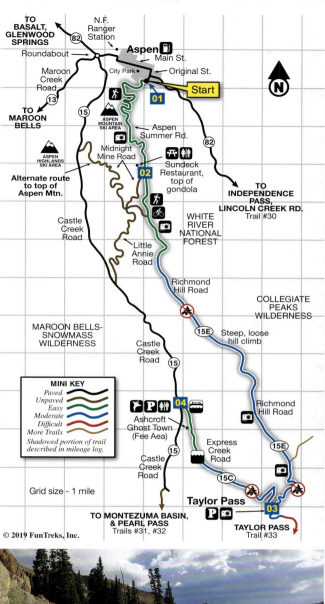

© 2019 FunTreks, Inc.

MINI KEY
Paved
Unpaved
Easy
Moderate
Difficult
More Trails
Shadowed portion of trail described in mileage log.

Grid size - 1 mile

Scenic views as you climb to Ruby Mine.

Narrow channels with fast-moving water.

Looking west at Grizzly Reservoir.

Historical Highlight: A plaque on Frenchman's Cabin says it was built in 1894. This cabin marks entry into the Lincoln Mining District. Silver was the primary ore mined here starting in the 1880s. Development of the area was hindered by the fact that ore had to be hauled all the way to Leadville. A resurgence in mining occurred in 1900 when the Ruby Mines and Development Company took over the operation. They built a 50-ton concentrating mill, then shipped the ore to nearby Aspen, which improved profits. Operations eventually shut down in 1912.

Overview: Road follows beautiful Lincoln Creek and is surrounded by wilderness. Stay on road at all times. Popular mountain biking, hiking and fishing area. Road accesses historic Lincoln Creek Mining District. Camp in one of 22 designated sites along trail or in two F.S. campgrounds. Swimming in Lincoln Creek is allowed but very dangerous. Open seasonally May 23 through September 15. Unlicensed vehicles are not allowed.

Rating: Moderate. The northern portion of this trail is easy. South of Grizzly Reservoir, the trail narrows and gets a bit rockier. The last 0.7 mile before Ruby Mine is rocky, narrow and steep.

Stats: Length: About 12 miles one way. Time: 3 to 4 hours. High point: 12,300 ft. Best time of year: July-Sept.

Current Conditions: White River N.F., Aspen R.D. Call (970) 925-3445.

Getting There: About 10 miles east of Aspen on Highway 82, turn south 0.3 mile east of mile marker 51 at sign for Lincoln Creek Road, F.S. 106.

MILEAGE LOG:

0.0 Zero trip odometer   [Rev. Miles]
Cross bridge and follow
road to right.   [11.7]
01 N39 07.253 W106 41.153

0.4 Stay left where road goes
right to Lincoln Gulch
Campground.   [11.3]

0.5 Hikers parking lot.   [11.2]

2.0 Camp spot #7 is near
beautiful rock-carved
section of Lincoln Creek.
    [9.7]

3.3 Bear left. Road to right
goes to hiking trail.   [8.4]
02 N39 05.690 W106 39.600

6.2 Grizzly Reservoir.   [5.5]

6.3 Pass dam and bear left
on lesser road.   [5.4]
03 N39 04.780 W106 36.823

6.6 Bear left after Portal
Campground. Road nar-
rows and gets rougher.
Pass Frenchman's Cabin
and enter historic Lincoln
Creek Mining District.
    [5.1]

10.0 Stay left. Right goes to
Petroleum Lake Hiking
Trailhead.   [1.7]

10.8 After John Nichols Cabin,
stay on road through
Ruby Townsite (private
property).   [0.9]

10.9 Turn left uphill on narrow
steep road.   [0.8]
04 N39 01.071 W106 36.481

11.7 Ruby Mine near wilderness boundary. Turn
around here.   [0.0]
05 N39 01.120 W106 36.142

Get FREE trail updates & GPS
downloads at www.FunTreks.com

Fishing at Grizzly Reservoir.

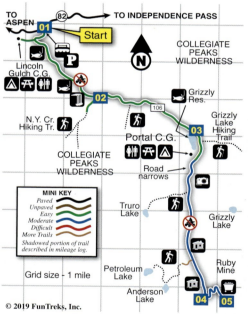

© 2019 FunTreks, Inc.

TO ASPEN — TO INDEPENDENCE PASS
82
Start
01
Lincoln Gulch C.G.
02
106
N.Y. Cr. Hiking Tr.
COLLEGIATE PEAKS WILDERNESS
COLLEGIATE PEAKS WILDERNESS
Grizzly Res.
Portal C.G.
03
Grizzly Lake Hiking Trail
Road narrows
Truro Lake
Grizzly Lake
Petroleum Lake
Anderson Lake
Ruby Mine
04 05

MINI KEY
Paved
Unpaved
Easy
Moderate
Difficult
More Trails
*Shadowed portion of trail
described in mileage log.*

Grid size - 1 mile

You'll pass several log cabins near the top.

Popular area for biking, hiking, canoeing.

Ruby Mine at end of trail (lower right).

Montezuma Basin

Narrow in places with tight switchbacks.

Waterfall just before Waypoint 02.

Historical Highlight: The basin above the parking lot operated as a small ski area for about 10 years starting in 1967. It had a vertical drop of just 200 feet and provided late season skiing, sometimes into July. It was primarily used as a racing and training camp. A rope tow serviced the area. Plans for a chair lift never materialized.

Overview: Follow old mining road to flat parking area above 12,700 feet. Rugged and beautiful route is mostly above timberline. Provides hiking access to two 14,000-ft. mountain peaks. Camping on lower portion of trail must be done in designated camping spots. Seasonal wildflowers. Open May 21 to October 22 depending on snow and mud conditions.

Rating: Difficult. Rating based on one tippy, rocky stretch of narrow shelf road near the top. Most of the road is fairly wide and moderate. Rocky spot after Waypoint 02 can get tougher later in the season. Stock vehicles should have high clearance, low-range gearing and skid plates. Novice drivers may find the last half mile intimidating.

Stats: Length: 5.1 miles. Time: 2 hours to go up and back. High point: 12,700 ft. Best time of year: Mid July-Sept.

Current Conditions: White River N.F., Aspen R.D. Call (970) 925-3445.

Getting There: From roundabout on Highway 82 west of Aspen, turn south on Castle Creek Road, F.S. 102. Follow paved road south about 13 miles and bear right at signs to Pearl Pass and Montezuma Basin.

86

0.0 Zero trip odometer [Rev. miles]
Follow signs south from small parking area near end of pavement of Castle Creek Road. [5.1]
01 N39 01.755 W106 48.466

1.3 After passing through area of designated camp spots, trail bends left and crosses Castle Creek next to foot bridge. [3.8]

2.8 Trail turns hard right after wooden bridge. Note waterfall above you. Steep and rocky through this section. Some SUV owners choose to park here and hike. [2.3]

3.0 Bear right. Left is Pearl Pass, Trail #32. [2.1]
02 N39 00.322 W106 50.287

3.2 After a couple of dispersed camp spots, pass through rocky section. [1.9]

4.7 Stay left. Go past Montezuma Mine. Road narrows to one lane and turns across face of mountain. [0.4]

5.1 Trail ends at parking area after short, rocky section. Plenty of space to turn around. [0.0]
03 N39 01.154 W106 51.293

Relax at the top and enjoy the views.

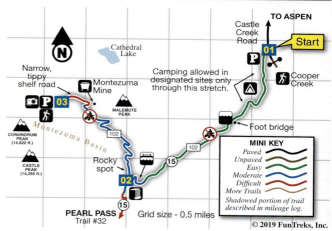

Cathedral Lake

Castle Creek Road

TO ASPEN

Start

01

Cooper Creek

Narrow, tippy shelf road

03

Montezuma Mine

Camping allowed in designated sites only through this stretch.

MALEMUTE PEAK

Foot bridge

Montezuma Basin

CONUNDRUM PEAK (14,022 ft.)

102

Rocky spot

CASTLE PEAK (14,265 ft.)

102

15

02

MINI KEY
Paved
Unpaved
Easy
Moderate
Difficult
More Trails
Shadowed portion of trail described in mileage log.

15

PEARL PASS Trail #32

Grid size - 0.5 miles

© 2019 FunTreks, Inc.

Parking area at end of trail. Difficult hike from here to Castle Peak at 14,265 ft.

Challenging rocky section on north side of Pearl Pass.

Snow can block this spot on north side of pass.

Historical Highlight: Few people know that mountain biking started in Crested Butte back in 1976, when a group of half-crazy bicyclists decided to ride their heavy, balloon-tired Schwinn bikes over Pearl Pass. Now there is an annual event in September called the Pearl Pass Tour. In one day, bikers ride from the town of Crested Butte to Aspen, a total of 38 miles. In 2009, the event was held on September 12. The date changes a bit each year, so you might want to find out the exact date before heading out.

Overview: Located between two of the most famous recreational areas in the state, this long trail offers an unmatched variety of different landscapes from rolling hillsides to challenging rock ledges. High elevation sections of the trail follow the border of the Maroon Bells-Snowmass Wilderness and pass through some of the most remote and strikingly beautiful areas of Colorado. Unlicensed vehicles are allowed on this trail between Wpt. 02 and 04 but must turn around at the pass. Closed between March 1 and May 27 depending on snow and mud conditions.

Rating: Difficult. Many boulder fields, steep climbs, water crossings and narrow shelf roads. These conditions are magnified by snow and ice that are present well into late summer at higher elevations. During years of heavy snowpack, the summit can be blocked for the entire year. Trail is not recommended for stock SUVs.

Stats: Length: 21.7 miles. Time: 3 to 5 hours. High point: 12,705 ft. Best time of year: Mid August-Sept.

Current Conditions: Gunnison N.F., Gunnison R.D. Call (970) 641-0471.

Getting There: **From Crested Butte:** From Highway 135 south of town, head northeast on Brush Creek Road, F.S. 738 (same road that goes to airport). **From Aspen:** From the roundabout on Highway 82 on the west side of Aspen, take paved Castle Creek Road, F.S. 102, south about 13 miles and turn right at sign for Pearl Pass.

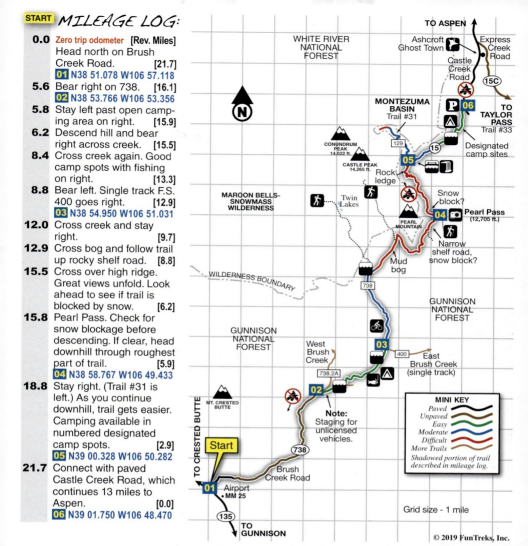

MILEAGE LOG:

START

0.0 Zero trip odometer **[Rev. Miles]** [21.7]
Head north on Brush Creek Road.
01 N38 51.078 W106 57.118

5.6 Bear right on 738. [16.1]
02 N38 53.766 W106 53.356

5.8 Stay left past open camping area on right. [15.9]

6.2 Descend hill and bear right across creek. [15.5]

8.4 Cross creek again. Good camp spots with fishing on right. [13.3]

8.8 Bear left. Single track F.S. 400 goes right. [12.9]
03 N38 54.950 W106 51.031

12.0 Cross creek and stay right. [9.7]

12.9 Cross bog and follow trail up rocky shelf road. [8.8]

15.5 Cross over high ridge. Great views unfold. Look ahead to see if trail is blocked by snow. [6.2]

15.8 Pearl Pass. Check for snow blockage before descending. If clear, head downhill through roughest part of trail. [5.9]
04 N38 58.767 W106 49.433

18.8 Stay right. (Trail #31 is left.) As you continue downhill, trail gets easier. Camping available in numbered designated camp spots. [2.9]
05 N39 00.328 W106 50.282

21.7 Connect with paved Castle Creek Road, which continues 13 miles to Aspen. [0.0]
06 N39 01.750 W106 48.470

WHITE RIVER NATIONAL FOREST

TO ASPEN

Ashcroft Ghost Town

Express Creek Road

Castle Creek Road

15C

06

TO TAYLOR PASS
Trail #33

MONTEZUMA BASIN
Trail #31

Designated camp sites

129

15

CONUNDRUM PEAK
14,022 ft.

CASTLE PEAK
14,265 ft.

Rock ledge

05

MAROON BELLS-SNOWMASS WILDERNESS

Twin Lakes

Snow block?

Pearl Pass
(12,705 ft.)
04

PEARL MOUNTAIN

Narrow shelf road, snow block?

Mud bog

WILDERNESS BOUNDARY

738

GUNNISON NATIONAL FOREST

GUNNISON NATIONAL FOREST

West Brush Creek

03

400

East Brush Creek
(single track)

738.2A

02

Note: Staging for unlicensed vehicles.

MT. CRESTED BUTTE

TO CRESTED BUTTE

Start

738

Brush Creek Road

01

Airport
• MM 25

135

TO GUNNISON

MINI KEY
Paved
Unpaved
Easy
Moderate
Difficult
More Trails
Shadowed portion of trail described in mileage log.

Grid size - 1 mile

© 2019 FunTreks, Inc.

Small area to park at Pearl Pass. Great views looking down from 12,705 ft.

Snow takes a while to melt at higher elevations.

Long, bumpy drive will test your suspension.

Ashcroft Ghost Town (fee area).

Historical Highlight: In the 1880s, Ashcroft was a major supply center for mining in the Aspen area. The road over Taylor Pass provided a way for stagecoaches and freight to come in from Buena Vista and Taylor Park. This road was quickly abandoned, however, as Aspen became the more important mining center and a new road was built over Independence Pass. Ashcroft's fate was sealed when railroads began serving Aspen in the late 1880s.

Overview: Shortest way to Taylor Park Reservoir from Aspen. Great views from Taylor Pass, but not much after that. This trail is one-third of popular loop that includes Trails #32, #33 and #34. It also connects to Trail #29. Unlicensed vehicles can run the trail in reverse from Taylor Park side but are not allowed to continue over the pass. Great camping for overnight trips available at Taylor Lake or Taylor River Road.

Rating: Difficult. Long section of bowling ball-size rocks is slow-going. Reverse direction is more challenging. Creek crossing has an obstacle that changes in difficulty. Fallen trees may block trail in early spring.

Stats: Length: 14.6 miles. Time: 2 to 3 hours. High point: 11,928 ft. Best time of year: Mid June-Sept.

Current Conditions: Mostly in Gunnison N.F., Gunnison R.D. Call (970) 641-0471.

Getting There: **From Aspen:** From the roundabout on Hwy. 82 west of Aspen, head south on paved Castle Creek Road, F.S. 102, about 11 miles and turn left on Express Creek Road just before Ashcroft Ghost Town. **From Crested Butte:** First drive Pearl Pass, Trail #32. Head north on Castle Creek Road about 2 miles and turn right on Express Creek Road. **From Taylor Park Reservoir:** Head northwest on Taylor River Road, F.S. 742, about 12 miles to Waypoint 04 and drive trail in reverse.

MILEAGE LOG:

0.0 Zero trip odometer [Rev. Miles]
Climb easy Express
Creek Road. As you ap-
proach Taylor Pass, the
road narrows and crosses
a shelf where it is tricky to
pass. **[14.6]**
01 N39 03.607 W106 48.050

4.8 Arrive at Taylor Pass.
(Note that Trail #29 goes
uphill to the left.) Bear
right and zigzag downhill
to Taylor Lake. Unlicensed
vehicles are now permit-
ted. **[9.8]**
02 N39 01.215 W106 45.345

5.4 Stay left where 761.1C
goes right. The rocky road
offers various choices, but
all are bone-jarring. **[9.2]**

7.1 Drop steeply into creek
and immediately bear
right then left, staying in
creek short distance. **[7.5]**

7.2 Exit creek, then cross it
again. **[7.4]**

8.8 Bear left on wider, flatter
Taylor River Road 742.
Stay on good road past
Dorchester Campground. **[5.8]**
03 N38 59.754 W106 42.209

14.6 Continuing straight takes
you to Taylor Park Res-
ervoir in about 12 miles.
Right goes to Italian
Creek, Trail #34, which
takes you to Hwy. 135
south of Crested Butte.
From there you can head
north and loop back to
Aspen via Pearl Pass,
Trail #32. South on 135
goes to Gunnison. **[0.0]**
04 N38 57.246 W106 37.287

Short section of the trail follows the creek.

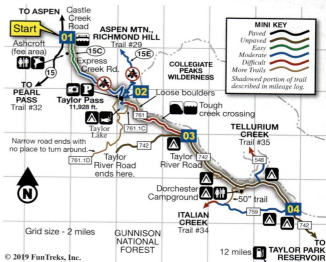

© 2019 FunTreks, Inc.

One of several small lakes above Taylor Lake where fishing is allowed. Fishing license required.

Rocky terrain most of the way.

American Flag Mountain.

Small cabin with "million dollar views."

Historical Highlight: *As mining boomed in Aspen, Crested Butte and Taylor Park in the early 1880s, roads connecting these areas were needed. Taylor Pass Road provided Aspen with access to Taylor Park, but it didn't help Crested Butte. Consequently, a road over Reno Divide was built soon after Taylor Pass. Both roads soon became obsolete when railroad service reached Aspen and Crested Butte. One hundred thirty years later, the roads remain open for recreational use. The 3-part loop of Trails 32, 33 and 34 remains one of the best 4WD trips in the USA.*

Overview: Both ends of the trail are popular recreation areas for hikers, bikers, fishermen, OHV and dirt bike riders. Many great places to camp along the trail. Side trip to American Flag Mountain has great views. The connecting Reno Divide portion is less traveled and very remote. Combine this trail with Pearl Pass and Taylor Pass to make a great loop. When Cement Creek is closed (March to May) use Reno Ridge Road to reach Taylor River Road.

Rating: Difficult. A narrow, remote road with steep climbs and potential mud bogs in wet weather. Becomes difficult in rainy weather especially in early part of summer. Aggressive tire tread is very important. Side trip to American Flag Mtn. is a steep climb up a slippery shale slope. Do not drive this trail alone. Upper Reno Divide 642 crosses a dangerous rocky ledge across talus slopes.

Stats: Length: 27 miles. Time: 3 to 5 hours. High point: 12,030 ft. Best time of year: Mid June-Sept.

Current Conditions: Gunnison N.F., Gunnison R.D. Call (970) 641-0471.

Getting There: From Taylor Park Reservoir: Take Taylor River Road, F.S. 742, north from reservoir about 12 miles and turn left on Italian Creek Road, F.S. 759. If you reach Dorchester Campground, you've gone too far. **From Crested Butte:** About 7 miles south of Crested Butte on Hwy. 135, head north on Cement Creek Road.

MILEAGE LOG:

0.0 Zero trip odometer [Rev. Miles]
Head west on 759 from Taylor River Road and pass through camping and fishing area. [14.1]
01 N38 57.246 W106 37.287

2.7 Road becomes 4-wheel-drive as you pass through opening in fence. You climb gradually through varied, but mostly easy terrain. [11.4]

6.5 Make hard right uphill to avoid cutting across private property. Follow signs to Cement Creek. [7.6]
02 N38 57.355 W106 43.472

7.2 Bear left downhill avoiding private property again. Pass old cabin and cross creek. [6.9]

7.5 Bear left at collapsed cabins through muddy section. [6.6]

7.6 Turn left and begin steep climb through muddy section. [6.5]

8.5 Bear right. [5.6]
03 N38 56.851 W106 43.428

8.6 Driver's choice. [5.5]

8.9 Turn right. (Great views from American Flag Mountain to left.) [5.2]

10.1 Stay left at important fork. Right is dangerous trip over Upper Reno Divide. [4.0]
04 N38 55.961 W106 44.391

14.1 Upper and lower roads merge back together. [0.0]

0.0 Zero trip odometer
Pass through gate and continue straight downhill on 759. (Alternate exit: turn left uphill on F.S. 759.1E, Reno Ridge Road, to reach Taylor River Road.) [12.9]
05 N38 54.453 W106 45.790

3.8 Turn left on Cement Creek Road 740. (Right is fun trip to Mt. Tilton.) [9.1]
06 N38 53.052 W106 47.463

9.5 Continue straight past Cement Creek C.G. [3.4]

12.9 The road becomes paved before reaching Highway 135. Right goes to Crested Butte; left goes to Almont then eventually Gunnison. [0.0]
07 N38 48.279 W106 53.408

50" width UTV attempts dangerous Upper Reno Ridge F.S. 642.

Not much room to pass between Waypoints 05 and 06.

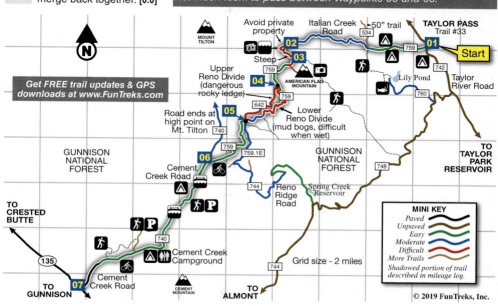

Get FREE trail updates & GPS downloads at www.FunTreks.com

MINI KEY
Paved
Unpaved
Easy
Moderate
Difficult
More Trails
Shadowed portion of trail described in mileage log.

Grid size - 2 miles

© 2019 FunTreks, Inc.

93

Great view from high point of trail at Waypoint 04.

First part of the trail is mostly wooded.

Have a camera ready to get shots like this.

Overview: Trail follows narrow corridor of open forest land cut through the Collegiate Peaks Wilderness. As you climb, views open up as you circle around a beautiful valley. Scenic high point with 360-degree views. Great trail for ATVs and UTVs. Stay on the established route at all times and under no circumstances enter the well-marked wilderness area.

Rating: Difficult. Moderately steep with embedded rock. Numerous crossings of Tellurium Creek are shallow except during periods of heavy runoff. Loop portion of trail has a couple of very steep rocky sections. The optional western loop is only for ATVs. Very steep and tippy in spots with loose talus and tight switchbacks.

Stats: Length: Round trip 12.4 miles. Time: 2 to 3 hours. High point: 12,270 ft. Best time of year: Mid July-Sept.

Current Conditions: Gunnison N.F., Gunnison R.D. Call (970) 641-0471.

Getting There: From Taylor Park Trading Post, head north 13.5 miles on Taylor River Road to well-marked Tellurium Creek Road 584 on right.

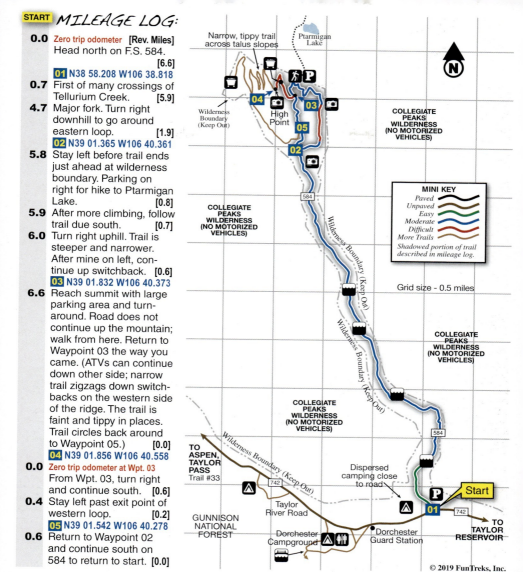

MILEAGE LOG:

START

0.0 Zero trip odometer [Rev. Miles]
Head north on F.S. 584. [6.6]
01 N38 58.208 W106 38.818

0.7 First of many crossings of Tellurium Creek. [5.9]

4.7 Major fork. Turn right downhill to go around eastern loop. [1.9]
02 N39 01.365 W106 40.361

5.8 Stay left before trail ends just ahead at wilderness boundary. Parking on right for hike to Ptarmigan Lake. [0.8]

5.9 After more climbing, follow trail due south. [0.7]

6.0 Turn right uphill. Trail is steeper and narrower. After mine on left, continue up switchback. [0.6]
03 N39 01.832 W106 40.373

6.6 Reach summit with large parking area and turn-around. Road does not continue up the mountain; walk from here. Return to Waypoint 03 the way you came. (ATVs can continue down other side; narrow trail zigzags down switchbacks on the western side of the ridge. The trail is faint and tippy in places. Trail circles back around to Waypoint 05.) [0.0]
04 N39 01.856 W106 40.558

0.0 Zero trip odometer at Wpt. 03.
From Wpt. 03, turn right and continue south. [0.6]

0.4 Stay left past exit point of western loop. [0.2]
05 N39 01.542 W106 40.278

0.6 Return to Waypoint 02 and continue south on 584 to return to start. [0.0]

Narrow, tippy trail across talus slopes

Ptarmigan Lake

Wilderness Boundary (Keep Out)

High Point

COLLEGIATE PEAKS WILDERNESS (NO MOTORIZED VEHICLES)

584

MINI KEY
Paved
Unpaved
Easy
Moderate
Difficult
More Trails
Shadowed portion of trail described in mileage log.

Grid size - 0.5 miles

COLLEGIATE PEAKS WILDERNESS (NO MOTORIZED VEHICLES)

Wilderness Boundary (Keep Out)

Wilderness Boundary (Keep Out)

COLLEGIATE PEAKS WILDERNESS (NO MOTORIZED VEHICLES)

584

COLLEGIATE PEAKS WILDERNESS (NO MOTORIZED VEHICLES)

TO ASPEN, TAYLOR PASS
Trail #33

Wilderness Boundary (Keep Out)

742

Dispersed camping close to road

GUNNISON NATIONAL FOREST

Taylor River Road

Dorchester Campground

Dorchester Guard Station

P

Start

01

742

TO TAYLOR RESERVOIR

© 2019 FunTreks, Inc.

Looking south into the valley below from Waypoint 03.

Green = Easy,   Blue = Moderate,   Red = Difficult, *= New

Buena Vista, Tincup, Sargents, Salida

Area 4 has changed considerably since the last edition of this book was published in 2010. Three trails that were moderate before—Tincup Pass, Hancock Pass, and Baldwin Lakes/Boulder Mountain—are now rated difficult.

A major landslide on Tomichi Pass has closed this trail indefinitely. Another landslide at the Palisades has closed the road to the southern side of the Alpine Tunnel. Future status of these trails remains unknown.

Despite these issues, the area is still one of the most popular four-wheeling destinations in Colorado. Trails around St. Elmo, Tincup and Pitkin constitute some of the highest and most spectacular passes and mountaintop destinations anywhere. Meanwhile, valley trails like Chinaman Gulch, Carnage Canyon and Fourmile remain popular wintertime destinations because they are seldom closed by snow.

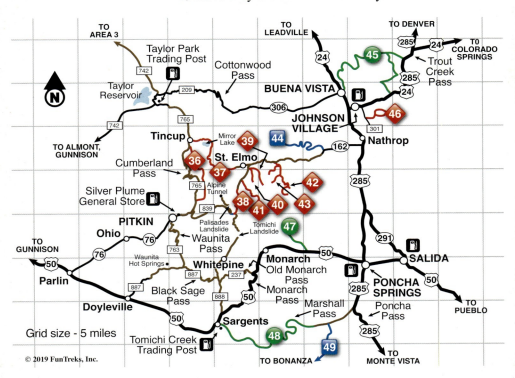

© 2019 FunTreks, Inc.

Open all year Chinaman Gulch, Trail #46, is rated difficult.

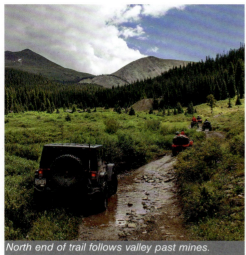
North end of trail follows valley past mines.

Tight through muddy forest.

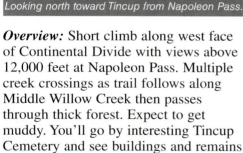
Looking north toward Tincup from Napoleon Pass.

One of many graves at the Tincup Cemetery.

Overview: Short climb along west face of Continental Divide with views above 12,000 feet at Napoleon Pass. Multiple creek crossings as trail follows along Middle Willow Creek then passes through thick forest. Expect to get muddy. You'll go by interesting Tincup Cemetery and see buildings and remains at Gold Cup Mine. No seasonal closures except by weather.

Rating: Difficult. No obstacles, just a mix of good-size rocks, big tree roots and mud. Trail follows creek, so it is rarely dry. Narrow sections are more difficult when wet and slippery. Don't hesitate to turn around if the slipperi-ness becomes dangerous. Stay on the trail and don't cut corners. Steep climb just before the pass may intimidate inexperienced drivers.

Stats: Length: 6.3 miles. Time: 2 to 3 hours. High point: 12,034 ft. Best time of year: Mid July-Sept.

Current Conditions: Gunnison N.F., Gunnison R.D. Call (970) 641-0471.

Getting There: We start at the White Church in Tincup, which can be reached via Trail #37 from St. Elmo or via F.S. 765 from the Taylor Park Trading Post at the Taylor Reservoir.

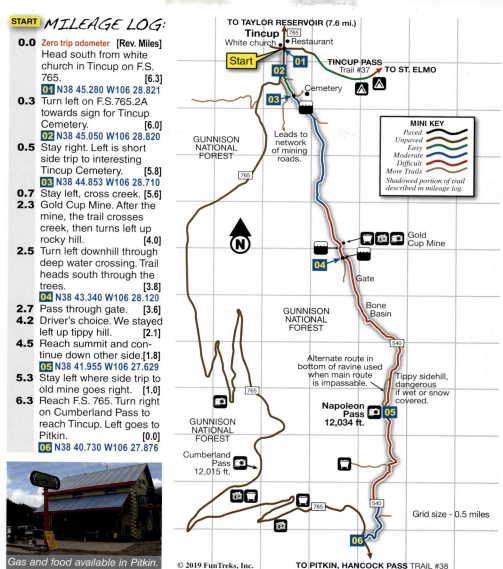

MILEAGE LOG:

START

0.0 Zero trip odometer [Rev. Miles]
Head south from white church in Tincup on F.S. 765. [6.3]
01 N38 45.280 W106 28.821

0.3 Turn left on F.S.765.2A towards sign for Tincup Cemetery. [6.0]
02 N38 45.050 W106 28.820

0.5 Stay right. Left is short side trip to interesting Tincup Cemetery. [5.8]
03 N38 44.853 W106 28.710

0.7 Stay left, cross creek. [5.6]

2.3 Gold Cup Mine. After the mine, the trail crosses creek, then turns left up rocky hill. [4.0]

2.5 Turn left downhill through deep water crossing. Trail heads south through the trees. [3.8]
04 N38 43.340 W106 28.120

2.7 Pass through gate. [3.6]

4.2 Driver's choice. We stayed left up tippy hill. [2.1]

4.5 Reach summit and continue down other side. [1.8]
05 N38 41.955 W106 27.629

5.3 Stay left where side trip to old mine goes right. [1.0]

6.3 Reach F.S. 765. Turn right on Cumberland Pass to reach Tincup. Left goes to Pitkin. [0.0]
06 N38 40.730 W106 27.876

Gas and food available in Pitkin.

TO TAYLOR RESERVOIR (7.6 mi.)

Tincup
White church • Restaurant
Start

01 **TINCUP PASS**
Trail #37 **TO ST. ELMO**

02

03 Cemetery

GUNNISON NATIONAL FOREST

Leads to network of mining roads.

765

MINI KEY
Paved
Unpaved
Easy
Moderate
Difficult
More Trails
Shadowed portion of trail described in mileage log.

Gold Cup Mine

04 Gate

GUNNISON NATIONAL FOREST

Bone Basin

540

Alternate route in bottom of ravine used when main route is impassable.

Tippy sidehill, dangerous if wet or snow covered.

765

Napoleon Pass 12,034 ft. **05**

GUNNISON NATIONAL FOREST

Cumberland Pass 12,015 ft.

765

540

Grid size - 0.5 miles

765

06

© 2019 FunTreks, Inc.

TO PITKIN, HANCOCK PASS TRAIL #38

Artifact at the Gold Cup Mine. Perhaps a drive wheel that was part of a steam engine.

99

It's a rocky and slow descent down north side of Tincup Pass.

Enjoying a sunset at camp spot along trail.

Historical Highlight: *St. Elmo was settled in 1878 and grew to a population of about 2,000. Like so many mining towns, the most prosperous businesses were saloons, dance halls and bawdy houses. In 1881, St. Elmo became an important railway stop. During the construction of the Alpine Tunnel, St. Elmo was a bustling supply center. When Mary Murphy Mine closed in 1920, St. Elmo was finished.*
    Contrary to popular belief, Tincup is not a ghost town. Most of the old cabins in town have been restored to their original condition and are occupied during the summer. No visit to Tincup is complete without a stop at the Tincup General Store.

Overview: A beautiful high-elevation route starting and ending at historic, quaint mountain towns. St. Elmo is one of the most popular ghost towns in Colorado. It has a few active businesses, including a general store and ATV rental. Tincup is a small residential community with many century-old buildings. Active summer businesses include the Tincup Store and Frenchy's Cafe. No seasonal gate closures.

Rating: Difficult. Sharp rocks near the top may cut tires. One short section of narrow shelf road often remains snow covered into early July. After the snow clears, this trail is suitable for SUVs with high clearance, low-range gearing, skid plates and good tires.

Stats: Length: Almost 13 miles. Time: 2 hours. High point: 12,154 ft. Best time of year: Mid July-early October.

Current Conditions: Gunnison and San Isabel N.F. Call Salida Ranger District at (719) 539-3591.

Getting There: From Johnson Village, head south on Highway 285 about 6 miles. Just past Nathrop, turn right on County Road 162. Go west 15.4 miles to parking area (with toilet) on left. Immediately after parking area, bear right following sign to St. Elmo. In center of town, turn right following sign to Tincup Pass. Cross wooden bridge and turn left. Head uphill on well-marked County Road 267.

MILEAGE LOG:

0.0 Zero trip odometer [Rev. Miles]
Wide road climbs steadily uphill and gets progressively rougher. Lots of good camp spots. [12.6]
`01` N38 42.237 W106 20.920

5.9 Climb switchbacks and cross narrow shelf road before reaching pass. Snow lingers here. Road gets rougher as you descend other side. [6.7]
`02` N38 42.544 W106 26.068

6.6 Stay left. Right is shorter but more difficult way down "Old Tincup." [6.0]
`03` N38 43.006 W106 26.165

7.5 Stay left. Old Tincup joins on right. [5.1]
`04` N38 43.276 W106 26.278

8.9 Follow rocky road around north side of lake. Can be covered in water in the spring. [3.7]

9.4 Parking lot at west end, continue downhill on wider F.S. 267. [3.2]
`05` N38 44.780 W106 25.861

12.6 You reach F.S. 765 in center of Tincup. Right goes to Taylor Park, left goes over Cumberland Pass to town of Pitkin. Both towns have gas and food. [0.0]
`06` N38 45.280 W106 28.810

Get FREE trail updates & GPS downloads at www.FunTreks.com

West end of St. Elmo remains a ghost town.

Road around Mirror Lake can flood in the spring.

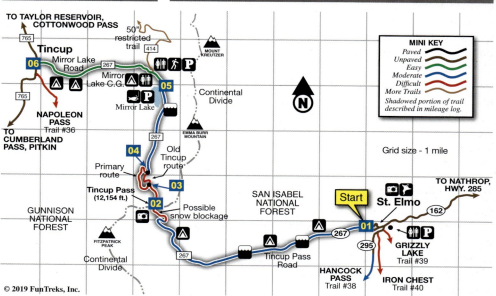

MINI KEY
Paved
Unpaved
Easy
Moderate
Difficult
More Trails
Shadowed portion of trail described in mileage log.

TO TAYLOR RESERVOIR, COTTONWOOD PASS
765
Tincup
Mirror Lake Road
50" restricted trail
414
MOUNT KREUTZER
267
`06`
`05`
Mirror Lake C.G.
Mirror Lake
Continental Divide
765
NAPOLEON PASS
Trail #36
TO CUMBERLAND PASS, PITKIN
EMMA BURR MOUNTAIN
267
`04`
Primary route
Old Tincup route
Grid size - 1 mile
Tincup Pass
(12,154 ft.)
`03`
`02`
Possible snow blockage
GUNNISON NATIONAL FOREST
SAN ISABEL NATIONAL FOREST
Start
St. Elmo
TO NATHROP, HWY. 285
162
FITZPATRICK PEAK
267
`01`
267
Tincup Pass Road
295
GRIZZLY LAKE
Trail #39
Continental Divide
HANCOCK PASS
Trail #38
IRON CHEST
Trail #40

© 2019 FunTreks, Inc.

Hancock Pass

F.S.266 winds down south side of Hancock Pass.

Upper portion is bumpy and slow.

Allie Belle Mine partially collapsed.

Historical Highlight: Hancock Road and the Alpine Tunnel Road were built along the original railroad grade that passed through the Alpine Tunnel in the 1880s. Several railroad structures still remain. Forest Road 839 was damaged at the Palisades by an avalanche in February 2016, and the road remains closed. It was hoped that Williams Pass Road would open as a way to reach tunnel, but so far, it's not.

Overview: Our route connects St. Elmo to Pitkin. Pass through the historic site of Hancock on way to 12,140-ft. Hancock Pass. After going over pass, you descend to bottom of Brittle Silver Basin, then continue down 839 past restored water tank. At Wpt. 07, turn left and exit through Pitkin on a long drive back to Hwy. 50. Or turn right and go over 12,015-ft. Cumberland Pass to Tincup, where you can return to St. Elmo over Tincup Pass, Trail #37. Very popular loop for OHVs. No seasonal closures except by snow.

Rating: Difficult. Most of the trail is easy wide road. At the pass, very rocky and slow-going, but okay for aggres-

sive stock SUVs with low range and skid plates. Do not attempt if snow is present.

Stats: Length: Almost 17 miles. Add 3 miles for side trip to Hancock Lake. Time: 3 to 4 hours. High point: 12,140 ft. Best time of year: July-early October.

Current Conditions: Gunnison and San Isabel N.F. Call (719) 539-3591.

Getting There: From Johnson Village, head south on Highway 285 about 6 miles. Just past Nathrop, turn right on County Road 162. Go west 15.4 miles to parking/staging area (with toilet) on left. Immediately after parking area, bear left on County Road 295.

102

MILEAGE LOG:

0.0 Zero trip odometer [Rev. Miles] Follow wide C.R. 295 south. [5.6]
01 N38 42.353 W106 20.410

2.7 Stay right around old railroad trestle then go straight past turn for Pomeroy Lakes. [2.9]

5.4 Arrive at Hancock Townsite marked on left. Hiking trail goes right to lower portal of Alpine Tunnel. Stay right after townsite and hiking. [0.2]
02 N38 38.416 W106 21.669

5.6 At clearing between large trees, the main trail goes

hard right up F.S. 299. Side trip to Hancock Lake goes straight 1.5 miles.[0.0]
03 N38 38.292 W106 21.679

0.0 Zero trip odometer From Waypoint 03, turn right on F.S. 299. [11.3]

1.5 Rocky road swings right and begins steep climb to Hancock Pass. [9.8]

2.2 Arrive at Hancock Pass and continue down other side. Road changes to Gunnison F.S. 266. [9.1]
04 N38 37.252 W106 22.485

3.1 Bear right on 888. Closed Tomichi Pass on left. [8.2]
05 N38 36.685 W106 22.711

3.7 Continue on F.S. 839.

Alpine Tunnel on right closed due to road damage from avalanche. [7.6]
06 N38 36.823 W106 23.397

4.8 Restored water tank on right. [6.5]

8.0 Water tank on right. [3.3]

11.3 Reach "T" intersection. Turn left to reach Pitkin (3 miles) quickest way to Highway 50. Right goes to Tincup (18 miles) over Cumberland Pass. [0.0]
07 N38 37.498 W106 28.555

Get FREE trail updates & GPS downloads at www.FunTreks.com

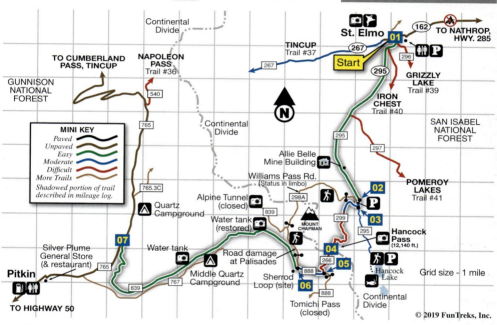

MINI KEY
Paved
Unpaved
Easy
Moderate
Difficult
More Trails
Shadowed portion of trail described in mileage log.

Continental Divide

TO CUMBERLAND PASS, TINCUP

NAPOLEON PASS Trail #36

GUNNISON NATIONAL FOREST

540
765
765.3C
765
839
767

Quartz Campground

Alpine Tunnel (closed)

Water tank (restored)

Middle Quartz Campground

Road damage at Palisades

Sherrod Loop (site)

Tomichi Pass (closed)

Continental Divide

TINCUP Trail #37

St. Elmo

Start

267
295
297
295
299
295
298A
839
888
266
888

Allie Belle Mine Building

Williams Pass Rd. (Status in limbo)

MOUNT CHAPMAN

162 TO NATHROP, HWY. 285

296

GRIZZLY LAKE Trail #39

IRON CHEST Trail #40

SAN ISABEL NATIONAL FOREST

POMEROY LAKES Trail #41

Hancock Pass (12,140 ft.)

Hancock Lake

Continental Divide

Grid size - 1 mile

© 2019 FunTreks, Inc.

Silver Plume General Store (& restaurant)

Water tank

Pitkin

TO HIGHWAY 50

Water tank restored by Jeep Club.

Popular Silver Plume Restaurant in Pitkin.

103

When you reach the parking area, take a short hike to this beautiful spot overlooking the lake.

Overview: Take your camera. The lake and surrounding mountains are gorgeous on a sunny day. Fish early in the day before the wind kicks up. Take insect repellent. Camp spots near the lake are limited in number. The obstacle at the start sometimes draws a crowd of spectators. Tough trail for ATVs and short, wheel-based vehicles. No seasonal closures except by snow.

Rating: Difficult. The toughest part of this trail is at the beginning where you must go over a very difficult rock obstacle immediately after a stream crossing. Do not attempt to make new routes around this spot. After the obstacle, a steep, loose-rock shelf road continues to be difficult a short distance. After that, the trail is mostly moderate with a few marginally difficult spots.

Stats: Length: 2.6 miles one way. Time: 1 hour. High point: 11,200 ft. Best time of year: Late June-Early Oct.

Current Conditions: San Isabel N.F., Salida R.D. Call (719) 539-3591.

Getting There: From Johnson Village, head south on Hwy. 285 about 6 miles. Just past Nathrop, turn right on C.R. 162. Go west 15.4 miles to parking area (with toilet) on left. Immediately after parking area, bear left on C.R. 295. Go 0.2 mile and watch for small road on left (unmarked F.S. 296) . A private drive next to trail entrance usually has "Keep Out" sign and chain across drive. Enter trail immediately left of sign.

MILEAGE LOG:

0.0 Zero trip odometer [Rev. Miles]
Drive short distance on F.S. 296 and watch for creek crossing on left. Avoid private property.[2.6]
01 N38 42.230 W106 20.613

0.2 Turn left and cross creek. Climb difficult ledges out of creek. Driver's choice within 100 feet or so; trail turns right uphill on steep, loose-rock shelf road.
[2.4]
02 N38 42.165 W106 20.468

0.9 Driver's choice. [1.7]

1.1 Cross creek again and pass cabin ruins. [1.5]

1.4 Pass roofless cabin on right. Muddy section follows, then talus slopes.
[1.2]

2.5 Bear left. Lake soon comes into view. [0.1]

2.6 Arrive at parking area. Lesser road on right goes to dispersed camp spots. Hiking path goes around lake to access fishing.[0.0]
03 N38 40.246 W106 20.075

Get FREE trail updates & GPS downloads at www.FunTreks.com

© 2019 FunTreks, Inc.

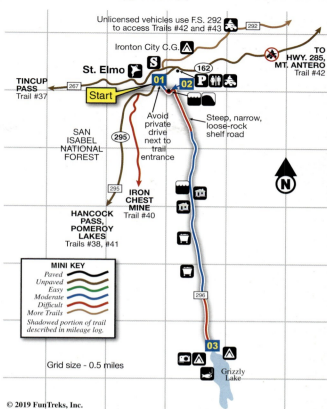

Unlicensed vehicles use F.S. 292 to access Trails #42 and #43

Ironton City C.G.

St. Elmo

TINCUP PASS Trail #37

Start

267

01 02

162

295

295

SAN ISABEL NATIONAL FOREST

IRON CHEST MINE Trail #40

HANCOCK PASS, POMEROY LAKES Trails #38, #41

292

TO HWY. 285, MT. ANTERO Trail #42

Avoid private drive next to trail entrance

Steep, narrow, loose-rock shelf road

N

296

03

Grizzly Lake

MINI KEY
Paved
Unpaved
Easy
Moderate
Difficult
More Trails
Shadowed portion of trail described in mileage log.

Grid size - 0.5 miles

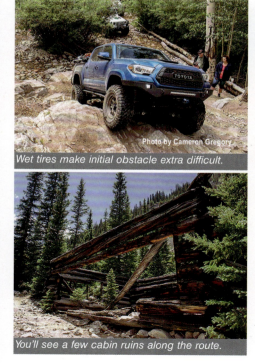

Wet tires make initial obstacle extra difficult.

Photo by Cameron Gregory

You'll see a few cabin ruins along the route.

Trail gets easier after this loose-rock shelf road.

105

Iron Chest Mine

Narrow shelf road has no room to pass. Make sure it is clear before proceeding.

Group enjoys lunch at Iron Chest Mine.

Historical Highlight: *The buildings at Iron Chest Mine are over 100 years old and are in relatively good condition given the 12,000-ft. altitude. A giant pulley lies on the ground in front of a large tram house with tram towers going down the mountain. Just over the high ridge above the mine is the Mary Murphy Mine, which can be reached via Pomeroy Lakes, Trail #41. Take a short 250-yard hike to the interesting Ghost House near start of trail. The cabin was built in 1886. Flattened tin cans were used as roof shingles.*

Overview: Classic hard-core trail with historic structures at Iron Chest Mine. Terrific views at top. Short walk to Ghost House at start. To keep this trail open, it is important to obey all signs and to stay out of mines and buildings.

Rating: Difficult. A short stretch of boulders at the beginning of the trail is brutal. After that, the trail continues as a narrow shelf road, often with small washouts. Snow can block trail late July.

Stats: Length: 2.7 miles one way. Time: 3 to 4 hours round trip. High point: near 12,000 feet. Best time of year: Mid July-early October.

Current Conditions: Although this trail is in the San Isabel National Forest, it is mostly on private property and is not considered a forest system road. It does not appear on an MVUM but has been open for years.

Getting There: From Johnson Village, head south on Hwy. 285 about 6 miles. Just past Nathrop, turn right on C.R. 162. Go west 15.4 miles to parking/staging area (with toilet) on left. Immediately after parking area, bear left on C.R. 295 where road forks right to St. Elmo. Watch for small road and parking area on left after 0.4 mile. (Don't confuse with Grizzly at 0.2 mile.)

MILEAGE LOG:

0.0 Zero trip odometer [Rev. Miles]
From small parking area, head east short distance, where trail turns right and begins climbing through difficult boulder field. Note on left the start of hiking trail to the historic Ghost House. [2.7]
01 N38 42.135 W108 20.787

0.3 Boulder field ends and trail winds tightly through the trees. [2.4]

1.7 After cabin, trail crosses narrow shelf road. Ice can block trail in July. [1.0]

2.3 Stay left where lesser road goes right. [0.4]
02 N38 40.714 W108 20.950

2.5 Driver's choice. [0.2]

2.7 Rocky climb ends at buildings of Iron Chest Mine. Turn around here. If you hike to top of ridge above mine, you'll see Mary Murphy Mine on the other side. [0.0]
03 N38 40.331 W108 20.947

Iron Chest is best known for this difficult boulder field.

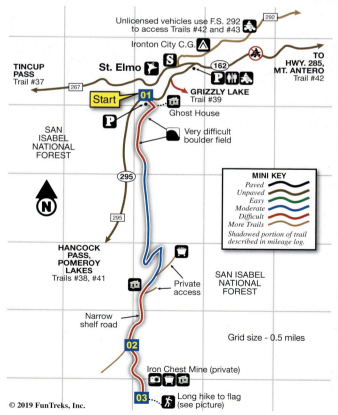

Unlicensed vehicles use F.S. 292 to access Trails #42 and #43

292

Ironton City C.G.

St. Elmo

S

162

TO HWY. 285, MT. ANTERO
Trail #42

TINCUP PASS
Trail #37

267

P

GRIZZLY LAKE
Trail #39

Start 01

Ghost House

P

Very difficult boulder field

SAN ISABEL NATIONAL FOREST

295

MINI KEY
Paved
Unpaved
Easy
Moderate
Difficult
More Trails
Shadowed portion of trail described in mileage log.

295

HANCOCK PASS, POMEROY LAKES
Trails #38, #41

Private access

SAN ISABEL NATIONAL FOREST

Narrow shelf road

Grid size - 0.5 miles

02

Iron Chest Mine (private)

03 Long hike to flag (see picture)

N

© 2019 FunTreks, Inc.

Do not enter structures.

Tough hike to flag from Wpt. 03.

Pomeroy Lakes

41

AREA 4 map on page 96

Building at Mary Murphy Mine has fallen down in recent years.

You pass this old boardinghouse at 0.7 mile.

Historical Highlight: *Mary Murphy Mine was a top producing mine that supported the town of Romley. The area flourished between 1870 and the early 1900s. The main part of Romley was located in a meadow below C.R. 295. Romley was also known as "Red Town," because all buildings in town were painted red with white trim. The railroad removed its tracks in 1926, but it was not until 1982 that the town was torn down by its owners.*

Overview: A significant number of mining structures remain, and most are on the lower, easier part of trail. You'll see many sightseers here. Fewer people venture up the harder parts of the trail to the Mary Murphy Mine and Lower Pomeroy Lake. No seasonal closures.

Rating: Difficult. Applies only to upper end of trails. The side trip to Mary Murphy Mine is a steep, narrow shelf road, but is relatively smooth. The only section not recommended for stock SUV is above Waypoint 03, where it is rocky and steep.

Stats: Length: 2.7 miles to lower lake,

add 0.6 mile for Mary Murphy Mine. Time: 2 to 3 hours. High point: 12,100 feet. Best time of year: July-Sept.

Current Conditions: San Isabel N.F., Salida R.D. Call (719) 539-3591.

Getting There: From Johnson Village, head south on Hwy. 285 about 6 miles. Just past Nathrop, turn right on C.R. 162. Go west 15.4 miles to parking/staging area (with toilet) on left. Immediately after parking area, bear left on C.R. 295. Go another 2.8 miles. Turn left at sign for Mary Murphy Mine after point where road dips to right to bypass old trestle.

MILEAGE LOG:

0.0 Zero trip odometer [Rev. Miles]
Head uphill on rocky
F.S. 297. [2.7]
01 N38 40.390 W106 22.004

0.7 Arrive at cluster of buildings. Boardinghouse on
right and Mary Murphy
Mill on left. [2.0]

0.9 Continue straight. [1.8]

1.1 Stay left. Private road
goes right. [1.6]

1.4 Bear right to reach Pomeroy Lakes. Left is side
trip to Mary Murphy Mine
described below. [1.3]
02 N38 39.588 W106 21.130

1.6 Interesting grave on right
next to road, followed by
road that joins on left.
 [1.1]

1.8 Turn sharply left up steep,
rocky road. Stock vehicles
may wish to park straight
ahead and hike from here.
 [0.9]
03 N38 39.311 W106 20.719

2.7 Trail ends at large flat
area to turn around. Hike
short distance to lower
lake or longer for upper
lake. [0.0]
04 N38 38.906 W106 20.381

0.0 Zero trip odometer
SIDE TRIP TO MINE:
Head northeast uphill on
road that soon becomes
narrow shelf road. [0.6]

0.6 Turn right then left up
steep hill to reach wide
area with turnaround.
Look around but don't get
too close. Leave every-
thing as you find it. [0.0]
05 N38 40.088 W106 21.064

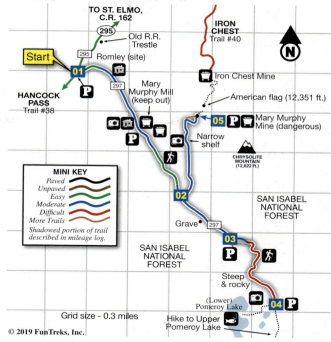

TO ST. ELMO, C.R. 162

IRON CHEST Trail #40

Old R.R. Trestle

Romley (site)

Start

HANCOCK PASS Trail #38

Mary Murphy Mill (keep out)

Iron Chest Mine

American flag (12,351 ft.)

Mary Murphy Mine (dangerous)

Narrow shelf

CHRYSOLITE MOUNTAIN (12,822 ft.)

MINI KEY
Paved
Unpaved
Easy
Moderate
Difficult
More Trails
Shadowed portion of trail described in mileage log.

SAN ISABEL NATIONAL FOREST

Grave

SAN ISABEL NATIONAL FOREST

Steep & rocky

(Lower) Pomeroy Lake

Grid size - 0.3 miles

Hike to Upper Pomeroy Lake

© 2019 FunTreks, Inc.

Wildflowers border Lower Pomeroy Lake.

The shelf road to Mary Murphy Mine is extremely narrow. Proceed with caution.

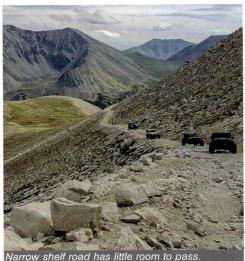
Narrow shelf road has little room to pass.

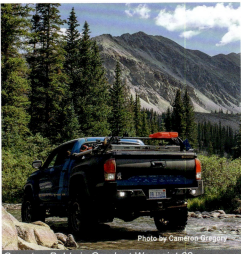
Photo by Cameron Gregory

Crossing Baldwin Creek at Waypoint 02.

Photo by Cameron Gregory

Summit at Waypoint 04.

Historical Highlight: At 14,269 feet, Mt. Antero is the 10th-highest peak in Colorado. The road up the mountain is relatively recent, built by a mining company in the early 1950s. Unlike most mining in the area, gold and silver were not the coveted ores. Rather, the mountain is known for aquamarine crystals. Although the area has proven itself commercially nonviable, prospectors and gem seekers continue to search for the valuable crystals, known to be primarily near the top. Everything left on the surface was picked clean long ago. Most of the area is open for hand digging; however, the work is difficult, with little chance of success. Only the hardy need apply. Source: www.buenavistagemworks.com

Overview: Incredibly high drive to near top of 14,000-ft. peak. Quiet camping at remote Browns Lake. Other roads to explore. Popular hiking and camping area. Campgrounds and private resorts along C.R. 162. Unlicensed vehicles stage at trailhead or St. Elmo and use F.S. 292. No seasonal closures.

Rating: Difficult. Extremely narrow shelf road with tight switchbacks. Small SUVs with low-range gearing and high clearance can drive all but last half mile to near top of Mt. Antero and Browns Lake. Oversize vehicles will have a hard time at switchbacks. Experienced drivers only. Avoid being at the top or stay in your vehicle if you see lightning in the area.

Stats: Length: 7.1 miles one way from C.R. 162 to Mt. Antero. Time: 3 to 4 hours. Add 2 hours for side trip to Browns Lake. High point: 13,750 ft. Best time of year: Mid July-Sept.

Current Conditions: San Isabel N.F., Salida R.D. Call (719) 539-3591.

Getting There: From Johnson Village, head south on Hwy. 285 about 6 miles. Just past Nathrop, turn west on C.R. 162 and go 12.3 miles to sign for Mt. Antero on left.

MILEAGE LOG:

0.0 Zero trip odometer [Rev. Miles]
MT. ANTERO:
Follow rocky F.S. 277 uphill. [7.1]
01 N38 42.600 W106 17.498

1.2 Continue straight. (Boulder Mountain is right. [5.9]

2.7 Turn left on F.S. 278 and cross Baldwin Creek. Straight is Baldwin Lk. [4.4]
02 N38 40.949 W106 16.375

4.2 Come out of trees and begin climbing narrow switchbacks. [2.9]

5.9 Turn left on 278.A. [1.2]
03 N38 39.706 W106 15.477

6.0 Stay left where 278.B goes right to Mt. White. [1.1]

6.5 Wide spot at fork. Stock vehicles should park here and walk to top. Hard-core vehicles with lockers can continue. [0.6]

7.1 Large flat area to park just below peak. Turn around here and visit Mt. White for more views, then return to Waypoint 03. [0.0]
04 N38 40.037 W106 14.977

0.0 Zero trip odometer
BROWNS LAKE:
From Waypoint 03, head south on F.S. 278. [3.5]

1.0 Bear left and descend rocky switchbacks. [2.5]

2.1 Stay left. Road weaves tightly through trees, then opens up. [1.4]

3.5 After rocky, steep section, you reach lake with good camping. [0.0]
05 N38 38.630 W106 14.738

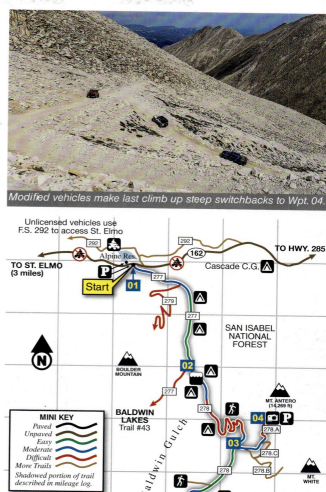

Modified vehicles make last climb up steep switchbacks to Wpt. 04.

Unlicensed vehicles use F.S. 292 to access St. Elmo

292

Alpine Res.

162

TO HWY. 285

TO ST. ELMO (3 miles)

Cascade C.G.

Start

01

277

279

277

SAN ISABEL NATIONAL FOREST

N

BOULDER MOUNTAIN

02

277

278

MT. ANTERO (14,269 ft)

BALDWIN LAKES Trail #43

04

278.A

03

278.C

278

278.B

MT. WHITE

MINI KEY
Paved
Unpaved
Easy
Moderate
Difficult
More Trails
Shadowed portion of trail described in mileage log.

05 Browns Lake

Baldwin Gulch

Grid size - 1 mile

© 2019 FunTreks, Inc.

Side trip on 278.B to Mt. White. Still had impressive views on this cloudy day.

You'll pass several smaller lakes before you reach Baldwin Lake at the top.

This is the toughest spot on the trail.

Look for these markers at start of trail.

Overview: Scenic, remote, lesser-traveled backroads are part of the highest OHV trail system in the U.S. Camp and fish at Baldwin Lakes, known for cutthroat trout. Narrowness of Boulder Mountain makes it ideal for ATVs and UTVs. Great views at the top. No seasonal closures except for snow.

Rating: Difficult: Rocky, narrow road suitable for aggressive, high-clearance SUVs with low range and skid plates. Boulder Mountain has two narrow, tippy spots on a shelf road. Oversize vehicles should not attempt. Snow melts late.

Stats: Baldwin Lakes: Length: 5 miles one way from C.R.162. Time: 3-4 hours. **Boulder Mountain:** Length: 5 miles one way from 277. Time: 2-3 hours. High point: 12,800 ft. Best time of year: July-Sept.

Current Conditions: San Isabel N.F., Salida R.D. Call (719) 539-3591.

Getting There: From Johnson Village, head south on Hwy. 285 about 6 miles. Just past Nathrop, turn west on C.R. 162 and go 12.3 miles. Turn left at markers for F.S. 277 and Mt. Antero.

0.0 Zero trip odometer [Rev. Miles]
BALDWIN LAKES:
Head uphill on 277.   [5.0]
`01` N38 42.599 W106 17.500

1.2 Continue straight. Boulder Mountain is right.   [3.8]
`02` N38 42.221 W106 16.487

2.7 Continue straight along creek. Mt. Antero is left across creek.   [2.3]
`03` N38 40.954 W106 16.373

3.6 Begin crossing rocky talus slopes.   [1.4]

4.2 Stay left. Closed road on right climbs to mine.   [0.8]
`04` N38 40.142 W106 17.496

4.7 Climb along right side of lakes. A few dispersed camping spots on left. [0.3]

5.0 Parking area. Hike ¼ mile to lake from here. Road that continues on right is not shown on MVUM. Turn around and return to Wpt. 02.   [0.0]
`05` N38 39.725 W106 18.094

0.0 Zero trip odometer
BOULDER MOUNTAIN:
Head west from Wpt. 02 up steep trail that winds tightly through trees.   [5.0]

0.9 Road joins on left at cabin ruin. Main road follows valley, then turns sharply right and begins series of narrow switchbacks.   [4.1]

3.0 Road gradually flattens out and gets easier.   [2.0]

5.0 Gentle climb with easy talus slopes end at small mine.   [0.0]
`06` N38 41.234 W106 17.388

MINI KEY
Paved
Unpaved
Easy
Moderate
Difficult
More Trails
Shadowed portion of trail described in mileage log.

Grid size - 1 mile

© 2019 FunTreks, Inc.

Don't go too early or you'll have to deal with lingering snow.

F.S. 279 ends here at top of Boulder Mountain at 12,800 feet.

Narrow and tippy F.S. 279.

On this June 14, we had to stop here and walk the last mile of the trail.

Passing is very tight in a few places.

Last mile is narrow and rough.

Overview: A popular 4x4 road because of its easy access. A relatively short drive to outstanding views even though the road does not go all the way to top. A few small camp spots along route. Unlicensed vehicles are allowed on F.S. 322 after forest boundary. You cannot park or unload in the parking area at the start; it's private property. Pick-up trucks hauling ATVs have the best chance of finding a place to park along the narrow road at the bottom. Road is closed Dec. 1 to April 15.

Rating: Moderate. Most of the road is easy except near the top where a narrow shelf road may intimidate novice drivers. Most stock, high-clearance 4x4 SUVs can do it. Low-range gearing is needed for steepest climbs. Snow may block trail at top as late as June or July.

Stats: Length: 5.4 miles. Time: 2 to 3 hours for round trip. High point: 12,300 ft. Best time of year: Late July-Sept.

Current Conditions: San Isabel N.F., Salida R.D. Call (719) 539-3591.

Getting There: From Johnson Village, head south on Hwy. 285 about 6 miles. Just past Nathrop, turn right on C.R. 162 and go 4.4 miles west to Mt. Princeton Hot Springs. Turn right uphill on C.R. 321. Stay on this paved road 1.2 miles and bear left on C.R. 322. Continue south, then west about a mile to entrance on right at Frontier Ranch.

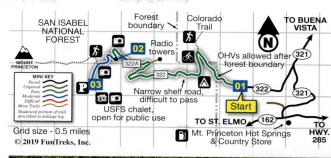

START *MILEAGE LOG:*

0.0 **Zero trip odometer** [Rev. Miles]
Stay right of Frontier Ranch gate and pass through parking area. Follow Mt. Princeton signs uphill on F.S. 322. [5.4]
01 N38 44.395 W106 10.509

1.1 Swing left where Colorado Trail goes right. As you climb, road comes out of trees along a narrow shelf road where it is difficult to pass. [4.3]

3.2 Stay left. Road on right goes to radio towers. [2.2]

4.2 Steeper road 322A is more chewed up. You may see passenger cars parked here. [1.2]
02 N38 44.710 W106 12.595

4.4 Last switchback before shelf road crosses face of mountain. Snow lingers here, sometimes into July. You may have to walk from here. [1.0]

5.4 Short, steep climb to right leads to small parking area at end of trail. Follow hiking trail short distance to interesting chalet owned by U.S. Forest Service. It's open to public. A hiking trail goes to the top of this 14,000-ft peak. [0.0]
03 N38 44.189 W106 12.824

Get FREE trail updates & GPS downloads at www.FunTreks.com

Grid size - 0.5 miles
© 2019 FunTreks, Inc.

Trail is popular with hikers and bikers. Drive with caution.

Chalet at end of trail.

Bear right here and pass through private parking lot.

Incredible views from dispersed camping areas along Shields Gulch south of Waypoint 02.

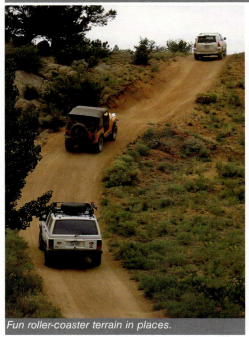
Fun roller-coaster terrain in places.

See small ghost town crossing Goddard Ranch.

Historical Highlight: *As you enter the area on F.S. 315, you'll see signs for the Midland Bike Trail on the left. This bike route follows an old railroad grade of the Colorado Midland R.R. that was active from 1887 to 1918. The railroad ran from Colorado Springs to New Castle on the Western Slope. New Castle produced coal and limestone, which was shipped to major mining centers, including Leadville. The railroad also carried passengers to Glenwood Hot Springs.*

Overview: Outstanding dispersed camping with incredible views of the Collegiate Peaks. Northwest corner of area has spaghetti-like network of roads that are fun to explore. Great area for ATVs, UTVs and dirt bikes. Seasonal gates close much of the area in winter and spring. Goddard Ranch is private property and is gated on each side during this same period. Open May 1 to Nov. 30.

Rating: Easy. Variety of conditions from graded roads to narrow, rutted and sandy roads. Steep in a few places.

Stats: Length: 24.7 miles. Time: 3 to 4 hours. High point: 9,800 ft. Best time of year: Mid May-Oct.

Current Conditions: San Isabel N.F., Salida R.D. Call (719) 539-3591.

Getting There: From Hwy. 24/285, at a point 5.5 miles east of Hwy. 24, turn north on F.S. Road 315, marked with a blue sign. Alternate entry point, on F.S. 311 at Trout Creek Pass, is located between mile markers 225 and 226. Look for large San Isabel National Forest sign.

116

MILEAGE LOG:

0.0 Zero trip odometer [Rev. Miles]
Follow wide, sandy 315 northwest uphill through Shields Gulch. [9.3]
01 N38 50.090 W106 01.380

1.8 Continue straight. Small road on left goes to great dispersed camping with views of valley. More camping follows. [7.5]

2.6 Bear right on 376. [6.7]
02 N38 51.488 W106 03.237

3.5 Stay right where 376B goes left. [5.8]

3.6 Stay left where 305 goes right. [5.7]

4.9 Take short hike up hillside on left to see mine. [4.4]
03 N38 52.277 W106 01.390

5.6 After mine on right, drop downhill into Chubb Park. [3.7]

6.7 Turn left on F.S. 309. [2.6]
04 N38 52.899 W105 59.811

9.3 You reach F.S. 311. Alternate entrance comes in from right. [0.0]
05 N38 54.844 W106 01.249

0.0 Zero trip odometer
Bear left on 311. After topping ridge, drop downhill and pass through Goddard Ranch with ghost town on left. Road closed 12/1 to 4/30. [6.4]

4.1 Bear left. [2.3]

4.2 Stay right where ATV trail goes left. [2.2]

4.9 Turn right on 373. [1.5]
06 N38 54.100 W106 05.372

6.3 Stay left. [0.1]

6.4 Stay left at intersection. Right dead ends at great view of Buena Vista and hiking trail. [0.0]
07 N38 54.789 W106 06.583

0.0 Zero trip odometer
Head south on 373. [9.0]

1.4 Continue straight. Left goes to camp spot. [7.6]

2.3 Continue straight on 375A following sandy wash. [6.7]

2.9 Stay right. Pass beaver ponds and culvert bridge over Fourmile Creek. [6.1]

3.9 Bear left on larger 375. Pass through good camping area. [5.1]
08 N38 53.986 W106 07.818

5.4 Continue straight where 376 joins on left. This is fun road that goes back to Shields Gulch. [3.6]
09 N38 53.056 W106 08.460

6.5 Turn left on wide 371 along railroad tracks. Follow it south into Buena Vista where it becomes North Colorado Ave. [2.5]
10 N38 52.471 W106 08.670

9.0 Turn right on main street to reach Hwy. 24. [0.0]

Mine shaft at Waypoint 03.

Toughest section of trail before Waypoint 03.

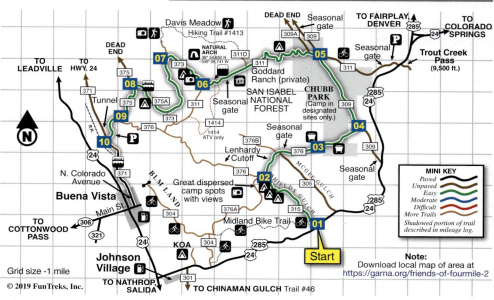

Grid size -1 mile

© 2019 FunTreks, Inc.

MINI KEY
Paved
Unpaved
Easy
Moderate
Difficult
More Trails
Shadowed portion of trail described in mileage log.

Note:
Download local map of area at
https://garna.org/friends-of-fourmile-2

Modified Jeep goes up easier spot on Waterfall.

Tight and twisty trail through here.

Trail coming down northern portion of loop.

Overview: One of the most popular motorized recreation spots in Colorado for both licensed and unlicensed vehicles. Minimal snow and close proximity to the Front Range makes it a popular winter destination. Carnage Canyon is a nationally recognized extreme trail.

A showcase area for extreme but responsible 4-wheeling. Stay on established routes at all times. Carry and use a spill kit if you attempt Carnage Canyon.

Rating: **Chinaman:** Difficult: Narrow and sandy with isolated rock obstacles, some with bypasses. Best suited for modified vehicles with large tires, lockers and skid plates. **Carnage:** An extreme trail for radically modified vehicles. Minimum 35-inch tires with lockers both ends. Be prepared to

winch, often. Expect mechanical failures and body damage.

Stats: **Chinaman:** Length: 7.1 miles round trip. Time: 2 to 4 hours. High point: 8,900 ft. **Carnage:** Length: 1 mile. Time: 2 to 5 hours. Open all year. Best time of year: May-Oct. Hot in summer.

Current Conditions: BLM Royal Gorge Field Office. Call (719) 539-7289.

Getting There: Take Hwy. 285 southwest from Denver or Hwy. 24 west from Colorado Springs. Turn left on C.R. 301 about a half mile before Johnson Village. Drive 1.6 miles south and look for gated road on left with BLM Chinaman Gulch sign. Drive in about 0.4 mile to parking area.

MILEAGE LOG:

0.0 *Zero trip odometer* [Rev. Miles]
CHINAMAN GULCH:
Head north along fence-
line. [5.4]
`01` N38 47.520 W106 05.133

0.2 At clearing, make hard
right up shelf road. [5.2]
`02` N38 47.736 W106 05.095

0.3 Gets very rocky. [5.1]
1.0 Make sharp left. Exit point
of Carnage on right. [4.4]
`03` N38 47.686 W106 04.460

1.4 Stay right. [4.0]
1.7 Bear right in sandy wash
and begin loop. [3.7]
`04` N38 48.207 W106 04.686

2.0 Optional Rockpile to right. [3.4]
2.6 The "Waterfall." Easier on
right side. Narrow, steep
canyon follows. [2.8]
`05` N38 47.885 W106 03.946

3.6 Stay left. (Trail 1423 goes
right to fun ATV, dirt bike
area. [1.8]
`06` N38 48.054 W106 03.221

3.6+ Optional Little Double
Whammy to right. More
obstacles without by-
passes follow. [1.8]

5.3 After narrow, rocky descent, bear left. [0.1]
`07` N38 48.296 W106 04.653

5.4 Return to start of loop at
Waypoint 04 and go out
the way you came in. [0.0]

0.0 *Zero trip odometer*
CARNAGE CANYON:
From parking area, head
east into sandy canyon.
Entrance, just ahead, is
well marked with warning
signs. Obstacles begin
immediately. Winch out at
end of canyon and bear
left.

1.0 Connect to Chinaman
Gulch at Waypoint 03. Left
returns to start.

Entrance to Carnage Canyon.

Heavily modified Tacoma climbs last obstacle before Waypoint 07.

TO HWY. 24,
JOHNSON
VILLAGE

MINI KEY
Paved
Unpaved
Easy
Moderate
Difficult
More Trails
*Shadowed portion of trail
described in mileage log.*

`07`
6044
`04`
CHINAMAN GULCH
Sandy
wash
Rockpile
(Optional)
BLM LAND

Rocky, steep
descent
Little
Double Whammy
(Optional)
BLM LAND
Tough
obstacle has
no bypass
`06`
1423
Narrow and tight
through trees
Rocky
`05`
6044
Waterfall
(Extreme to left,
moderate to right.)

301
BLM LAND
`02`
`03`
6042
Gate
6043
Gate
`01`
P
Start
CARNAGE CANYON
Extreme 4x4 Trail
Colorado
Detention
Facility

Grid size - 0.2 miles

N

119

North Fork Reservoir at dam. Note lingering snow in late June.

Overview: The road is fairly bumpy and mostly in the trees until you get to the North Fork Reservoir. This is a popular fishing lake, and camp spots go quickly in this fee campground. Reservations are recommended on weekends. There are many excellent dispersed camp spots along the route, some near scenic McCoy Creek. Two significant waterfalls are shown on map. Open to unlicensed vehicles after the forest boundary. There is a parking area used for staging where the dirt road begins prior to the forest boundary. We saw no signs prohibiting riding this short section of county road, but this could change. Trail is open all year, weather permitting.

Rating: Easy. Bumpy embedded rock requires high clearance. Four-wheel drive and low range recommended after North Fork Reservoir.

Stats: Length: About 8 miles depending on where you turn around at Billings Lake. Time: 2-3 hours for round trip. High point: 11,900 ft. Best time of year: July to early October.

Current Conditions: San Isabel N.F., Salida R.D. Call (719) 539-3591.

Getting There: Head west on Highway 50 from Salida towards Monarch Pass. Bear right on paved C.R. 240 about a half mile west of mile marker 211, north of Maysville. Follow this paved road north 3.1 miles until it changes to dirt, then continue 0.7 mile to start of trail at Angel of Shavano Campground.

MILEAGE LOG:

Zero trip odometer [Rev. Miles]

0.0 Angel of Shavano Group Picnic Ground, Campground and hiking trailhead. C.R. 240 becomes F.S. 240. [7.8]
01 N38 35.057 W106 13.167

0.2 Dispersed camp spot by waterfall on right. Many good dispersed camp spots follow. [7.6]

2.7 Hidden waterfall on left. Walk short distance to edge of canyon. Caution: High cliffs. [5.1]
02 N38 35.735 W106 15.686

6.2 Stay right uphill for Billings Lake. Left goes to popular North Fork Reservoir and fee campground. [1.6]
03 N38 36.676 W106 18.924

7.4 Gated fork to left goes toward Billings Lake. Good dispersed camp spots scattered around. [0.4]
04 N38 37.443 W106 19.554

7.8 Road continues around lake past various mines. It appears to loop all the way back, but a gate prevents completing loop. You must turn around at some point. The road gets rougher, but it's fun. [0.0]

Get FREE trail updates & GPS downloads at www.FunTreks.com

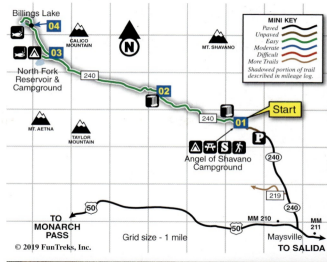

Billings Lake

MINI KEY
Paved
Unpaved
Easy
Moderate
Difficult
More Trails
Shadowed portion of trail described in mileage log.

CALICO MOUNTAIN
MT. SHAVANO
North Fork Reservoir & Campground
240
02
Start
01
MT. AETNA
TAYLOR MOUNTAIN
240
Angel of Shavano Campground
240
219
TO MONARCH PASS
50
MM 210
50
240
MM 211
Maysville
Grid size - 1 mile
TO SALIDA

© 2019 FunTreks, Inc.

Many free dispersed camp spots along F.S. 240.

Look for waterfall at Wpt. 02.

Billings Lake in late July. Stay on designated routes.

121

Poncha Creek Road climbs through thick aspens, a great trip for fall color.

Marshall Pass at 10,842 feet.

Historical Highlight: *In the 1920s, the town of Shirley was a transfer point for silver, zinc, lead and copper ores that arrived via aerial tram from the Rawley Mine in Bonanza, located over the mountains to the south (see Trail #49). From Shirley, the ore was loaded onto railcars of the Denver and Rio Grande Western Railroad and hauled over Marshall Pass to smelters in Leadville. The main road over Marshall Pass follows the old railroad grade. Shirley died in 1930 when the Rawley Mine shut down.*

Overview: A popular camping and fishing area with several Forest Service campgrounds around O'Haver Lake. Poncha Creek Road offers a better backcountry experience with stream fishing and dispersed camping next to the water. Great fall color with lots of aspens. Parking lots near Shirley Townsite and Marshall Pass provide convenient staging for unlicensed vehicles, which are not allowed on county roads entering and leaving the area. Road closed March 1 to May 1.

Rating: Easy. Marshall Pass can be reached from either side via well-graded, 2-wheel-drive roads F.S. 243 and F.S. 200. The route shown here bypasses 200 and takes you up the east side along parallel Poncha Creek Road, F.S. 203. This 4-wheel-drive road is less traveled with fewer motorists. Suitable for any SUV with low range gearing and high clearance.

Stats: Length: 27 miles. Time: 3 to 4 hours. High point: 10,842 ft. Best time of year: Mid June-Oct.

Current Conditions: San Isabel N.F., Salida R.D. Call (719) 539-3591.

Getting There: Take Hwy. 285 south from Poncha Springs about 5 miles. Turn right on well-marked C.R. 200 and follow signs to Marshall Pass.

MILEAGE LOG:

0.0 Zero trip odometer [Rev. Miles]
Head west on wide, graded C.R. 200. [10.3]
`01` N38 26.894 W106 06.414

2.3 Continue straight. Kiosks on left explain history of the area. Right is easiest way to O'Haver Lake and Marshall Pass. [8.0]

2.4 Large parking lot and staging area on left with toilet. Bear right. [7.9]

3.1 Cross one-lane bridge and turn left on 203. Pass through area of dispersed camping popular for fishing along creek. [7.2]
`02` N38 24.934 W106 08.300

5.6 Continue straight past Starvation Creek Hiking Trailhead on left. Road gets rougher as it begins to climb more. [4.7]
`03` N38 23.899 W106 10.404

7.3 Continue straight. Road to left goes downhill to camp spot along creek. [3.0]

9.7 Stay right where 203A goes left. [0.6]

10.2 Flat area near Marshall Pass. Right goes direct to C.R. 200. To reach Marshall Pass, continue west short distance, then bear right downhill. [0.1]

10.3 Arrive at Marshall Pass parking area with camping spots and hiking. [0.0]
`04` N38 23.496 W106 14.890

0.0 Zero trip odometer
Head down west side of pass on wide, smooth F.S. 243. Note black soot along sides of road as you are following an old railroad grade. [16.7]

11.3 Stay left on F.S. 243 where wide road joins on right. [5.4]
`05` N38 22.200 W106 20.610

16.7 Follow super-wide gravel road into Sargents at Highway 50. Trading post has gas. [0.0]
`06` N38 24.430 W106 24.920

Get FREE trail updates & GPS downloads at www.FunTreks.com

Tomichi Creek Trading Post at Sargents has gas.

Low-clearance vehicle navigates toughest part of trail.

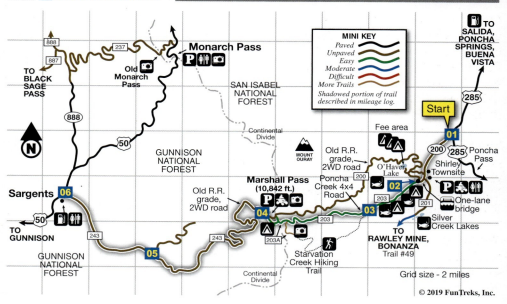

MINI KEY
Paved
Unpaved
Easy
Moderate
Difficult
More Trails
Shadowed portion of trail described in mileage log.

Monarch Pass
Old Monarch Pass

TO BLACK SAGE PASS

SAN ISABEL NATIONAL FOREST

Continental Divide

MOUNT OURAY

GUNNISON NATIONAL FOREST

Fee area
Old R.R. grade, 2WD road
O'Haver Lake
Poncha Creek 4x4 Road

TO SALIDA, PONCHA SPRINGS, BUENA VISTA

Start

Poncha Pass
Shirley Townsite
One-lane bridge
Silver Creek Lakes

Marshall Pass (10,842 ft.)
Old R.R. grade, 2WD road

Sargents `06`
TO GUNNISON

GUNNISON NATIONAL FOREST

Starvation Creek Hiking Trail

TO RAWLEY MINE, BONANZA Trail #49

Continental Divide

Grid size - 2 miles

© 2019 FunTreks, Inc.

Rawley Mine, Bonanza

AREA 4 map on page 96

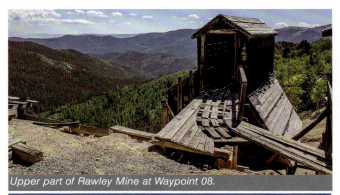
Upper part of Rawley Mine at Waypoint 08.

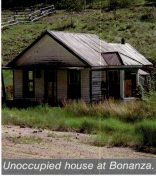
Unoccupied house at Bonanza.

Narrow shelf road no problem for a UTV.

Historical Highlight: *Bonanza was a town of 500 people in the early 1880s, with over 100 buildings, including 6 saloons, a drugstore, post office, hardware store, school, town hall, furniture store and 2 hotels. As the silver mines faded, the population dropped to below 100. A second boom occurred in the 1920s with the discovery of new ore at the Rawley Mine. At that time, a cable tram was built to carry ore to a mill in Shirley. Bonanza faded away in the 1930s, and much was destroyed by fire in 1937. A few residents still remain.*

Overview: This is a fun trip with lots of standing mine buildings, especially at the Rawley Mine. See historic town of Bonanza, but respect privacy of the few residents that remain. Plenty of trails to explore including alternate return route shown on map but not described in text. Although route-finding is tricky, it's worth the effort if you seek more adventure. Closed March 15 to May 15.

Rating: Moderate. Most of this route is easy; however, the climb starting at Waypoint 02 is extremely narrow in places and requires low range. If you encounter another vehicle, you may have to back up a considerable distance. Alternate return route has a few moderately rocky spots, but is otherwise easy.

Stats: Length: About 36 miles. Time: 4 to 6 hours. High point: 11,200 ft. Best time of year: Mid June-early Oct.

Current Conditions: Rio Grande and San Isabel N.F. Call (719) 539-3591.

Getting There: Take Hwy. 285 south from Poncha Springs about 5 miles. Turn right on well-marked C.R. 200 and go 2.3 miles to information kiosk on left. Stay left and continue short distance to parking lot on left.

You can also reach Bonanza from the south via County Road LL-56. It starts from Highway 285 just north of Villa Grove. If you are driving Hayden Pass, Trail #97, you can add Trail #48 to make a great loop back to Salida.

MILEAGE LOG:

START

0.0 Zero trip odometer **[Rev. Miles]**
Head south on wide, graded 201 from parking lot. **[14.9]**
01 N38 25.203 W106 07.756

2.9 Road gets rougher, stay right. **[12.0]**

5.4 Hard left uphill at sign for Toll Road Gulch. **[9.5]**
02 N38 21.816 W106 10.632

9.2 Cross talus ledge road with views. **[5.7]**

11.0 Stay right downhill. **[3.9]**

12.1 Continue straight on 869. Left is alternate return route shown on map. **[2.8]**
03 N38 19.716 W106 08.740

13.0 Stay right. **[1.9]**

13.2 Picnic tables with modern vault toilet. **[1.7]**

14.0 Continue straight to town of Bonanza. **[0.9]**
04 N38 18.402 W106 08.831

14.9 Bonanza. Turn around here and return to Waypoint 04. **[0.0]**
05 N38 17.658 W106 08.562

0.0 Zero trip odometer
Coming from Bonanza, turn right at Wpt. 04. **[3.2]**

0.8 Hard left up tight switchback. Right is interesting but difficult back way to Rawley Mines. **[2.4]**

1.0 Hard right uphill on 890. Left goes to 869. **[2.2]**
06 N38 18.684 W106 08.450

2.2 Hard left uphill. Straight downhill is lower part of Rawley Mine. **[1.0]**
07 N38 19.302 W106 07.545

3.0 Turn right on lesser road. Main road 890 continues to left to Round Mtn. **[0.2]**

3.2 Arrive at upper Rawley Mine. **[0.0]**
08 N38 19.536 W106 07.507
Explore other roads around mines, then return to Waypoint 06, where a right turn will take you back the way you came. Turning left at Waypoint 06 will take you back to Bonanza, where you can continue south about 15 miles on a good road to Highway 285 near Villa Grove.

Several water crossings as you climb to the shelf road.

MINI KEY
Paved
Unpaved
Easy
Moderate
Difficult
More Trails
Shadowed portion of trail described in mileage log.

TO SALIDA, PONCHA SPRINGS, BUENA VISTA

200
285

Shirley Townsite (Information kiosk)

Poncha Pass

O'Haver Lake

Start 01

200

203

SAN ISABEL NATIONAL FOREST

5325

TO VILLA GROVE

878

5325

Moderate rocky descent

201.B

Follow signs to Silver Creek

MARSHALL PASS VIA PONCHA CREEK Trail #48

N38° 24.122 W106° 07.664

201

Private drive

5325

5330

N38° 23.167 W106° 04.743

RIO GRANDE NATIONAL FOREST

876

To camping and Hwy. 285

Alternate way back to start is fun but route-finding is complex.

Road follows Clover Creek starting here.

890

890

02

Narrow

ROUND MOUNTAIN

Shelf road

876

Rawley Mines with standing structures

Enter Rio Grande National Forest

869

Muddy

Superior Mill (site)

03

08

07

Whale Mine

892

Whale Hill over 12,000 ft.

869

890

Superior Mine

862

06

04

RIO GRANDE NATIONAL FOREST

Exchequer Townsite and cemetery

Information board explains history.

Grid size - 1 mile

Bonanza 05

TO VILLA GROVE, HWY. 285

© 2019 FunTreks, Inc.

Green = Easy, Blue = Moderate, Red = Difficult

Vail, Leadville, Fairplay

Many of the trails in Area 5 were originally built as mining roads during the boom years of the 1880s and 1890s. Some trails, like Mosquito Pass, were abandoned within a short time of their construction and replaced by fast-developing railroads. Much of Hagerman Pass Road follows an old railroad grade left from the first standard gauge railroad built across the Continental Divide. It is hard to imagine that today's little-used Weston Pass was once a busy stagecoach route hauling thousands of people and tons of supplies into Leadville. For a truly amazing hard-core experience, check out impressive Holy Cross, considered by us to be one of the best trails in Colorado.

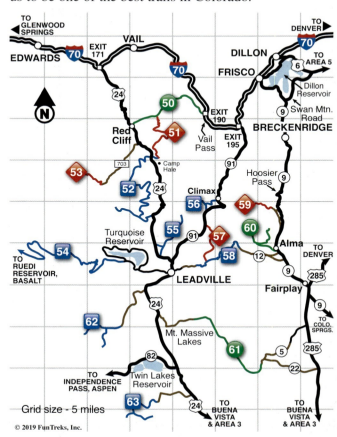

Grid size - 5 miles

© 2019 FunTreks, Inc.

Early obstacle on Holy Cross, Trail #53, rated difficult.

East side is quite easy after it dries out in the summer. Mount Holy Cross can be seen top center.

UTV heads east through forest gate coming uphill from Red Cliff.

Historical Highlight: Shrine Pass was the primary route over the Gore Mountains before the construction of Interstate 70 in the 1970s. Today it's a popular cross-country ski and snowmobiling area located south of the Vail Ski Area. Mount of the Holy Cross was dedicated as a national monument in 1929, but later lost that status.

Overview: Views of Mt. Holy Cross from the west side of Shrine Pass. Short walk to observation deck (handicap accessible). Popular area for mountain biking and hiking. Snow can block road even in July. Great wildflowers and fall color. Open to unlicensed vehicles between Waypoints 02 and 05 from June 21 to November 22.

Rating: Easy. Suitable for passenger cars to the observation deck. Road gets narrower and rougher as you descend towards Red Cliff. Can get muddy and 4-wheel drive may be necessary.

Stats: Length: 11.2 miles. Time: 1 hour. High point: 11,089 ft. Best time of year: Mid July-early Oct.

Current Conditions: White River N.F. Holy Cross R.D. Call (970) 827-5715.

Getting There: Get off Interstate 70 at exit 190 between Copper Mountain and Vail. Continue straight (west) on Shrine Pass Road where paved road turns left for the rest area.

MILEAGE LOG:

0.0 Zero trip odometer [Rev. Miles] Head west from freeway on wide dirt road. [11.2]
01 N39 31.774 W106 13.082

2.3 Large parking lot on left at Shrine Pass. Popular hiking and biking trails depart from this area. Vault toilet. [8.9]
02 N39 32.770 W106 14.477

3.7 Small parking lot on left with toilet. Take short walk from here to observation deck to see Mount Holy Cross. [7.5]
03 N39 33.606 W106 15.352

3.8 Continue straight where Lime Creek Road goes right. This road is wide and easy and offers some dispersed camping. Dead-ends in 5.0 miles. [7.4]

8.7 Small wooden bridge on left goes to McAllister Gulch, Trail #51. [2.5]
04 N39 31.422 W106 19.534

11.0 As you enter Red Cliff, pass over bridge where pavement begins. [0.2]

11.2 Arrive at "T" intersection in town. Turn right and climb High Road to Hwy. 24. At 24, turn left for Leadville; right for Minturn and back to I-70 west of Vail. [0.0]
05 N39 30.804 W106 22.085

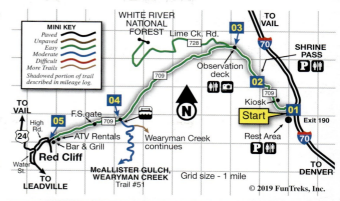

MINI KEY
Paved
Unpaved
Easy
Moderate
Difficult
More Trails
Shadowed portion of trail described in mileage log.

WHITE RIVER NATIONAL FOREST
Lime Ck. Rd.
728
709
Observation deck
TO VAIL
03
TO VAIL
SHRINE PASS
70
02
709
Kiosk
Start
01
Exit 190
04
F.S. gate
709
05
High Rd.
24
ATV Rentals
Bar & Grill
Wearyman Creek continues
Rest Area
TO DENVER
TO VAIL
Red Cliff
Water St.
TO LEADVILLE
McALLISTER GULCH, WEARYMAN CREEK
Trail #51
Grid size - 1 mile
© 2019 FunTreks, Inc.

View of Mount Holy Cross from the observation deck.

CAUTION
HISTORIC MILITARY WEAPONS AREA
DO NOT TOUCH OR REMOVE UNKNOWN OBJECTS

FIRE RESTRICTIONS

Information kiosk and warning signs at east end of trail just up the hill from rest area.

129

Easy stretch of road across Hornsilver Mountain.

Looking down on Camp Hale.

Left at Wpt. 05 follows narrow creek to Wpt. 06.

Historical Highlight: Camp Hale was established in 1942 as a winter training post for the army. At its peak, the camp housed about 16,000 soldiers, 14,000 of whom were members of the famous 10th Mountain Division. In addition to barracks, the post included mess halls, a hospital, chapel, fire station, post exchange, stockade, ski shop, bakery and an ice-making plant. Information boards are located on Highway 24 and throughout the area.

Overview: Trail begins at historic Camp Hale, climbs to top of Resolution Mountain, then descends to Shrine Pass Road via Wearyman Creek. Panoramic views of mountains including Mt. Holy Cross. Fee camping at south end of Camp Hale. No dispersed camping in Camp Hale. Optional: At Wpt. 05, turn right up Wearyman Creek to Ptarmigan Pass to make a loop. Open from June 21 to November 22.

Rating: Mostly moderate, except for one steep, rocky spot pictured on opposite page. Most stock 4x4s can get up it when dry with an experienced driver. Option: turn right at Wpt. 05 (see map).

Stats: Length: 12.7 miles. Time: 2 to 3 hours. High point: 11,900 ft. Best time of year: Mid July-early Oct.

Current Conditions: White River N.F. Holy Cross R.D. Call (970) 827-5715.

Getting There: From Leadville: Take Hwy. 24 north from Leadville about 17 miles to entrance of Camp Hale. **From Shrine Pass Road:** See directions for Trail #50.

MILEAGE LOG:

0.0 Zero trip odometer **[Rev. Miles]**
Head east into Camp Hale crossing bridge. **[6.0]**
01 N39 26.118 W106 19.529

0.5 Turn left at "T" intersection where 714 goes right. **[5.5]**

1.2 Cross culvert then turn left on 708. (Right goes to Ptarmigan Pass and eventually connects to Waypoint 05 after driving Wearyman Creek.) **[4.8]**
02 N39 26.880 W106 19.147

2.0 After passing dispersed camp spot, turn right along Eagle River. **[4.0]**

2.5 Turn right uphill on single lane road that crosses hillside. Stay right past private residence and climb through trees. **[3.5]**
03 N39 27.744 W106 19.797

5.5 Steep climb with challenging section before coming out of trees. **[0.5]**

5.9 Turn right uphill on steep and narrow road to top of Resolution Mountain. **[0.1]**
04 N39 29.256 W106 17.861

6.0 Turn around at top and return to Wpt. 04. **[0.0]**

0.0 Zero trip odometer
From Waypoint 04, continue north. **[6.2]**

2.3 Stay right. **[3.9]**

4.2 Continue straight. **[2.0]**

5.3 Turn left and follow in and out of narrow creek. **[0.9]**
05 N39 31.217 W106 18.896

6.2 Shrine Pass Road. Left goes to Red Cliff, right to I-70, exit 190. **[0.0]**
06 N39 31.405 W106 19.510

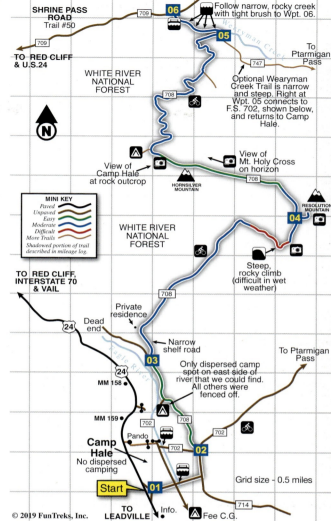

SHRINE PASS ROAD
Trail #50

Follow narrow, rocky creek with tight brush to Wpt. 06.

TO RED CLIFF & U.S. 24

WHITE RIVER NATIONAL FOREST

To Ptarmigan Pass

Optional Wearyman Creek Trail is narrow and steep. Right at Wpt. 05 connects to F.S. 702, shown below, and returns to Camp Hale.

View of Mt. Holy Cross on horizon

View of Camp Hale at rock outcrop

HORNSILVER MOUNTAIN

RESOLUTION MOUNTAIN

MINI KEY
Paved
Unpaved
Easy
Moderate
Difficult
More Trails
Shadowed portion of trail described in mileage log.

WHITE RIVER NATIONAL FOREST

Steep, rocky climb (difficult in wet weather)

TO RED CLIFF, INTERSTATE 70 & VAIL

Private residence

Dead end

Narrow shelf road

To Ptarmigan Pass

Only dispersed camp spot on east side of river that we could find. All others were fenced off.

Eagle River

MM 158

MM 159

Camp Hale
No dispersed camping

Pando

Grid size - 0.5 miles

Start

© 2019 FunTreks, Inc.

TO LEADVILLE

Info.

Fee C.G.

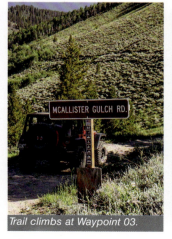
MCALLISTER GULCH RD.
Trail climbs at Waypoint 03.

This steep, rocky climb is why we rated the trail difficult (see map).

Fishing at Slide Lake. Homestake Peak can be seen in the distance.

Wurtz Ditch. Caution: Steep embankments on each side of road.

Point of Interest: Wurtz Ditch, a diversion dam, collects surface water that flows down the mountainside. The road across the top of the dam seems to be flat, but actually climbs a few hundred feet over its 10.5-mile length when heading north. Because it is smooth and relatively flat, it is a popular mountain bike trail for beginners. Please be alert for mountain bikers and hikers as you go around many blind curves.

Overview: The drive to Slide Lake is the main feature of this trip. A rough but manageable climb takes you to a pristine lake surrounded by beautiful mountains, including 13,215-ft. Homestake Peak. We're showing Wurtz Ditch (also spelled Wurts or Wuritz) as an optional side trip. It's an interesting curiosity, but a fairly long and uneventful drive if you go all the way to the end. There are several wide spots where you can turn around along the way. F.S. 145 opens July 2 or when the road dries out. Watch for hikers and mountain bikers, especially on F.S. 705.

Rating: Moderate. This rating applies to Slide Lake only. Good size embedded rock with several steep sections that will toss you around if you drive too fast. Go slow with careful tire placement. Suitable for high-clearance, aggressive stock 4x4 SUVs. F.S. 705 is very easy.

Stats: Length: 4.2 miles one way to Slide Lake. Time: Allow 1½ to 2 hours to reach lake. High point: 11,600 ft. Best time of year: July through Sept.

Current Conditions: San Isabel N.F., Leadville R.D. Call (719) 486-0749.

Getting There: Drive north from Leadville on Highway 24 about 7 miles and turn left on C.R. 19 between mile markers 168 and 167.

MILEAGE LOG:

0.0 Zero trip odometer [Rev. Miles]
Head west on C.R. 19
from Highway 24. [4.2]
01 N39 20.834 W106 19.944

0.9 Turn right on F.S. 100
(Still a wide road. Several
spots along this road are
wide enough to park a
hauling trailer, or you can
find room around Way-
point 03.) [3.3]
02 N39 20.878 W106 20.715

1.5 Continue straight and follow sign for F.S. 145 past
a private building on the
left. [2.7]
03 N39 21.246 W106 21.164

3.9 Continue straight. Path
on left goes to 10th Mtn.
Division Hut. [0.3]

4.2 Road ends at picnic table.
Easy half-mile hike to
lake. After hike, return to
Waypoint 03. [0.0]
04 N39 22.333 W106 23.355

0.0 Zero trip odometer at Wpt. 03
(Optional side trip.) From
Waypoint 03, cross small
bridge and follow 705
north along the ditch.

10.5 Easy part of F.S. 705
ends at turnaround.
Return the way you came.
(Note: F.S. 705 continues
as a steep, rough and
sometimes muddy 4WD
road and eventually con-
nects to No Name Road,
which returns to Highway
24 after a long, uneventful
drive.

Road is rough and slow-going. Relax and take your time.

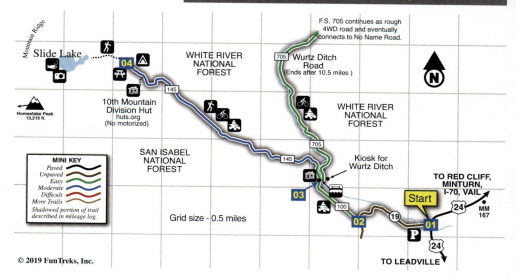

Mountain Ridge

Slide Lake

04

WHITE RIVER
NATIONAL
FOREST

F.S. 705 continues as rough
4WD road and eventually
connects to No Name Road.

705 Wurtz Ditch
Road
(Ends after 10.5 miles)

WHITE RIVER
NATIONAL
FOREST

Homestake Peak
13,215 ft.

10th Mountain
Division Hut
huts.org
(No motorized)

145

705

145

SAN ISABEL
NATIONAL
FOREST

Kiosk for
Wurtz Ditch

TO RED CLIFF,
MINTURN,
I-70, VAIL

MINI KEY
Paved
Unpaved
Easy
Moderate
Difficult
More Trails
*Shadowed portion of trail
described in mileage log.*

03

100

Start

24

MM
167

Grid size - 0.5 miles

02

19

01

P

24

TO LEADVILLE

Large boulders at French Creek are extra difficult with wet tires.

Cleveland Rock is extreme.

Most people have lunch at Holy Cross City and head back down.

Historical Highlight: *Holy Cross City once had a population of about 300 people, a school and a hotel. Look around and you should be able to count about 17 foundations along with a dwindling number of cabins. The town survived only a few short years during the 1880s.*

Overview: Many consider this the best hard-core trail in Colorado, replete with stunning scenery, historical points of interest and thrilling obstacles. Heavy traffic on weekends often means waiting awhile at obstacles like French Creek. Cleveland Rock is very extreme. Most visit the city, then head back down. Open to unlicensed vehicles from June 21 to November 22.

Rating: Difficult. One of the most difficult in the state, offering nonstop challenges. Minimum 33-inch tires, differential lockers and winch. Bring spare parts and don't go alone.

Stats: Length: 3.8 miles one way to Holy Cross City; 11 miles round trip. Time: 5 to 7 hours or more. High point: 11,500 ft. Best time: July-early Oct.

Current Conditions: White River N.F. Holy Cross R.D. Call (970) 827-5715.

Getting There: Find Homestake Road, F.S. 703, off Highway 24 between mile markers 156 and 157. The turn is on the south side of the road a few miles north of Camp Hale and about 20 miles north of Leadville. Drive south 7.3 miles past Gold Park F.S. Campground to the well-marked trail on right.

MILEAGE LOG:

0.0 Zero trip odometer   [Rev. Miles]
Head uphill on F.S. 759, one-way through this section. Difficult spots begin immediately.   [3.7]
01 N39 24.192 W106 26.616

1.3 Continue straight. You'll return to this point and exit here. If you've had trouble getting this far, exit now. The trail gets much more difficult.   [2.4]
02 N39 24.595 W106 27.318

1.5 Obstacle.   [2.2]
2.5 Obstacle.   [1.2]
2.8 French Creek. If you can't get through in two or three attempts, winch or take a strap if people are waiting.   [0.9]
03 N39 25.240 W106 28.515

3.2 Awkward ledge with tree root. Rollovers are possible here.   [0.5]

3.7 After rocky climb past mining debris, bear right to reach Holy Cross City in about 400 feet.   [0.0]
04 N39 24.888 W106 28.740
To reach Cleveland Rock, stay left at Waypoint 04, then turn right in a few hundred feet. Or go into Holy Cross City and turn left, then right at top of hill. Trail ends at wilderness boundary soon after Cleveland Rock. Hike to great fishing lakes.

When done, return the way you came to EXIT ROUTE at Waypoint 02.

0.0 Zero trip odometer
At Waypoint 02, turn right and leave trail.   [4.4]
0.8 Stay left.   [3.6]
1.8 Go through parking area for Fancy Creek Hiking Trail and turn left.   [2.6]
05 N39 23.437 W106 28.230

4.0 Turn left on Homestake Road 703.   [0.4]
06 N39 23.894 W106 26.629

4.4 Return to starting point of trail at Waypoint 01. Straight takes you back to Highway 24.   [0.0]

Mine ruins near top.

French Creek can get congested on weekends.

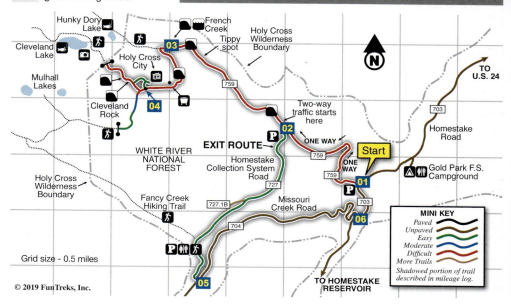

Hunky Dory Lake
Cleveland Lake
Mulhall Lakes
Holy Cross City
Cleveland Rock
04
Holy Cross Wilderness Boundary
WHITE RIVER NATIONAL FOREST
Fancy Creek Hiking Trail
03
French Creek
Tippy spot
Holy Cross Wilderness Boundary
759
Two-way traffic starts here
02
P
ONE WAY
759
EXIT ROUTE
Homestake Collection System Road
727
727.1B
704
Missouri Creek Road
05
N
TO U.S. 24
703
Homestake Road
Gold Park F.S. Campground
ONE WAY
759
Start
P
703
01
06
TO HOMESTAKE RESERVOIR

Grid size - 0.5 miles

MINI KEY
Paved
Unpaved
Easy
Moderate
Difficult
More Trails
Shadowed portion of trail described in mileage log.

© 2019 FunTreks, Inc.

View of Turquoise Reservoir as you climb the east side towards the pass.

Steeper spots are chewed up and rutted.

Historical Highlight: *The Hagerman Tunnel was completed in 1886 and connected Colorado Springs to Aspen. The railroad was the first standard gauge railroad to cross the Continental Divide. Due to high maintenance costs, the Busk-Ivanhoe Tunnel was built at a lower altitude seven years later. It too proved to be impractical and was later bought by mining magnate Albert Carlton. He renamed the tunnel after himself and converted it to automobile use. It served as such between 1924 and 1937. A third tunnel, the Charles H. Boustead Tunnel, was built in the 1960s by the Corps of Engineers to divert water from the Fryingpan Wilderness to the Turquoise Reservoir.*

Overview: With three outstanding wilderness areas as a backdrop, Turquoise Reservoir serves as a focal point for many recreational activities, especially fishing. Great hiking trails, including the Colorado Trail, crisscross the area. In addition, you can see two historically significant railroad tunnels. To make a long day out of it, you can continue another 43 miles past Ruedi Reservoir to Highway 82 at Basalt and return to Leadville via Independence Pass.

Rating: Moderate. This road has gotten rougher since our last edition was published in 2010. We encountered larger embedded rock and deeper ruts. Unless the road is improved by future maintenance, you'll need high ground clearance and 4-wheel drive. A passenger car won't be adequate.

Stats: Length: 11.6 miles as described here. Time: Allow 3-4 hours for round trip if you turn around at Wpt. 04. High point: 11,925 ft. Best time of year: June-Late September.

Current Conditions: East side: San Isabel N.F., Leadville R.D. Call (719) 486-0749. West side: White River N.F., Summer map of Aspen-Sopris R.D. Call (970) 963-2266.

Getting There: Take 6th St. west from Leadville and bear right on paved C.R. 4. Continue another 3.5 miles until the road forks south of Turquoise Reservoir. Bear left over the dam and continue around the south side of the lake. After another 3.5 miles, stay left on C.R. 4 where paved C.R. 9 continues around reservoir.

MILEAGE LOG:

0.0 Zero trip odometer [Rev. Miles]
Continue uphill on gravel
road, C.R. 4 [11.6]
01 N39 16.113 W106 25.044

3.6 Road narrows and turns
sharply right past parking
and sealed entrance to
Carlton Tunnel. [8.0]
02 N39 14.886 W106 28.212

4.6 Kiosk and parking. Hiking
trail follows railroad grade
to Hagerman Tunnel. [7.0]

5.0 Road turns left uphill and
gets rougher. [6.6]

7.9 Cross summit and descend other side. [3.7]
03 N39 15.790 W106 28.874

10.9 Cross water diversion
ditch on diagonal. [0.7]

11.6 Intersect with F.S. 527
on left. This road goes
to Ivanhoe Lake along
original railroad grade that
comes out of other end of
Carlton Tunnel. This side
road continues past the
tunnel to Lily Pad Lake
and another hiking trail.
Turn around here or read
below. [0.0]
04 N39 17.530 W106 31.668
North on 532 continues
another 43 miles (32
miles is paved) past
Ruedi Reservoir to Basalt
and Highway 82. The road
runs along the Frying-
pan River, a fisherman's
paradise.

Looking southeast from the dam at Ivanhoe Lake

View as you start down the west side. Road stays rough.

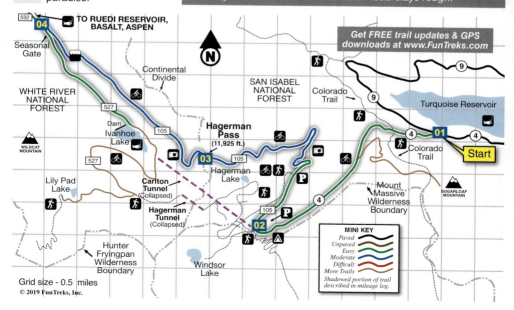

Get FREE trail updates & GPS downloads at www.FunTreks.com

532 **04** TO RUEDI RESERVOIR, BASALT, ASPEN

Seasonal Gate

Continental Divide

WHITE RIVER NATIONAL FOREST

SAN ISABEL NATIONAL FOREST

Colorado Trail

9

9

Turquoise Reservoir

527

Dam
Ivanhoe Lake

105

WILDCAT MOUNTAIN

527

Hagerman Pass
(11,925 ft.)

03 105

Hagerman Lake

4

Colorado Trail

Start

01

4

Lily Pad Lake

527

Carlton Tunnel
(Collapsed)

Hagerman Tunnel
(Collapsed)

105

02

P

P

Mount Massive Wilderness Boundary

SUGARLOAF MOUNTAIN

Hunter Fryingpan Wilderness Boundary

Windsor Lake

MINI KEY
Paved
Unpaved
Easy
Moderate
Difficult
More Trails
Shadowed portion of trail described in mileage log.

Grid size - 0.5 miles
© 2019 FunTreks, Inc.

137

Climbing to timberline. Turquoise Lake can be seen in distance.

Descending from Buckeye Peak across open tundra.

SUV starts down steep section.

Overview: A quick, fun getaway just north of Leadville. Mount Zion is about two-thirds of the way up the trail and has distant views of Leadville and Turquoise Lake. Mount Zion is barely noticeable as you drive across it. Best views are at end of road near Buckeye Peak. F.S. 109 has no seasonal closures; F.S. 189 does not open until June 30.

Rating: Moderate. Last time we drove this trail, it was fairly easy due to recent maintenance. This time we encountered a steep, rocky, loose hill that we rated as moderate. Most stock, high-clearance 4x4 SUVs should still be able to handle this trail with an experienced driver.

Stats: Length: 12.5 miles round trip as described. Time: 2-3 hours. High point: 12,350 ft. Best time of year: July-Sept.

Current Conditions: San Isabel N.F., Leadville R.D. Call (719) 486-0749.

Getting There: Head north out of Leadville on Highway 24. Just north of town after last gas station, stay left on 24 where Highway 91 goes straight (it's easy to miss this turn). Go 1.4 miles and turn right on unmarked dirt road. Road is not obvious because it crosses an open dirt area. Dispersed camping is allowed farther back in the trees after F.S. 109 splits to the left.

MILEAGE LOG:

0.0 Zero trip odometer [Rev. miles]
Head north across open area. F.S. 109 is not marked until you drive in a short distance. [6.5]
01 N39 16.376 W106 18.663

0.1 Bear left on F.S. 109. Dispersed camping in trees on right. [6.4]

0.2 Turn left uphill through seasonal gate. Climb and weave uphill through forest. [6.3]

2.5 Continue straight where 189 goes left. You'll return here later. [4.0]
02 N39 17.930 W106 17.673

2.9 Climb steep, rocky, loose section, then stay right past cell tower. [3.6]

4.1 Rocky climb with views of Leadville to right. You are crossing Mt. Zion, but it is not obvious. [2.4]
03 N39 18.596 W106 16.663

6.5 After long climb across open area, trail ends at high viewpoint just below Buckeye Peak. Turn around and return to Waypoint 02. [0.0]
04 N39 20.335 W106 15.339

0.0 Zero trip odometer at Wpt. 02
Coming downhill, turn right on 189 and pass through gate. (See seasonal closure.) [2.0]

2.0 After descending through aspens on a narrow, rutted, and often muddy road, you pass through another gate to a county road. Turn left to get back to Highway 24. [0.0]
05 N39 17.970 W106 19.543

Get FREE trail updates & GPS downloads at www.FunTreks.com

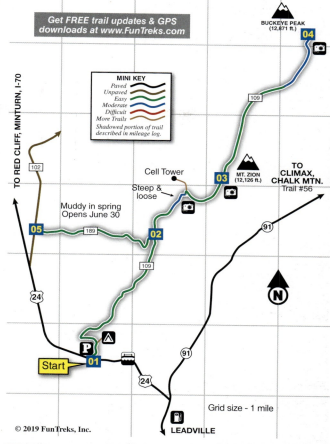

MINI KEY
Paved
Unpaved
Easy
Moderate
Difficult
More Trails
Shadowed portion of trail described in mileage log

TO RED CLIFF, MINTURN, I-70

Cell Tower

Steep & loose

Muddy in spring Opens June 30

BUCKEYE PEAK (12,871 ft.)

MT. ZION (12,126 ft.)

TO CLIMAX, CHALK MTN. Trail #56

N

Start

Grid size - 1 mile

© 2019 FunTreks, Inc.

LEADVILLE

F.S. 189 is narrow and twisty.

Trail ends just below Buckeye Peak.

Chalk Mountain

Looking down from the overlook at Highway 91, Fremont Pass and the Climax Mine.

Trail starts here across from mile marker 8.

Road is steep and rutted in places.

Overview: This is a short, fun, drive to a great overlook. Take binoculars and a camera. It's a great spot to relax and have a picnic. The start is above 10,000 feet, so it doesn't take long to reach tundra above timberline. Stay on the trail at all times. No seasonal closures, but expect snow to block the road early.

Rating: Moderate. Narrow and steep with intermittent loose, rocky sections. One spot with rock ledges. Chewed-up spots will likely get worse. High ground clearance and 4-wheel drive required.

Stats: Length: Round trip 6.4 miles. Time: Allow about 2 hours total driving time to get up and back with capable vehicle. High point: 12,000 ft. Best time of year: July-mid September.

Current Conditions: San Isabel N.F., Leadville R.D. Call (719) 486-0749.

Getting There: Head north from Leadville 8 miles on Highway 91 towards Fremont Pass. Turn into parking area on left side of road immediately after mile marker 8.

MILEAGE LOG:

0.0 Zero trip odometer **[Rev. Miles]**
Head north from parking area and stay left uphill where road joins on right from Hwy. 91. **[3.2]**
01 N39 21.129 W106 13.139

0.3 Make hard left at switchback. Climb steep switchbacks with water bars.**[2.9]**

0.5 Road levels out a bit. **[2.7]**

1.1 Bear right. Rough road to left is not shown on MVUM. It eventually dead- ends after a couple of miles. **[2.1]**
02 N39 21.897 W106 13.007

1.3 Steep, loose, chewed-up section. This spot could worsen over time. **[1.9]**

1.6 Road swings left up some rocky ledges, then road gets easier as it twists and undulates across the tundra. **[1.6]**

2.4 Bear right at triangular intersection and head south over flat area. **[0.8]**
03 N39 22.569 W106 12.289

3.1 Road descends steeply down short hill. **[0.1]**

3.2 Road ends at rock outcrop and beautiful overlook. Great spot for a picnic. Caution: Watch your kids and dogs at cliff edges. **[0.0]**
04 N39 22.000 W106 11.915

Get FREE trail updates & GPS downloads at www.FunTreks.com

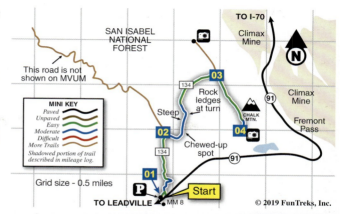

TO I-70
Climax Mine
SAN ISABEL NATIONAL FOREST
This road is not shown on MVUM
Climax Mine
Fremont Pass

MINI KEY
Paved
Unpaved
Easy
Moderate
Difficult
More Trails
Shadowed portion of trail described in mileage log.

Grid size - 0.5 miles

134
03
Steep
Rock ledges at turn
CHALK MTN.
02
04
Chewed-up spot
134
91
01
P
Start
TO LEADVILLE MM 8
91

© 2019 FunTreks, Inc.

Plenty of room for several vehicles to park at the overlook.

Narrow two-track in places is fun to drive as it twists and undulates up the mountain.

Trail narrows and gets rockier as it enters forest.

Starting down Birdseye Gulch after Wpt. 03.

Historical Highlight: As you drive to start of trail from Leadville, you'll see signs on left for the "Matchless Mine Tour." It takes less than an hour, but is extremely informative. They tell the story of Baby Doe Tabor, who for many years lived a rich and famous life as the wife of millionaire Horace Tabor, founder of the Matchless Mine, which largely was responsible for the development of Leadville. The tour starts in Baby Doe's shack where she died penniless and alone on Mar. 7, 1935. The shack is the original, with her pictures still hanging on the walls.

Overview: This trail is a side trip off Mosquito Pass, Trail #58. Its reputation for difficulty has been largely based on a short section of mud bogs that, at one time, were almost impossible to get across. Recent repairs by the 4WD community have improved conditions for this spot. If you get lucky, you might see a tourist train at Waypoint 04. Unlicensed vehicles usually enter from the north end off Hwy. 91 because of a large parking area next to the road.

Rating: Difficult. The road is steep and very rocky in spots due to erosion. Although we cannot recommend this trail for stock SUVs, more aggressive models with skilled drivers can do it.

Stats: Length: 6.3 miles. Time: About 3 hours. High point: 12,100 ft. Best time of year: July-September.

Current Conditions: Pike and San Isabel N.F., Leadville R.D. Call (719) 486-0749.

Getting There: From Leadville: From Hwy. 24 in downtown Leadville, head east on 7th Street, and it becomes County Road 3. Go by Matchless Mine and continue after pavement ends. Continue straight at 1.8 miles, then bear left at 2.7 miles. Bear left at 4.1 miles at unofficial parking area. Take left fork next to gated road that goes into private Diamond Mine.

To start at north end: Take Hwy. 91 north from Leadville to parking lot on right 0.3 mile after mile marker 5.

MILEAGE LOG:

0.0 Zero trip odometer [Rev. Miles]
Head uphill on steep rocky road. Try to avoid shortcuts. [1.9]
01 N39 15.560 W106 13.114

1.6 Cut back to left for Birdseye Gulch. [0.3]
02 N39 16.149 W106 11.796

1.9 Turn right downhill for Birdseye Gulch. Straight is interesting side trip to top of Prospect Mtn. near 12,500 ft. [0.0]
03 N39 16.199 W106 12.018

0.0 Zero trip odometer
From Waypoint 03, head north. Road is fairly level at first, but soon drops steeply downhill. This section can be difficult due to erosion. Avoid making new paths; turn around if your vehicle is not capable. [4.4]

1.2 Cross where old mud bog was repaired. [3.2]

1.4 Rocky road narrows with tippy, steep spots. [3.0]

2.2 Continue straight after coming down rocky hill. Ignore lesser roads. [2.2]

2.9 Cross train tracks. Watch for tourist train out of Leadville. [1.5]
04 N39 18.230 W106 12.950

4.3 Stay left where private drive joins on right. [0.1]

4.4 Reach end of trail at parking lot next to Hwy. 91.[0.0]
05 N39 18.902 W106 13.498

Get FREE trail updates & GPS downloads at www.FunTreks.com

Tippy spot with no bypass.

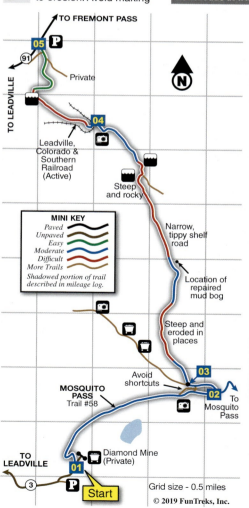

TO FREMONT PASS

91

TO LEADVILLE

Private

05 P

04

Leadville, Colorado & Southern Railroad (Active)

Steep and rocky

N

MINI KEY
Paved
Unpaved
Easy
Moderate
Difficult
More Trails
Shadowed portion of trail described in mileage log.

Narrow, tippy shelf road

Location of repaired mud bog

Steep and eroded in places

Avoid shortcuts

03

02 To Mosquito Pass

MOSQUITO PASS
Trail #58

Diamond Mine (Private)

TO LEADVILLE

3

01 P **Start**

Grid size - 0.5 miles

© 2019 FunTreks, Inc.

Watch for tourist train at Waypoint 04.

Avoid making new paths; stay on the trail.

Thick wildflowers starting up west side of pass.

North London Mine on east side.

Historical Highlight: This short-lived trail was actively used in the 1870s as the quickest way to reach western mining activities. Like so many of these high pass roads, travelers eventually found it easier to take longer but lower routes like Weston Pass. In the late 1870s, Leadville was the most famous silver mining camp in the world, and by the 1890s, it was the second-largest city in Colorado. Today, Leadville is home to the National Mining Museum.

The headstone at the summit honors Father Dyer, "The Snowshoe Itinerant." Starting in 1861, he spent 29 years preaching at mining camps along the mountains. He became a legend by carrying mail and gold across the pass sometimes twice a day. At least one trip took him 3 days to dig through the snow.

Overview: Highest pass road in Colorado open to motorized travel. Views from the 13,185 ft. summit are impressive on a clear day. Very interesting mine structures on the east side. Connects to difficult Birdseye Gulch, Trail #57. Spend some time in Leadville; it's a great historic town.

Rating: Moderate. The upper portion of the trail is narrow and rocky on both sides of pass but suitable for aggressive, high-clearance, stock SUVs with low range. Road is closed when blocked by snow, which can occur well into late summer following a hard winter.

Stats: Length: 10.8 miles. Time: 2 to 3 hours. High point: 13,185 ft. Best time of year: August-September.

Current Conditions: Pike and San Isabel N.F., Leadville R.D. Call (719) 486-0749.

Getting There: From Leadville: From Hwy. 24 in downtown Leadville, head east on 7th Street, and it becomes County Road 3. Go by Matchless Mine and continue after pavement ends. Continue straight at 1.8 miles, then bear left at 2.7 miles. Bear left at 4.1 miles at unofficial parking area. Take left fork next to gated road that goes into private Diamond Mine. **From Alma:** From Hwy. 9 south of Alma, head west on either County Road 10 or 12. Continue on C.R. 12 after two roads merge.

MILEAGE LOG:

START

0.0 Zero trip odometer **[Rev. Miles]**
Head uphill on main steep rocky road. **[6.6]**
01 N39 15.575 W106 13.110

1.6 Stay right as roads go left to Birdseye Gulch. Road soon starts up narrow ledge road. **[5.0]**
02 N39 16.151 W106 11.791

2.2 Bear right at tight turn where lesser road goes straight. **[4.4]**

2.7 Continue straight. **[3.9]**

3.2 Arrive at Mosquito Pass and continue down other side towards Fairplay. **[3.4]**
03 N39 16.863 W106 11.161

4.2 Stay left where F.S. 41 goes right. **[2.4]**

4.6 Pass through cut in rock and descend ridge. **[2.0]**

4.8 North London Mine on right. Great photos. Don't enter structures. **[1.8]**

6.0 Turn right where lesser 856 goes left. **[0.6]**
04 N39 17.979 W106 09.210

6.6 Road on right goes to North London Mill. **[0.0]**
05 N39 17.576 W106 08.920

0.0 Zero trip odometer
Continue east from Wpt. 05 on C.R. 12. **[4.2]**

1.9 Continue straight where 419 joins on right. No unlicensed vehicles allowed east of this point. **[2.3]**
06 N39 16.706 W106 07.333

3.9 Slow down through residential community of Park City. **[0.3]**

4.2 Driver's choice. Left goes to Highway 9 at Alma. Right goes to Highway 9 towards Fairplay. **[0.0]**
07 N39 16.716 W106 05.226

Get FREE trail updates & GPS downloads at www.FunTreks.com

Marker for Father Dyer at pass.

Use small side road to access North London Mill on east side.

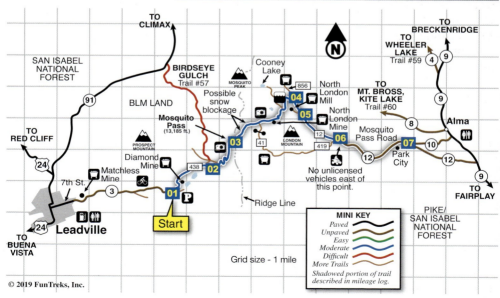

Shelf roads are wide with room to pass.

© 2019 FunTreks, Inc.

145

Looking back down the valley with Hoosier Pass in the background.

Passing under Magnolia Mill.

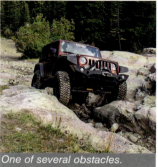

One of several obstacles.

Historical Highlight: In the 1860s, a town called Montgomery filled the mouth of this massive valley at the base of Mt. Lincoln. At its peak, the town consisted of over 150 cabins and buildings, which are now buried under the waters of Montgomery Reservoir. The only thing left standing is the Magnolia Mill. You can't miss it because the trail passes directly under it. The metal construction of the building would suggest that it was modernized and used at a later date.

Overview: Trail climbs up a beautiful valley to a high mountain lake with waterfall. Pass directly under historic Magnolia Mill. Gorgeous seasonal wildflowers. Fun during early-season runoff. Take a fishing pole.

Rating: Difficult. Several large rock obstacles require careful tire placement. Very narrow in spots with tight brush that can scratch paint, especially when squeezing by other vehicles. Water rushes down the trail during early-season snowmelt. Last mile climbs Bowling Ball Hill to lake. Airing down helps to avoid sliding sideways.

Stats: Length: 3.2 miles. Time: 3 to 4 hours. High point: 12,200 ft. Best time of year: Mid July-early Oct.

Current Conditions: Pike-San Isabel N.F., South Park R.D. Call (719) 836-2031.

Getting There: Head west on County Road 4 from Highway 9. County Road 4 comes in from two different points off Highway 9. Northern point is one mile south of Hoosier Pass, which is south of Breckenridge. Southern point is about 2 miles north of Alma. The roads merge before Montgomery Reservoir. Follow road around northwest side of reservoir until road narrows and turns uphill to right.

MILEAGE LOG:

START

0.0 Zero trip odometer [Rev. Miles]
Bear right up a couple of rocky switchbacks and pass under Magnolia Mill. Note impressive waterfall behind mill. **[3.2]**
01 N39 21.438 W106 04.945

0.6 Large rock obstacle followed by narrow trail with tight brush. **[2.6]**

2.2 Cross potentially deep mud hole. **[1.0]**

2.7 Stay right and climb Bowling Ball Hill. **[0.5]**

2.9 Turn right uphill at rocky ledge. **[0.3]**
02 N39 21.874 W106 07.588

3.2 Trail ends at parking area below Wheeler Lake. Stay out of mud. Return the way you came. **[0.0]**
03 N39 22.104 W106 07.687

Get FREE trail updates & GPS downloads at www.FunTreks.com

Wheeler Lake

Steep

Bowling Ball Hill

PIKE NATIONAL FOREST

408

Start

01

Montgomery Reservoir

Magnolia Mill

N

TO BRECKENRIDGE

9

Hoosier Pass (11,514 ft.)

4

4

9

TO RT. 9

TO ALMA

MT. LINCOLN

MINI KEY
Paved
Unpaved
Easy
Moderate
Difficult
More Trails
Shadowed portion of trail described in mileage log.

Grid size - 0.5 miles

© 2019 FunTreks, Inc.

Brush is tight.

Magnolia Mill is in good shape. Look for waterfall behind mill.

Vehicles gather at parking area near the lake. Bring a fishing pole.

147

Hiking trail at Windy Ridge.

Historical Highlight: In addition to being the highest incorporated town in North America at 10,578 ft., Alma has a rich mining history. In the 1870s, the general area around Alma, called the Mosquito Range Mining District, had a population of about 10,000 people (today the population is about 250). Mines were everywhere, spread from Mosquito Pass to Mt. Lincoln, Mt. Democrat and Mt. Bross. Many buildings in Alma have been recognized for their historical significance, including the Alma Town Hall, which is a registered state historical site. The Paris Mill was built in 1895. Ore came by tram buckets from the Paris Mine high up on Mt. Bross. The town of Alma has a couple of authentic restaurants and bars and is a popular stop for skiers heading into the mountains. Make sure to observe the speed limit through town—law enforcement is frequently waiting at one end of town or the other.

A 1000-year-old bristlecone pine tree.

Overview: This description covers the lower portion of Mt. Bross to Windy Ridge Bristlecone Pine Scenic Area and Kite Lake (a different Kite Lake than Trail #19). Some roads above Wpt. 04 are now showing as legal on 2019 MVUM (check latest map). See 1,000-year-old trees at Windy Ridge. Kite Lake offers three "fourteener" hiking trails: Mt. Lincoln, Mt. Democrat and Mt. Bross. If you want to experience an authentic Colorado town, take a few minutes to walk through Alma.

Rating: Easy. Lower portion of road, when dry, is suitable for passenger cars.

Upper sections are steep and rough. High clearance is recommended.

Stats: Length: Windy Ridge is 6.4 miles from Alma; Kite Lake is 5.5 miles from Alma. Time: 2-4 hours. High point: 12,000 ft. Best time of year: July-Sept.

Current Conditions: Pike-San Isabel N.F., South Park R.D. Call (719) 836-2031.

Getting There: Take Hwy. 9 south from Breckenridge or north from Fairplay to small town of Alma. Turn west on Buckskin Road (County Road 8).

MILEAGE LOG:

START

0.0 Zero trip odometer [Rev. Miles]
Head west on Buckskin Road. **[2.8]**
01 N39 17.034 W106 03.774

2.8 Arrive at intersection with Dolly Varden Road just after Paris Mill. **[0.0]**
02 N39 17.803 W106 06.483

0.0 Zero trip odometer
WINDY RIDGE:
Turn right on Dolly Varden Road, C.R. 787. **[3.6]**

2.9 Bear left uphill at Mineral Park Mine. **[0.7]**

3.1 Stay right where tougher 857 goes left. **[0.5]**
03 N39 19.103 W106 05.104

3.6 Arrive at Windy Ridge. Tour site then return to Waypoint 02. **[0.0]**
04 N39 19.282 W106 04.859

0.0 Zero trip odometer
KITE LAKE:
From Wpt. 02, continue north on Buckskin Road. After Sweet Home Mine, road gets rougher, especially as you approach Kite Lake. **[2.7]**

1.6 Continue straight. **[1.1]**

2.7 Arrive at Kite Lake and campground. Hiking trail departs to three different 14,000-ft. peaks. **[0.0]**
05 N39 19.660 W106 07.748

Get FREE trail updates & GPS downloads at www.FunTreks.com

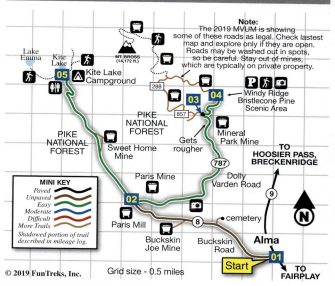

Wide shelf road to Windy Ridge.

Note:
The 2019 MVUM is showing some of these roads as legal. Check lastest map and explore only if they are open. Roads may be washed out in spots, so be careful. Stay out of mines, which are typically on private property.

Lake Emma

Kite Lake

05 Kite Lake Campground

MT. BROSS (14,172 ft.)

288

857

Windy Ridge Bristlecone Pine Scenic Area

03 **04**

PIKE NATIONAL FOREST

PIKE NATIONAL FOREST

Sweet Home Mine

Gets rougher

Mineral Park Mine

787

Paris Mine

Dolly Varden Road

TO HOOSIER PASS, BRECKENRIDGE

9

MINI KEY
Paved
Unpaved
Easy
Moderate
Difficult
More Trails
Shadowed portion of trail described in mileage log.

02

Paris Mill

Buckskin Joe Mine

8

cemetery

Buckskin Road

N

Alma

01

Start

TO FAIRPLAY

© 2019 FunTreks, Inc.   Grid size - 0.5 miles

The campground at Kite Lake is primitive. Hike to three different 14,000-ft. peaks from here.

149

West side of pass is rougher than east side. As you descend, Mt. Massive can be seen in the distance.

This sign marks the pass.

WESTON PASS
ELEVATION 11,921 FEET
SAN ISABEL   PIKE
National Forest   National Forest

Historical Highlight: In the 1860s and 1870s, Weston Pass was a busy toll road for freight wagons and stagecoaches. At its peak, the road was used by hundreds each day. When the railroads reached Leadville in the early 1880s, use of the road declined rapidly. The numbered wagon-wheel signs along the road are part of an auto tour. A flyer for the tour can be picked up at forest ranger stations in Fairplay and Leadville or download from the Forest Service website.

Overview: Pleasant drive over relatively low pass. Forest campground and many great dispersed camp spots along South Fork of South Platte River and Big Union Creek. Several hiking trails lead to the nearby Buffalo Peaks Wilderness. Wildflowers. Good fall color. Alternate climb to pass on F.S. 162 adds a little fun. Open all year weather permitting.

Rating: Easy. Suitable for passenger cars in good weather on the east side. High clearance and 4-wheel drive is needed on the west side.

Stats: Length: 19.5 miles. Time: About 2 hours. High point: 11,921 ft. Best time of year: Mid June-Early Oct.

Current Conditions: East side: Pike-San Isabel N.F., South Park R.D. Call (719) 836-2031. West side: Leadville R.D. Call (719) 486-0749.

Getting There: **From Fairplay:** Take Hwy. 285 south 4.7 miles and turn right on C.R. 5 between mile markers 178 and 179. Follow this road southwest 7.0 miles and stay right on C.R. 22. (If coming from the south on Highway 285, turn left on C.R. 22 between mile markers 173 and 172. Travel west 7.1 miles and turn left where C.R. 5 joins on right.) **From Leadville:** Take Hwy. 24 south about 7 miles and turn left on C.R. 7 to Mt. Massive Lakes. Follow reverse mileage.

START

MILEAGE LOG:

0.0 Zero trip odometer [Rev. Miles]
Continue southwest on County Road 22. [19.5]
01 N39 05.888 W106 05.322

0.6 Continue straight. Sheep Creek Drive on right. [18.9]

3.0 Rich Creek Hiking Trail on left. [16.5]

4.1 Weston Pass Campground on left, followed by several dispersed camp spots along river. [15.4]

7.0 Main road continues straight. Right on F.S. 162 is slightly more difficult, but more scenic. [12.5]

8.0 Main road continues straight. Right is F.S. 161, a short connector route to F.S. 162. [11.5]

8.8 Cross Weston Pass and begin rougher descent

down other side. Many good dispersed camp spots along creek. [10.7]
02 N39 07.885 W106 10.931

13.1 Continue straight on main road past camp spots. Largest mountain ahead is Mt. Massive. [6.4]

17.3 Pavement begins and passes through residential area. [2.2]

19.5 Highway 24. Right goes to Leadville in 7 miles. [0.0]
03 N39 10.594 W106 19.323

Road climbs toward pass on east side.

F.S.162 is an alternate way to reach the pass. It's very scenic and just slightly rougher than C.R. 22.

151

Champion Mill remains in relatively good condition.

Water here was about 30 inches deep on our last trip in 2010.

Historical Highlight: Like many mines in Colorado, the Champion Mine started operation back in the late 1800s. However, its most productive period was in later years between 1906 and 1919. The mine was reopened again in 1921 and finally shut down for the last time in 1940. Although the mill could collapse at any time, it presently is in remarkably good shape. Much of the milling equipment still remains inside. In addition to the mill, tram towers remain on the mountainside.

Overview: Located between Mount Massive and Mount Elbert, this trail climbs to one of the largest and best-preserved mill structures in Colorado. Views in every direction near the top. Terrain is exciting and challenging after Wpt. 02. Water crossings are fun but can be deep. Area before Wpt. 02 sees heavy traffic by hikers. Two popular fourteener hiking trails depart from campgrounds. No seasonal closures.

Rating: Moderate. Mostly smooth with occasional rocky sections. In the spring, water crossings may be too deep to safely cross. High-clearance stock SUVs can drive F.S. 110. Side trip on F.S. 110J has one difficult spot, but there's a good place to turn around if you don't want to drive up it.

Stats: Length: Round trip 15 miles. Time: 2 to 3 hours. High point: 11,580 ft. Best time of year: July-Sept.

Current Conditions: San Isabel N.F., Leadville R.D. Call (719) 486-0749.

Getting There: Just south of Leadville on Highway 24, turn west on paved C.R. 300 one-tenth mile south of mile marker 180. Go 0.8 mile and turn left on C.R. 11. Go another 1.2 miles and turn right on dirt road (still C.R. 11). Continue another 3.4 miles to parking area used for dispersed camping.

MILEAGE LOG:

0.0 Zero trip odometer [Rev. Miles] From parking area, continue south on C.R. 11. [7.4]
01 N39 10.033 W106 23.499

0.7 Halfmoon C.G. [6.7]

1.3 Emerald Lake Picnic Area (fee required). [6.1]

1.8 Mt. Elbert Trailhead and campground. [5.6]

2.2 Mt. Massive Hiking Trailhead. [5.2]

2.6 Road narrows, gets rougher and climbs. [4.8]

4.2 Stay right heading west uphill on F.S. 110. Left is a fun side trip to an obstacle. (When we drove this, we were allowed to drive the obstacle, but not to Iron Mike Mine per 2016 MVUM.) [3.2]
02 N39 09.036 W106 27.325

4.7 Water crossing. [2.7]

5.8 Water crossing. (Depending on the season, this section could be anything from a shallow creek to a deep lake.) [1.6]

6.7 Pass cabin on left. [0.7]

6.9 Stay right at fork. [0.5]

7.4 Seasonal gate. Champion Mill can be seen directly ahead. Walk if gate is closed. Road to left goes to Champion Mine near top of Mount Champion. This road is not shown on Forest Service MVUM. Look around, then return the way you came. [0.0]
03 N39 08.280 W106 30.063

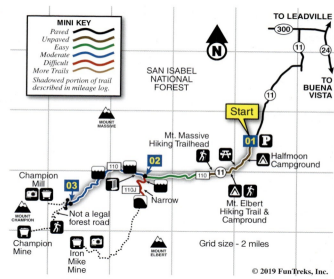

MINI KEY
Paved
Unpaved
Easy
Moderate
Difficult
More Trails
Shadowed portion of trail described in mileage log.

TO LEADVILLE
300
11
24
TO BUENA VISTA
11
11

SAN ISABEL NATIONAL FOREST

MOUNT MASSIVE

Start
01 P
Halfmoon Campground
Mt. Massive Hiking Trailhead
110
02
110
11
Champion Mill
03
110J
Narrow
Not a legal forest road
MOUNT CHAMPION
Mt. Elbert Hiking Trail & Campround
Champion Mine
Iron Mike Mine
MOUNT ELBERT

Grid size - 2 miles

© 2019 FunTreks, Inc.

First half of drive follows alongside Halfmoon Creek.

Water crossings after Wpt. 02.

Old vehicle next to Champion Mill at top. Please do not vandalize.

Lost Canyon

63

C.R. 398 starts here.

View of Lost Canyon from camp spot at 2.4 miles.

At Waypoint 02, stay right.

Missouri Mountain seen through window from cabin after Wpt. 05.

Overview: Trail looks down on Lost Canyon from high point near top of Quail Mountain. Views in all directions from overlooks include Twin Lakes Reservoir, Mt. Elbert and Clear Creek Reservoir. Great camping and mountain biking on lower portion. Accesses Cache Creek, a very popular gold-panning area open to the public. Trail crosses private land, stay on the correct trail and don't make shortcuts. There are other 4WD roads to explore on east side of Arkansas River from C.R. 397. No seasonal closures except by weather.

Rating: Moderate. After Waypoint 02, road narrows and is steep in spots. Intermittent rocky sections. Aggressive, high-clearance SUVs only. Road shown on map west of Wpt. 05 has a difficult section not suitable for stock vehicles.

Stats: Length: 7.6 miles one way. Add side trips. Time: About 3-5 hours. High point: 12,500 ft. Best time of year: Mid July-Sept.

Current Conditions: San Isabel N.F., Leadville R.D. Call (719) 486-0749.

Getting There: From town of Granite, on Highway 24, about halfway between Buena Vista and Leadville, head uphill on County Road 398, which departs immediately behind the Sage Outdoor Adventure Store on west side of Highway 24 (limited hours in the summer). Stay on County Road 398 for 2.8 miles until you reach fork where F.S. 399 goes right and F.S. 398 goes left. Parking and staging allowed here, We suggest going another 0.9 mile for camping (see picture).

START MILEAGE LOG:

0.0 Zero trip odometer [Rev. Miles] Stay left and begin easy climb up F.S. 398. [7.6]
01 N39 03.298 W106 18.696

0.9 Flat area popular for camping. [6.7]

2.4 At switchback, look for camp spot to left with rock outcrop, great view. [5.2]

4.1 Follow main road hard right past private property. [3.5]

5.0 Road narrows and climbs more steeply. [2.6]

5.1 At log cabin ruin, stay right uphill to views. Left is private drive. [2.5]
02 N39 02.280 W106 20.421

5.6 Roads come back together at log cabin. Stay right uphill at every choice. All roads to left go to active Gold Basin Mine. [2.0]
03 N39 02.416 W106 20.794

6.8 After steep section, road levels off and forks. Stay left. Two roads of triangle intersection go right to overlooks. [0.8]
04 N39 01.991 W106 21.821

7.4 Stay left. Right is difficult climb to 360° view. [0.2]
05 N39 01.530 W106 21.726

7.6 Cabin ruins. Goat trail behind cabins leads to Columbine Mine. Road continues another 3.2 miles to overlook of Clear Creek Reservoir. One very steep spot is not for beginners. Check latest MVUM for legality of route. [0.0]

From Waypoint 05, road continues 3 miles east past cabin ruins.

Popular dispersed camping area at 0.9 mile.

Network of roads between Waypoints 02 and 03. Stay right uphill.

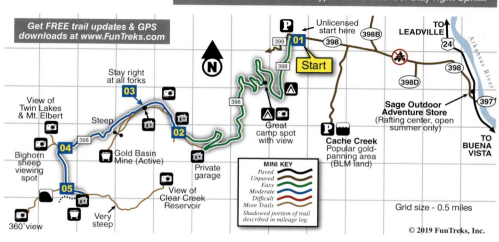

Get FREE trail updates & GPS downloads at www.FunTreks.com

Stay right at all forks

View of Twin Lakes & Mt. Elbert

Steep

03

02

04

398

Gold Basin Mine (Active)

Bighorn sheep viewing spot

05

360° view

Very steep

View of Clear Creek Reservoir

Private garage

Great camp spot with view

399

398

01 Start

398B

Unlicensed start here

398

398D

TO LEADVILLE

24

Arkansas River

398

397

Sage Outdoor Adventure Store (Rafting center, open summer only)

TO BUENA VISTA

Cache Creek Popular gold-panning area (BLM land)

MINI KEY
Paved
Unpaved
Easy
Moderate
Difficult
More Trails
Shadowed portion of trail described in mileage log.

Grid size - 0.5 miles

© 2019 FunTreks, Inc.

Idaho Springs, Bailey, Breckenridge, Montezuma

Area 6 has many outstanding trails with the added benefit of being relatively close to Denver. Many trails are tucked between major ski areas where jaw-dropping scenery is the norm. Trail #79 actually goes up the center of Peak 10 of the Breckenridge Ski Area.

We quickly noticed on our redrive that quite a few trails had gotten more difficult. As a result, we upped the rating of five trails from moderate to difficult. Depending on your vehicle, this is a plus for some drivers and a bummer for others. Either way, however, everyone should find lots of trails to suit their fancy.

One trail needs special mention—Saxon Mountain, Trail #66. We've rated it difficult, not because it is that hard to drive, but because it's prone to serious rock slides. Even though it's a county road, we consider it very dangerous until the worst spots get fixed.

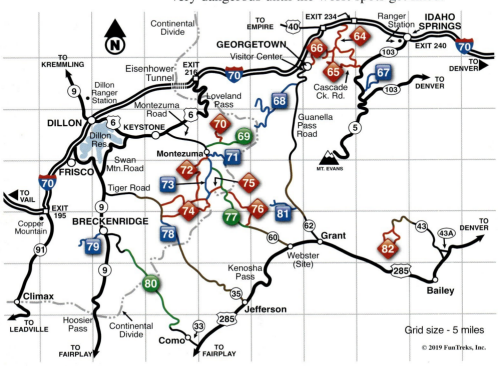

Grid size - 5 miles

© 2019 FunTreks, Inc.

Nearing the top of Saints John, Trail #72, rated difficult.

Spring Creek

64

Obstacle #1, extreme articulation tester!

Obstacle #2, easiest of the bunch.

Obstacle #3 changes constantly.

Obstacle #4, the Rock Garden, never ends.

Overview: Due to its close proximity to Denver, this trail sees very heavy use. In the last few years, many large boulders have been exposed, creating near extreme conditions. A previously seldom-used side road at the bottom has now become the main trail. This section features a daunting challenge. The Rock Garden (challenge #4), has multiple obstacles that seem to have no end. Great views looking down on I-70 and Georgetown. No seasonal closures except by weather.

Rating: Difficult. Short sections of moderate road connect a series of steep boulder challenges. Highly modified vehicles only. Lockers are a must. Unlicensed vehicles are allowed, but getting an ATV or UTV up this trail would be quite an accomplishment.

Stats: Length: 5 miles. Time: 2 to 4 hours depending on vehicle capability. High point: 11,050 ft. Best time of year: Late June-early October.

Current Conditions: Arapaho N.F., Clear Creek R.D. Call (303) 567-3000.

Getting There: Get off Interstate 70 at Downieville exit 234 west of Idaho Springs. Go west on the access road. It starts on the north side and passes under the freeway. At 1.1 miles from the exit, turn left on Alvarado Road. Cross the bridge and immediately pull over to the left.

MILEAGE LOG:

0.0 Zero trip odometer [Rev. Miles]
Head east uphill on what starts as a residential road. **[5.0]**
`01` N39 45.779 W105 38.009

0.2 Continue straight to go up obstacle #1. Switchback to right is bypass. **[4.8]**

0.5 Road curves south to bottom of obstacle on your right. Select a line. **[4.5]**

0.6 At top of obstacle #1, turn left and continue uphill on 712.2J. **[4.4]**
`02` N39 45.667 W105 37.654

1.1 Turn right uphill on lesser road marked 712.2J. Left on more traveled road goes to camp spots and rejoins trail. **[3.9]**
`03` N39 45.457 W105 37.805

1.7 Swing left uphill at obstacle #2. View right. **[3.3]**

2.2 Sharp switchback to left. More to come. **[2.8]**

2.5 Turn left uphill on shortcut. Main trail is left but is narrow with trees. **[2.5]**

3.5 Turn hard left up boulders of obstacle #3, then stay left again. **[1.5]**
`04` N39 44.880 W105 38.593

4.3 Start of Rock Garden, obstacle #4. **[0.7]**
`05` N39 44.338 W105 38.468

5.0 Intersect with 712.1. **[0.0]**
`06` N39 43.923 W105 38.721
Choices from here:
A. Return the way you came. **B.** Turn right and go down Saxon Mountain to Georgetown, Trail #66.
C. Go right or left following map for Cascade Creek, Trail #65.

View of I-70 below from Obstacle #2.

The trail.

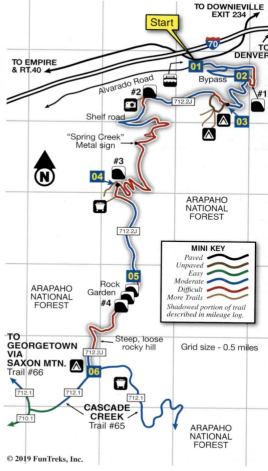

MINI KEY
Paved
Unpaved
Easy
Moderate
Difficult
More Trails
Shadowed portion of trail described in mileage log.

Grid size - 0.5 miles

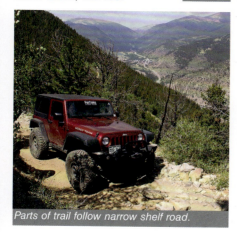

Parts of trail follow narrow shelf road.

© 2019 FunTreks, Inc.

159

Section between Waypoints 02 and 08 was slow-going for our stock Wrangler Sport with street tires.

Tow vehicles will have to climb steep hill to get to this parking spot.

Historical Highlight: *Hidden in the trees just south of Waypoint 04 is the townsite of Lamartine. A faint road 727.1B leads to it. A small town of about 500 mine workers lived here in the late 1890s to service the Lamartine Mine, shown on map. Just a few logs remain from a couple of cabins. If you look closely as you drive the trails, you'll see remains of many other mines in the area.*

Overview: This loop passes through a network of mountain roads between Georgetown and Idaho Springs. It is surrounded by residential property on all sides. We've chosen to enter via Cascade Creek Road because it passes less private property and offers a little parking for unlicensed vehicles. This loop can also be accessed from Saxon Road, Trail #66, and Ute Creek Road. No seasonal closures except by weather.

Rating: Difficult. Mostly moderate except for the western half of Cascade Creek Road 710.1. This part has loose boulders and tricky ledges. Harder going uphill in reverse direction. We

did it in our stock Wrangler Sport going downhill, but it was a challenge.

Stats: Length: 12.2 miles. Time: 2 to 3 hours. High point: 11,050 ft. Best time of year: Late June-early October.

Current Conditions: Arapaho N.F., Clear Creek R.D. Call (303) 567-3000.

Getting There: Get off I-70 at Idaho Springs, Exit 240. Head south on Route 103 towards Mt. Evans. Turn right on Cascade Creek Road about a half mile past mile marker 5. There's a small area to park along 103 before you turn and more parking 0.4 mile up the trail.

MILEAGE LOG:

0.0 Zero trip odometer **[Rev. Miles]**
Head uphill on Cascade Creek Road 116. **[4.4]**
`01` **N39 42.380 W105 36.330**

0.4 Closed shooting area. Some parking on left. **[4.0]**

1.2 Hard right uphill on 710.1C. **[3.2]**
`02` **N39 42.691 W105 37.532**

1.9 Hard right up switchback at flat mine area. **[2.5]**

2.2 Continue straight. Road joins on left. **[2.2]**

2.4 Bear left uphill on Ute Creek Road 118. **[2.0]**
`03` **N39 43.227 W105 37.121**

2.7 Turn right uphill on 712.2A at boulder. **[1.7]**

4.4 At top of hill, turn left on 712.1. **[0.0]**
`04` **N39 43.899 W105 37.055**

0.0 Zero trip odometer
From Wpt. 04, head west on 712.1. **[2.5]**

1.1 Stay right. Left is shortcut downhill to Wpt. 08. **[1.4]**
`05` **N39 43.583 W105 38.088**

1.6 Stay left where 712.2G goes right. **[0.9]**

1.8 Stay right where 712.2I goes left to mine. **[0.7]**

2.3 Continue straight where 712.2G rejoins. **[0.2]**

2.5 Continue straight. Right downhill is difficult Spring Creek, Trail #64. **[0.0]**
`06` **N39 43.920 W105 38.720**

0.0 Zero trip odometer
From Wpt. 06, continue southwest on 712.1. **[5.2]**

0.6 Bear left. (Right goes to Trail #66.) Within 200 ft., stay left again downhill on 710.1. **[4.6]**
`07` **N39 43.640 W105 39.270**

1.6 Make a hard left on 710.1 where 710.1A goes straight. **[3.6]**

2.4 Turn right downhill on 710.1 and enter trees. Left goes back to Waypoint 05 on 712.2B. **[2.8]**
`08` **N39 42.875 W105 39.110**

4.0 Return to Waypoint 02 and stay right. **[1.2]**

5.2 Return to start of trail at Highway 103. **[0.0]**

Get FREE trail updates & GPS downloads at www.FunTreks.com

Mine building next to road.

View from mine along F.S. 710.1C.

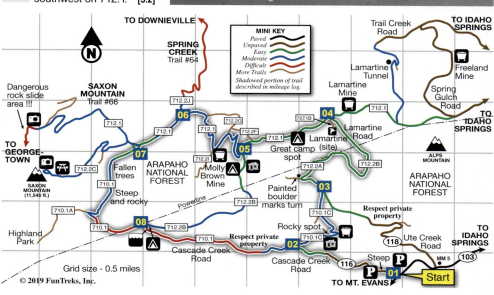

© 2019 FunTreks, Inc.

161

Barely got over this rockslide at 3.5 miles. Very scary spot!

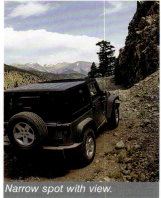

Narrow spot with view.

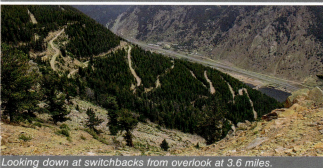

Looking down at switchbacks from overlook at 3.6 miles.

Historical Highlight: *Silver was first discovered on top of Saxon Mountain in 1866. Production continued for many years with several changes in ownership of the mine. At some point, the main vein was considered lost and each new owner thought he could find it. The last owner, Walter Berry of Pittsburgh, Pa., spent 15 years looking for the vein, but gave up in 1951. He tried again in 1968 with newer technology, but still had no luck. Some still believe a rich silver vein is there, waiting to be discovered.*

Overview: Great views of Georgetown and I-70 corridor. Mt. Evans can be seen from the top on a clear day. Endless switchbacks are impressive. Don't miss historic Georgetown and the visitor center. Parking space is limited at the trailhead. To drive trail from top down, go up Cascade Creek, Trail #65. No seasonal closures, but avoid if snow covered or after periods of heavy rain when rockslides are more likely.

Rating: Difficult. We last drove this road on July 5, 2018. At that time, the road was nearly impassable due to several rockslides. By the time you read this, we hope repairs have been made to the road. If not, this road should be considered VERY DANGEROUS. We got through in our stock Wrangler Sport,

but it was challenging in spots.

Stats: Length: 6.3 miles. Time: 1 hour to top with capable vehicle. High point: 11,400 ft. Best time of year: Late June-September.

Current Conditions: Upper portion is in Arapaho N.F., Clear Creek R.D. Call (303) 567-3000. Balance is Clear Creek County Road 712.

Getting There: Get off Interstate 70 at Georgetown exit 228. Head due east through roundabout to Main Street and turn left. Main Street becomes dirt and runs into entrance to Saxon Mountain Road after a half mile. Continue up the road another quarter mile to sign. Stay right avoiding residential driveways.

0.0 Zero trip odometer [Rev. Miles] Stay right uphill. There is a small, rocky area to park at first switchback. Road is wide enough to park partway up, but it's very rough if you are towing a trailer. [6.3]
01 N39 43.359 W105 41.389

1.5 Road on right goes to flat area to camp. [4.8]

1.6 Narrow spot with view. (See photo at left.) [4.7]

1.8 Stay right where road on left goes downhill. [4.5]

1.9 Large boulder blocked trail. Not easy to get around. [4.4]

2.1 Stay right. Left goes to huge dumping of large drain pipes. [4.2]

2.3 Stay right uphill. [4.0]

2.7 Follow switchback hard left through tight boulder field. Difficult section begins here. [3.6]

3.1 Continue uphill. Road on right goes to ruins of small cabins. [3.2]

3.3 Another large boulder to get around. Dangerous rock slide area. [3.0]

3.5 Near impassable spot due to large rock slide at narrow point. Very dangerous. [2.8]

3.6 Overlook. Worst part of trail is over. [2.7]

3.8 Stay right uphill where large road goes left downhill. [2.5]
02 N39 43.800 W105 40.360

4.5 Cabin ruin on right. [1.8]

4.6 Fence opening at forest boundary. Road becomes F.S. 712.1. Sign explains

trail is adopted by NAXJA, North American XJ Association. [1.7]

5.3 Stay right uphill on F.S. 712.2C. Left goes to Cascade Creek, Trail #65, and Spring Creek, Trail #64. [1.0]
03 N39 43.664 W105 39.403

6.3 Road ends at small loop at top of Saxon Mountain where you'll find picnic tables and camp spots. Stay away from cell towers hidden in the trees. [0.0]
04 N39 43.355 W105 40.283
Return the way you came or go back to Waypoint 03 and turn right. From here you can go down Cascade Creek or very difficult Spring Creek.

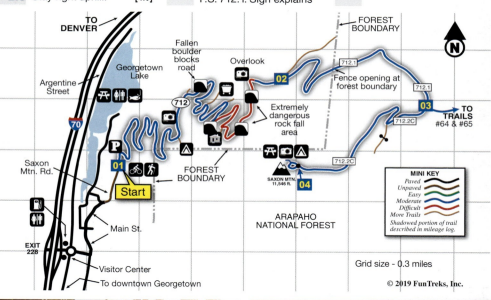

Just enough room to get around fallen boulder.

One of several picnic spots at the top.

© 2019 FunTreks, Inc.

163

View of Mt. Evans from camp spot at top of mountain just north of Waypoint 04.

Start of trail is hard to see coming up Hwy.103

Open area at top of trail.

Overview: A short fun loop with several side roads to explore. Seasonally open to unlicensed vehicles June 15 through Dec. 15. Gate is locked the rest of the year. Broad views from top of mountain at Wpt. 04. Dispersed camping allowed along entire route. Parking along Highway 103 near start of trail. Before or after you drive this trail, consider a trip to Echo Lake and Mt. Evans, just another 2.5 miles past the trailhead on Highway 103.

Rating: Moderate. Much of this trail is easy; however, the eastern side of the main loop has gotten chewed up with large ruts in a few places. It could become difficult in the future. Side trip on 246.1B is very steep and narrow at the north end.

Stats: Length: Round trip is 5.3 miles. Time: 2-3 hours. High point: 10,300 ft. Best time to go: Late June-mid October.

Current Conditions: Arapaho N.F., Clear Creek R.D. Call (303) 567-3000.

Getting There: Get off I-70 at Idaho Springs, Exit 240, following signs to Mt. Evans. Follow Highway 103 south. Turn very sharp left on dirt road 0.3 mile after mile marker 10. Hard to see this road until after you go past it.

MILEAGE LOG:

START

0.0 Zero trip odometer [Rev. Miles]
Head uphill through seasonal gate. [1.3]
01 N39 40.847 W105 36.294

0.6 Bear left on 246.1A. [0.7]
02 N39 41.171 W105 36.195

0.9 Ignore road on left. [0.4]

1.0 Stay right. Side trip to left on 246.1B is fun, but all roads dead-end at bottom of long hill. [0.3]
03 N39 41.335 W105 35.857

1.1 Continue straight. (246.1B rejoins on left.) [0.2]

1.3 Arrive at clearing at top of mountain where loop begins. [0.0]

0.0 Zero trip odometer at Wpt. 04
Stay left to go around loop clockwise. [2.7]
04 N39 41.504 W105 35.704

0.1 Continue straight. Camp spot uphill to left. [2.6]

0.5 Stay right. [2.2]

0.9 Low point of loop. Camp spot in meadow to left. Trail turns right and begins long climb. [1.8]
05 N39 41.952 W105 35.293

1.3 Steep, chewed up spot will test articulation. [1.4]

1.9 Steep with deep ruts. [0.8]

2.0 Stay right. [0.7]

2.3 Stay right. Left connects to 246.1, but is not on MVUM. [0.4]

2.5 Great camp spot on right with view. [0.2]

2.6 Stay right and return to Waypoint 04. Difficult road on left is not on MVUM. [0.1]

2.7 Complete loop at Waypoint 04. Turn left and go out the way you came in on 246.1A. [0.0]

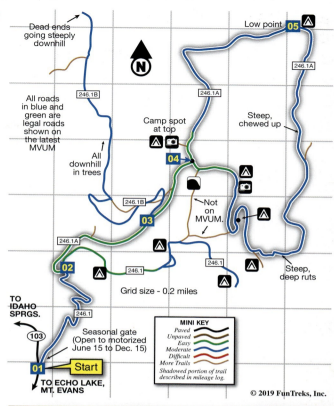

Dead ends going steeply downhill

Low point **05**

246.1A

All roads in blue and green are legal roads shown on the latest MVUM

Camp spot at top

Steep, chewed up

All downhill in trees

246.1B

04

246.1A

03

Not on MVUM.

246.1B

246.1A

02

Steep, deep ruts

246.1

246.1

TO IDAHO SPRGS.

Grid size - 0.2 miles

103

246.1

Seasonal gate (Open to motorized June 15 to Dec. 15)

01 **Start**

TO ECHO LAKE, MT. EVANS

MINI KEY
Paved
Unpaved
Easy
Moderate
Difficult
More Trails
Shadowed portion of trail described in mileage log.

© 2019 FunTreks, Inc.

Front Range 4x4 Adopt-a-Road.

Steep, deep ruts test articulation along eastern side of loop.

Great views at McClellan Mountain Waypoint 07.

Rocky spot on way to Wpt. 04.

Santiago Mine (temporarily closed). Photo taken 2004.

Historical Highlight: *Not much remains of the town of Waldorf. In the 1860s, it had the highest post office in the United States at 11,666 ft. The railroad that ran to Waldorf, in addition to carrying freight, also carried tourists. In 1905, the railroad was extended to the top of McClellan Mountain and was known as the Stairway to the Stars. At the top, tourists were given a tour of the Ice Palace, an old mining tunnel filled with ice formations. F.S. 248.1 follows the old railroad grade. If you wonder how the trains made the tight turns at the switchbacks, they didn't. They continued past the turn, then backed up, alternating forwards and backwards up the mountainside.*

Overview: Incredible views from 13,132-ft. Argentine Pass and top of McClellan Mountain. Recent soil tests have temporarily closed historic buildings at Santiago Mine and Ghost Town, but plans to reopen by 2020 are underway. Many legal side roads to explore. Numerous tourist attractions in quaint Georgetown. No seasonal closures.

Rating: Moderate. Rocky at the start and very narrow at the top of Argentine Pass with one moderate ledge. Much of the lower route is easy unless you take alternate route 248.1B along creek. Need aggressive stock SUV with low range and high clearance.

Stats: Length: 6 miles to Waldorf. Add 2.3 miles for Argentine and 4 miles for McClellan. Time: 4 to 6 hours. High point: 13,132 ft. Best time of year: Mid July-Sept.

Current Conditions: Arapaho N.F., Clear Creek R.D. Call (303) 567-3000.

Getting There: Get off I-70 at Exit 228 and follow signs west through town towards Guanella Pass. As you climb out of town, continue 2.7 miles. When a tight switchback swings left, watch for narrow road on right. Sign once said "Waldorf," but new construction may have changed that. Follow F.S. 248.1.

MILEAGE LOG:

0.0 Zero trip odometer **[Rev. Miles]**
Head uphill on 248.1. **[6.0]**
01 N39 40.991 W105 42.170

0.4 Stay right uphill at switchback. Designated camping on the right. **[5.6]**

0.9 Stay right up switchback. Road to left is 248.1B. This is an alternate route along the creek and is more difficult. **[5.1]**

1.2 Stay left at switchback and continue to follow 248.1 southwest above creek. **[4.8]**

3.6 Stay right. Left goes downhill to 248.1B. **[2.4]**
02 N39 39.988 W105 44.377

6.0 Important fork. Flat area ahead is Waldorf site; only mine tailings remain. **[0.0]**
03 N39 38.270 W105 45.900

0.0 Zero trip odometer
ARGENTINE PASS:
At Waypoint 03, cross Waldorf site to narrow road on other side. **[2.3]**

0.3 Stay right uphill. **[2.0]**

0.5 Stay left. **[1.8]**

0.9 Stay right uphill. **[1.4]**

2.3 Argentine Pass. View of Peru Creek below. Return to Waypoint 03. **[0.0]**
04 N39 37.528 W105 46.933

0.0 Zero trip odometer
MCCLELLAN MTN:
At Waypoint 03, continue north on 248.1. Avoid roads that branch off at switchbacks. **[4.0]**

0.7 Stay right uphill on 248.1. Left on F.S. 248.2C goes to Santiago Mine and Ghost Town (closed for repairs). **[3.3]**
05 N39 38.826 W105 45.722

1.3 Stay left up first switchback. **[2.7]**

1.9 Turn right. **[2.1]**

2.6 Bear left after switchback. (Straight dead-ends at overlook of I-70 in about 2 more miles. We did not drive this road. **[1.4]**
06 N39 39.869 W105 46.348

4.0 Road ends at cliff edge with view of Grays and Torreys Peaks. Small space to turn around. **[0.0]**
07 N39 39.062 W105 46.649
On return trip, take opportunity to explore many legal side roads.

Looking down from Argentine Pass at Peru Creek, Trail #69.

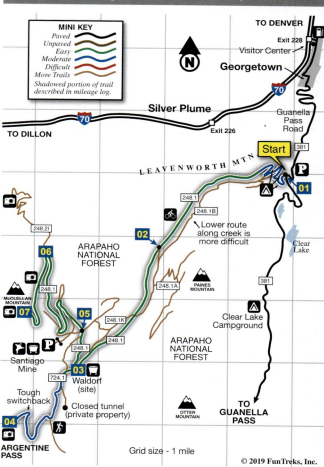

MINI KEY
Paved
Unpaved
Easy
Moderate
Difficult
More Trails
Shadowed portion of trail described in mileage log.

TO DENVER
Exit 228
Visitor Center
Georgetown
I-70
Silver Plume
Guanella Pass Road
TO DILLON
I-70
Exit 226
Start
381
P
LEAVENWORTH MTN
248.1
248.1B
Lower route along creek is more difficult
01
Clear Lake
248.2I
ARAPAHO NATIONAL FOREST
02
248.1A
PAINES MOUNTAIN
381
06
248.1
McCLELLAN MOUNTAIN
07
05
248.1K
248.1
Clear Lake Campground
ARAPAHO NATIONAL FOREST
P
Santiago Mine
724.1
03
Waldorf (site)
Tough switchback
Closed tunnel (private property)
04
OTTER MOUNTAIN
TO GUANELLA PASS
ARGENTINE PASS
Grid size - 1 mile
© 2019 FunTreks, Inc.

167

Peru Creek Road 260, when dry, is easy and scenic all the way.

Sign at start of trail (2018).

Parking lot at end of F.S. 260 (Wpt.04). Hike from here.

Historical Highlight: The Pennsylvania Mine was a rich producer of gold and silver, with its best year occurring in 1893, the year of the great silver crash. It continued to operate through the crash, producing $3 million in total earnings between 1893 and 1898. It has been a major polluter of water in the area, and clean-up efforts, which have closed the trail intermittently in recent years, are now complete.

Overview: Easy road accesses great camping, hiking and historic structures. Side trip up Cinnamon Gulch reaches a dramatic viewpoint at a tram house. See Chihuahua Gulch, Trail #70, for more difficult side trip. A sign at the start of trail says unlicensed vehicles are allowed on all of 260, but the 2016 MVUM shows unlicensed are allowed starting after 2 miles at Warden Gulch. Check future MVUMs for possible changes. Seasonally closed to all OHVs Nov. 23 to May 20 or until dry.

Rating: Easy. Forest Road 260 can be driven in a high-clearance two-wheel-drive vehicle when dry. You'll want 4-wheel drive for side roads.

Stats: Length: 10.2 miles in and out as described here. Time: 2-3 hours. High point: 11,250 ft. Best time: July-Sept.

Current Conditions: White River N.F., Dillon R.D. Call (970) 468-5400.

Getting There: Get off Route 6 just east of the Keystone Ski Area, following signs to Montezuma Road. There is an exit ramp for eastbound traffic, but westbound traffic must turn left at Gondola Road and backtrack to Montezuma Road (see map detail). Head south on Montezuma Road 4.5 miles along the Snake River. When the road curves hard left, immediately turn left into a fenced parking area.

MILEAGE LOG:

0.0 Zero trip odometer [Rev. Miles]
PERU CREEK:
Head north, then east on county road which soon becomes F.S. 260. [4.6]
01 N39 35.530 W105 52.259

2.0 Continue straight. Warden Gulch 265 goes right. [2.6]

2.1 Continue straight. Chihuahua Gulch, Trail #70, is on the left. [2.5]
02 N39 36.026 W105 50.291

3.7 Continue straight. Cinnamon Gulch is to right (described below). [0.9]
03 N39 36.160 W105 48.795

4.6 Trail ends at parking lot for Argentine Pass and Horseshoe Basin Hiking Trails. Return to Wpt. 03. [0.0]
04 N39 36.558 W105 47.955

0.0 Zero trip odometer at Wpt. 03
CINNAMON GULCH:
From Waypoint 03, head south across creek. [0.5]

0.1 Bear left. Right goes to Pennsylvania Mill. [0.4]

0.2 Bear right past Pennsylvania Mine. Road climbs to right. [0.3]

0.5 Rough road goes left to great photo spot at tram house. [0.0]
05 N39 35.855 W105 48.815
Road continues south uphill from Wpt. 05 and ends in about 0.7 mile.

Take first right at bottom of F.S. 262 to see Pennsylvania Mill.

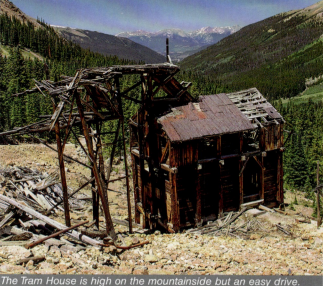

The Tram House is high on the mountainside but an easy drive.

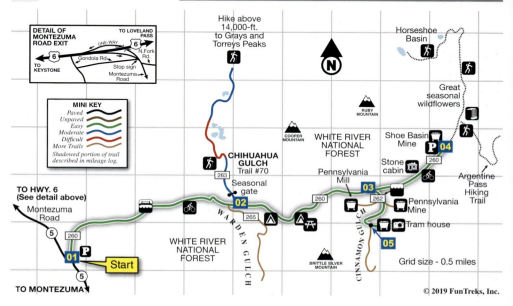

DETAIL OF MONTEZUMA ROAD EXIT
TO LOVELAND PASS
ONE-WAY
6
N.Fork Rd.
6
Gondola Rd.
TO KEYSTONE
Stop sign
Montezuma Road

MINI KEY
Paved
Unpaved
Easy
Moderate
Difficult
More Trails
Shadowed portion of trail described in mileage log.

Hike above 14,000-ft. to Grays and Torreys Peaks

Horseshoe Basin

Great seasonal wildflowers

RUBY MOUNTAIN

COOPER MOUNTAIN

WHITE RIVER NATIONAL FOREST

Shoe Basin Mine

P 04
260

CHIHUAHUA GULCH Trail #70
263
Seasonal gate
02
265

Pennsylvania Mill
03
260
262

Stone cabin

Pennsylvania Mine

Tram house
05

TO HWY. 6 (See detail above)
Montezuma Road
5
260
01 **P**
Start
5

WHITE RIVER NATIONAL FOREST

WARDEN GULCH

BRITTLE SILVER MOUNTAIN

CINNAMON GULCH

Argentine Pass Hiking Trail

Grid size - 0.5 miles

TO MONTEZUMA

© 2019 FunTreks, Inc.

First water crossing.

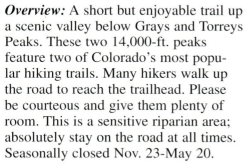

Looking down valley from second water crossing.

Wet area with tight brush on upper part of trail.

Overview: A short but enjoyable trail up a scenic valley below Grays and Torreys Peaks. These two 14,000-ft. peaks feature two of Colorado's most popular hiking trails. Many hikers walk up the road to reach the trailhead. Please be courteous and give them plenty of room. This is a sensitive riparian area; absolutely stay on the road at all times. Seasonally closed Nov. 23-May 20.

Rating: Difficult. Mostly moderate, but a couple of boulder fields we rank as marginally difficult. We did it in our stock Wrangler without lockers, but it took some very careful tire placement. Tight brush in places.

Stats: Length: 2.0 miles one way. Time: 2-3 hours for round trip. High point: 11,200 ft. Best time: Mid July-October.

Current Conditions: White River N.F., Dillon R.D. Call (970) 468-5400.

Getting There: Get off Route 6 just east of the Keystone Ski Area, following signs to Montezuma Road. There is an exit ramp for eastbound traffic, but westbound traffic must turn left at Gondola Road and backtrack to Montezuma Road (see map detail for Trail #69). Head south on Montezuma Road 4.5 miles along the Snake River. When the road curves hard left, immediately turn left into a fenced parking area. Follow Road 260 north then east 2.1 miles to Chihuahua Gulch on left.

MILEAGE LOG:

0.0 Zero trip odometer [Rev. Miles]
Head north uphill on steep road that passes through talus field. **[2.0]**
01 N39 36.027 W105 50.292

0.6 Climb small rocky ledge and stay left. Camp spots in this area. Difficult rocky section follows. **[1.4]**

0.7 Circle downhill and cross creek. Road heads north along rocky hillside above creek. **[1.3]**

1.2 Cross section of corduroy road. **[0.8]**
02 N39 36.858 W105 50.666

1.4 Cross creek again. Very scenic spot looking south down valley. **[0.6]**

1.8 Stay left. Camp spot to right. **[0.2]**

1.9 Stay left again. Don't drive up creek. **[0.1]**

2.0 Trail ends at parking area for popular hiking trail to Grays and Torreys Peaks. Turn around here. **[0.0]**
03 N39 37.371 W105 50.368

Family camps on right at 0.6 mile in stock Toyota 4Runner.

FREE trail updates & GPS downloads at www. funtreks.com

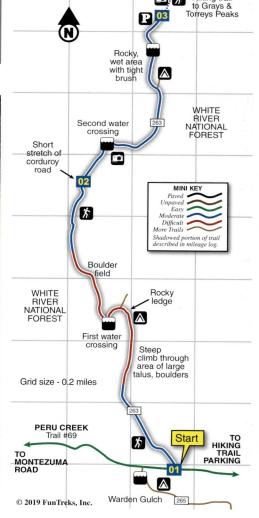

MINI KEY
Paved
Unpaved
Easy
Moderate
Difficult
More Trails
Shadowed portion of trail described in mileage log.

Hiking trail to Grays & Torreys Peaks

Rocky, wet area with tight brush

WHITE RIVER NATIONAL FOREST

263

Second water crossing

Short stretch of corduroy road

02

Boulder field

Rocky ledge

WHITE RIVER NATIONAL FOREST

First water crossing

Steep climb through area of large talus, boulders

Grid size - 0.2 miles

263

PERU CREEK
Trail #69

Start

TO HIKING TRAIL PARKING

TO MONTEZUMA ROAD

Warden Gulch

265

01

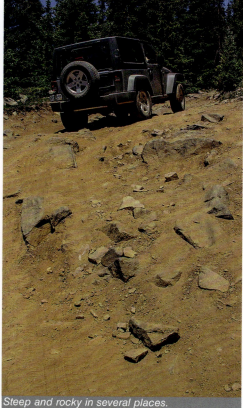
Steep and rocky in several places.

© 2019 FunTreks, Inc.

Breckenridge Ski Area in distance, Glacier Ridge right center. Road lower right is F.S. 275.1C.

Road narrows as you near the timberline.

Tight switchbacks are chewed up in places.

Overview: Climbs above 13,000 ft. with stunning panoramic views, including Breckenridge Ski Area, Grays Peak, Peru Creek, Webster Pass and Radical Hill. Unlicensed vehicles are no longer allowed on this trail. Seasonally closed Nov. 23 to May 20.

Rating: Moderate: This trail is very steep, narrow and quite rocky in spots. We don't rate it difficult, but it comes very close. Not recommended for novice drivers or anyone afraid of high narrow shelf roads.

Stats: Length: Round trip 9 miles. Time: 2 hours. High point: 13,120 ft. Best time of year: Mid July-Sept.

Current Conditions: White River N.F., Dillon R.D. Call (970) 468-5400.

Getting There: Get off Route 6 just east of the Keystone Ski Area, following signs to Montezuma Road. There is an exit ramp for eastbound traffic, but westbound traffic must turn left at Gondola Road and backtrack to Montezuma Road (See map detail of exit.) Head south on Montezuma Road 5.2 miles where pavement ends. Continue into town of Montezuma on dirt road to stop sign and turn left uphill on 3rd Street (not marked). Warning: Go slow in town to minimize dust or suffer the wrath of local residents. Do not park on the streets.

MILEAGE LOG:

START

0.0 Zero trip odometer **[Rev. Miles]**
Follow easy road through residential area and climb through forest. **[4.5]**
01 N39 34.915 W105 52.091

0.7 Private residence on the left. Continue climbing and follow main road right. **[3.8]**

2.7 Climb out of trees. Road is narrow and rocky and somewhat V-shaped. **[1.8]**

2.9 Mine on right. Turn hard left up tight switchback. This is perhaps the toughest spot as it is steep and quite chewed up. **[1.6]**

3.4 Top of ridge. Look east below for view of Peru Creek, Trail #69. Road continues to climb very steeply, but is not quite as rough. **[1.1]**

3.8 Bear left staying on F.S. 264. Right dead-ends at Sansfield Mine. Near top of mountain road levels off. **[0.7]**
02 N39 34.669 W105 50.369

4.5 We stopped here, although narrow shelf road continued a bit farther. Looking southwest you can see Webster Pass and Radical Hill from this point. **[0.0]**
03 N39 34.205 W105 50.266

Starting down switchbacks from about Waypoint 02.

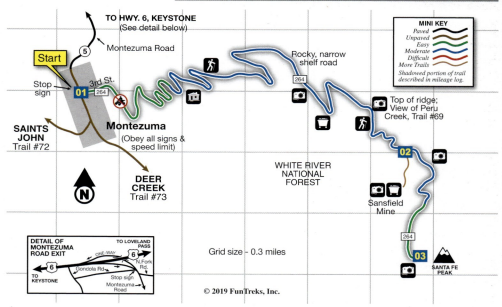

TO HWY. 6, KEYSTONE
(See detail below)

Montezuma Road

Start

Stop sign

3rd St.

01 264

Rocky, narrow shelf road

264

Top of ridge;
View of Peru
Creek, Trail #69

02

MINI KEY
Paved
Unpaved
Easy
Moderate
Difficult
More Trails
Shadowed portion of trail described in mileage log.

SAINTS JOHN
Trail #72

Montezuma
(Obey all signs & speed limit)

WHITE RIVER
NATIONAL
FOREST

Sansfield Mine

DEER CREEK
Trail #73

264

03

SANTA FE PEAK

N

DETAIL OF MONTEZUMA ROAD EXIT

TO LOVELAND PASS

ONE-WAY

6

N. Fork Rd.

Gondola Rd.

Stop sign

Montezuma Road

TO KEYSTONE

6

Grid size - 0.3 miles

© 2019 FunTreks, Inc.

173

Hair-raising steep descent down narrow ridge.

4WD club enjoys lunch near General Teller Mine.

Common sight along upper parts of trail.

Cabins and wildflowers at Wild Irishman Mine.

Historical Highlight: The town of Saints John was active during the 1870s and early 1880s. Even before the silver crash of 1893, the town had gone under. Foundations of a large mill still remain at the site. A restored private cabin you pass was originally the house of the mine supervisor. The company that owned the mine didn't allow saloons, so miners headed down the hill to Montezuma, which had many saloons and brothels. Wild Irishman Mine was never more than a camp and was active in the 1870s.

Overview: Memorable climb with stunning scenery, historic mine buildings and real adventure. Connects to a network of outstanding high-elevation trails. Mountain goats often seen at the top. Great area for ATVs, UTVs and dirt bikes. Large staging area on C.R. 5 (see Trail # 73). So far, the town of Montezuma has been allowing unlicensed vehicles to come into town, but this could change if abuses occur. Please ride slowly through town to minimize dust. Seasonally open 5/21 to 11/22.

Rating: Difficult: Very steep with loose rock in places. Experienced drivers in aggressive stock SUVs can do it in direction described here. Low-range gearing a must. Differential lockers recommended to drive in reverse direction.

Stats: Length: 6.5 miles one way. Time: 2-3 hours. High point: 12,335 ft. Best time of year: Mid July-Sept.

Current Conditions: White River N.F., Dillon R.D. Call (970) 468-5400.

Getting There: Get off Route 6 at east end of Keystone Ski Area following signs to Montezuma Road. (See map detail of exit.) Head south on Montezuma Road 5.2 miles where pavement ends. Continue into town of Montezuma on dirt road to Saints John Road on right (F.S. 275).

MILEAGE LOG:

0.0 Zero trip odometer **[Rev. Miles]** Head west uphill on F.S. 275 from center of Montezuma. **[6.5]**

01 N39 34.805 W105 52.059

0.05 Pass through private property. Stay on road at all times. **[6.45]**

0.1 Official F.S. sign shows unlicensed vehicles allowed on 275. **[6.4]**

0.5 Stay left on 275. Road on right is not on MVUM. **[6.0]**

1.3 Weave through Saints John Townsite. **[5.2]**

1.4 Turn hard right, cross creek, then swing left past private cabin. **[5.1]**

1.8 Cross creek. **[4.7]**

1.9 Seasonal gate. **[4.6]**

2.2 Stay left. Lesser road to right. **[4.3]**

2.9 Pullover on left for cabins at Wild Irishman Mine. Hike downhill short distance to cabins. **[3.6]**

3.1 Follow switchback to right past Wild Irishman Mine. Very steep and rocky. **[3.4]**

3.5 Continue straight where shortcut to 275.1B goes left. **[3.0]**

3.7 Continue straight where 275.1B joins on left. **[2.8]**

02 N39 33.413 W105 52.932

3.8 Shed and General Teller Mine on left. **[2.7]**

4.4 Steep rocky downhill. Lockers recommended in reverse direction. **[2.1]**

4.6 Continue straight past 275.1C on left. Fun side trip. Road 275 continues rough and rocky. **[1.9]**

03 N39 32.864 W105 53.125

6.5 "T" intersection near edge of cliff has amazing views. Watch for mountain goats in this area. **[0.0]**

04 N39 31.381 W105 52.923 Shortest and easiest way to get down the mountain is via Deer Creek, Trail #73, using reverse directions. Turn left then stay left following F.S. 5. Right at Waypoint 04 returns to Breckenridge via difficult North & Middle Fork of the Swan River, Trail #74.

Map labels

DETAIL OF MONTEZUMA ROAD EXIT

TO LOVELAND PASS

ONE-WAY

N.Fork Rd.

Gondola Rd.

Stop sign

TO KEYSTONE

Montezuma Road

TO HWY. 6, KEYSTONE (See detail at left.)

Montezuma Road

SANTA FE PEAK Trail #71

Montezuma

So far, unlicensed vehicles have been allowed to ride into town. Go slow. NO DUST!

SAINTS JOHN CREEK

Saints John Townsite

Seasonal forest gate

Wild Irishman Mine

Large parking & staging area

S

TO RADICAL HILL Trail #75, WEBSTER PASS Trail #77

Steep, narrow switchbacks

GLACIER MOUNTAIN

General Teller Mine

DEER CREEK Trail #73

DEER CREEK

Steep, loose rock hill

WHITE RIVER NATIONAL FOREST

MINI KEY
Paved
Unpaved
Easy
Moderate
Difficult
More Trails
Shadowed portion of trail described in mileage log.

Rough road

DEER CREEK Trail #73

TELLER MOUNTAIN

TO WEBSTER PASS Trail #77

Watch for mountain goats.

RADICAL HILL Trail #75

Grid size - 0.5 miles

© 2019 FunTreks, Inc.

TO NORTH FORK OF SWAN RIVER Trail #74

Watch for mountain goats.

Steep hill

TO MIDDLE FORK OF SWAN RIVER Trail #74

Longtime users of FunTreks' books were happy to meet the author.

This vehicle is coming down the trail with 2.7 miles to go to reach the bottom.

Family in SUV stops for a picnic along the route.

Historical Highlight: Montezuma was established in 1865 when silver was discovered at nearby Argentine Pass. By 1890, the population grew to nearly 10,000. When the silver boom ended in 1893, the town quickly faded away. Today the town is often described as a ghost town; however, more than 50 people still live here. The Montezuma schoolhouse is one of several original structures. At this writing, unlicensed vehicles are allowed to ride in town. But to maintain this privilege, it is critical that everyone goes slowly and avoids kicking up clouds of dust. Also, do not park in town; use the staging area shown on our map.

Overview: We've found this to be the easiest and quickest 4x4 route to the higher elevations south of Montezuma and Breckenridge. The scenery at the top is some of the best in Colorado. Mountain goats are often seen at the top hanging around cliff edges. This trail can be combined with difficult Saints John, Trail #72, to form a spectacular loop. Seasonally closed Nov. 23 to May 20 according to sign on trail.

Rating: Moderate: The road is narrow, steep and rocky in a few places, but doable in a high-clearance 4x4 SUV with low-range gearing. Conditions have gotten slightly more difficult the last few years, and it's possible the rat-

ing may someday become difficult.

Stats: Length: 4.6 miles one way. Time: 1½ to 2 hours one way. High point: 12,600 ft. Best time: Mid July-Sept.

Current Conditions: White River N.F., Dillon R.D. Call (970) 468-5400.

Getting There: Get off Route 6 at east end of Keystone Ski Area following signs to Montezuma Road. (See map detail of exit.) Head south on Montezuma Road 5.2 miles where pavement ends. Continue south through town on wide dirt road, C.R. 5, another 1.5 miles to large parking lot and staging area shown on map.

176

MILEAGE LOG:

0.0 **Zero trip odometer** [Rev. Miles]
From staging area, head south uphill on well-defined road. Ignore lesser roads that branch off. **[4.6]**
01 **N39 33.841 W105 51.634**

0.5 Pass through area of beaver ponds and dispersed camp spots. **[4.1]**

0.8 Seasonal gate. **[3.8]**

0.9 Continue straight. Unmarked road on right. **[3.7]**

1.3 F.A. 289 joins on right. **[3.3]**

1.4 Continue straight where F.S. 290 goes left. **[3.2]**

2.7 Climb above treeline and zigzag up a couple of long switchbacks. **[1.9]**

3.2 Stay right on F.S. 5. Left goes to difficult Radical Hill, Trail #75. **[1.4]**
02 **N39 31.653 W105 51.935**

3.3 Stay right. Left is a second chance to go to Radical Hill. **[1.3]**

3.8 Turn right on F.S. 275 that connects to Saints John, Trail #72. Straight goes to Middle Fork of the Swan River, Trail #74. **[0.8]**
03 **N39 31.255 W105 52.136**

4.6 Driver's choice. Right goes down Saints John, Trail #72. Straight goes to North Fork of the Swan River, Trail #74. **[0.0]**
04 **N39 31.381 W105 52.911**

Get FREE trail updates & GPS downloads at www.FunTreks.com

© 2019 FunTreks, Inc.

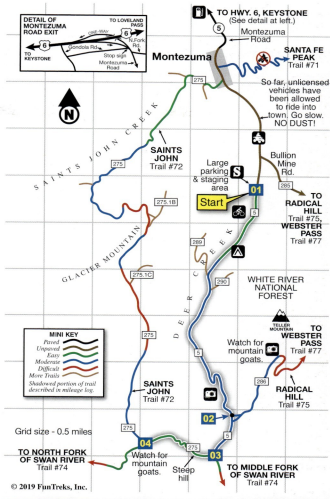

DETAIL OF MONTEZUMA ROAD EXIT
TO LOVELAND PASS
ONE-WAY
6
N.Fork Rd.
Gondola Rd.
Stop sign
TO KEYSTONE
6
Montezuma Road

TO HWY. 6, KEYSTONE (See detail at left.)
5
Montezuma Road

SANTA FE PEAK Trail #71

Montezuma

So far, unlicensed vehicles have been allowed to ride into town. Go slow. NO DUST!

Bullion Mine Rd.

285

TO RADICAL HILL Trail #75, **WEBSTER PASS** Trail #77

275

SAINTS JOHN Trail #72

275.1B

Large parking & staging area

Start

01

5

289

290

275

275.1C

275

SAINTS JOHN Trail #72

275

DEER CREEK

WHITE RIVER NATIONAL FOREST

TELLER Mountain

TO WEBSTER PASS Trail #77

Watch for mountain goats.

5

286

RADICAL HILL Trail #75

02

5

GLACIER MOUNTAIN

SAINTS JOHN CREEK

MINI KEY
Paved
Unpaved
Easy
Moderate
Difficult
More Trails
Shadowed portion of trail described in mileage log.

Grid size - 0.5 miles

04

TO NORTH FORK OF SWAN RIVER Trail #74

Watch for mountain goats.

Steep hill

275

03

TO MIDDLE FORK OF SWAN RIVER Trail #74

N

DEER CREEK ROAD #5
OPEN TO

OPEN TO — NOV. 23 THRU MAY 20

SEASONAL CLOSURES

NOV 23-MAY 20 OR UNTIL ROAD IS DRY

Open to unlicensed as posted.

Steep and rough in places. Our stock Jeep had no problems.

Author and his brother enjoy a meal on Wise Mountain.

Goats relaxing in the sun.

Popular loop for side-by-sides.

Historical Highlight: *The piles of rock seen along Tiger Road are from dredge mining that took place between 1898 and 1942. Large barges created their own deep ponds as they sucked silt and rock from the bottom of the Swan and Blue Rivers. Parts of an old dredge barge can be seen in a pond along Tiger Road 2.5 miles east of Highway 9.*

Swandyke was an active mining town between 1898 and 1910 with a population near 500. The town was a stage stop for passengers coming over Georgia Pass. Businesses included a saloon, barber shop, butcher shop and blacksmith shop.

Overview: Several well-preserved cabins along route, including one with full roof at top of Wise Mountain. Breathtaking views above timberline. Entire trail is open to unlicensed vehicles. Trail provides access to Trails #72, 73, 75-78. Open seasonally from May 21 to November 22.

Rating: Difficult. Steep, loose and rocky climbs on North Fork. The upper section of the Middle Fork is very narrow, rocky and steep in places. Early season conditions, when snow lingers on the trail, can create difficult and potentially dangerous situations. When dry, trail is usually suitable for aggressive stock SUVs with high ground clearance and low-range gearing, but use careful judgment if conditions deteriorate.

Stats: Length: 13.8-mile loop. Time: 3 to 4 hours. High point: 12,600 ft. Best time of year: Mid July-Sept.

Current Conditions: White River N.F., Dillon R.D. Call (970) 468-5400.

Getting There: From Highway 9 about 3 miles north of Breckenridge, head east on well-marked Tiger Road. Follow sign for golf course. Continue east after the pavement ends on a well-graded gravel road. Watch for staging area on right after about 4.8 miles. Continue another mile to start of North Fork route on left just before heavy wooden bridge.

START **MILEAGE LOG:**

0.0 *Zero trip odometer* [Rev. Miles]
NORTH FORK:
Head northeast uphill from Tiger Road. [6.4]
01 N39 30.787 W105 56.823

0.6 Cross open area and bear left uphill on F.S. 354. [5.8]
02 N39 30.982 W105 56.254

1.8 Continue straight on lesser road. Closed road goes left. [4.6]

2.3 Turn right on lesser road before cabin ruins and cross North Fork of Swan River. Road narrows and gets steeper. [4.1]
03 N39 31.622 W105 54.818

3.7 Turn right at "T" intersection to see cabin at top of Wise Mountain. [2.7]
04 N39 30.798 W105 54.168

3.8 Turn around at cabin. [2.6]

4.0 Return to Waypoint 04 and continue uphill. [2.4]

4.6 Driver's choice up extremely steep hill. [1.8]

5.6 Stay right along ridge. Left is Saints John, Trail #72. [0.8]
05 N39 31.376 W105 52.925

6.4 Arrive at intersection with Deer Creek, Trail #73, on left. [0.0]
06 N39 31.251 W105 52.142

Zero trip odometer
0.0 **MIDDLE FORK:**
From Wpt. 06, turn right (south) on F.S. 5. [7.4]

0.6 Driver's choice. [6.8]

0.7 Bear right downhill on F.S. 6. (Left dead ends at high scenic point not on 2016 MVUM.) [6.7]
07 N39 30.806 W105 51.748

1.1 Stay left as road goes right. [6.3]

1.2 Challenging downhill section with driver's choices. Stay left towards cabin for easiest route. [6.2]

2.5 Turn left. [4.9]

2.9 Cabin marks location of historic Swandyke. [4.5]

3.2 Stay left. [4.2]

3.5 Stay right downhill. Left is difficult #10 Hill and connects to top of Georgia Pass, Trail #78. [3.9]
08 N39 30.166 W105 54.072

4.1 Stay left downhill. [3.3]

6.1 Turn right on main Tiger Road to reach start of trail. Straight crosses creek and connects to Georgia Pass, Trail #78. [1.3]
09 N39 29.746 W105 56.699

7.4 Arrive back at beginning of trail at Waypoint 01. [0.0]

Looking down at Wise Mountain with ski runs in distance.

Washed-out section of trail.

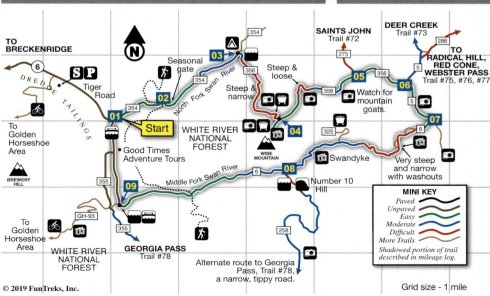

TO BRECKENRIDGE

TO RADICAL HILL, RED CONE, WEBSTER PASS
Trail #75, #76, #77

SAINTS JOHN Trail #72

DEER CREEK Trail #73

Tiger Road

Seasonal gate

North Fork Swan River

Steep & loose

Steep & narrow

Watch for mountain goats.

Start

WHITE RIVER NATIONAL FOREST

WISE MOUNTAIN

Very steep and narrow with washouts

Good Times Adventure Tours

Middle Fork Swan River

Swandyke

Number 10 Hill

To Golden Horseshoe Area

BREWERY HILL

To Golden Horseshoe Area

WHITE RIVER NATIONAL FOREST

GEORGIA PASS Trail #78

Alternate route to Georgia Pass, Trail #78, a narrow, tippy road.

MINI KEY
Paved
Unpaved
Easy
Moderate
Difficult
More Trails
Shadowed portion of trail described in mileage log.

© 2019 FunTreks, Inc.

Grid size - 1 mile

179

Not for stock vehicles. Red Cone, Trail #76, and Webster Pass, Trail #77, in the background.

Mountain goats didn't seem bothered too much.

Shelf road is not one way.

Overview: A short, white-knuckle climb to an outstanding view above 12,600 feet. Most people combine this trail with others in the area to make loop routes. Great area for ATVs, UTVs and dirt bikes. Seasonally open 5/21 to 11/22.

Rating: Difficult. Very tippy, narrow and steep with several challenging rocky sections. Vehicles wider than 74 inches will find the last section of the climb especially nerve-racking as a small rock wall forces you toward the edge of the shelf road. Snow may block trail into mid summer.

Stats: Length: Hill by itself is only 1.7 miles. Base of hill is 3.7 miles from Montezuma. Time: Less than an hour for just the hill. Add several hours to get there and return depending upon where you start and end. High point: 12,600 ft. Best time of year: Late July-Sept.

Current Conditions: White River N.F., Dillon R.D. Call (970) 468-5400.

Getting There: Get off Route 6 at east end of Keystone Ski Area following signs to Montezuma Road. (See map detail of exit.) Head south on Montezuma Road 5.2 miles where pavement ends. Continue into town of Montezuma. Unlicensed vehicles can stage south of Waypoint 02.

You can also reach the bottom of Radical Hill from the south via Red Cone, Trail #76, or Webster Pass, Trail #77.

MILEAGE LOG:

0.0 Zero trip odometer **[Rev. Miles]**
Continue south through Montezuma on main road towards Deer Creek. **[3.7]**
01 N39 34.821 W105 52.057

1.1 Turn left toward Webster Pass. **[2.6]**
02 N39 34.083 W105 51.619

1.4 Continue straight. **[2.3]**

1.6 Continue straight after seasonal gate, trail swings right and crosses Snake River. **[2.1]**

3.7 Turn right for Radical Hill and Deer Creek. **[0.0]**
03 N39 32.294 W105 50.504

0.0 Zero trip odometer
From Waypoint 03, head uphill on F.S. 286. **[2.5]**

0.8 Continue uphill; several challenging rocky sections with no bypasses. **[1.7]**

1.1 Stay right. Narrow, tippy trail climbs steeply. Lesser road goes left to tiny cabin with views. **[1.4]**

1.7 Reach top of hill. (Watch for mountain goats.) Continue gradually down other side of mountain on rocky road. **[0.8]**
04 N39 32.170 W105 51.384

2.5 At Trail #73. Right goes downhill on Deer Creek. Left connects to North & Middle Fork of the Swan River, Trail #74. **[0.0]**
05 N39 31.667 W105 51.801

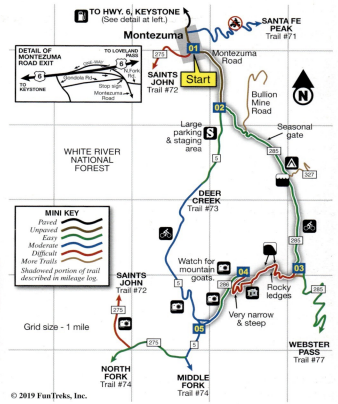

TO HWY. 6, KEYSTONE (See detail at left.)

Montezuma

SANTA FE PEAK Trail #71

DETAIL OF MONTEZUMA ROAD EXIT
TO LOVELAND PASS
ONE-WAY
6
TO KEYSTONE
6
Gondola Rd.
N.Fork Rd.
Stop sign
Montezuma Road

275

SAINTS JOHN Trail #72

Start

01

Montezuma Road

02

Bullion Mine Road

N

Large parking & staging area **S**

Seasonal gate

WHITE RIVER NATIONAL FOREST

5

285

327

285

DEER CREEK Trail #73

MINI KEY
Paved
Unpaved
Easy
Moderate
Difficult
More Trails
Shadowed portion of trail described in mileage log.

285

03

5

Watch for mountain goats.

5

04

286

Rocky ledges

285

SAINTS JOHN Trail #72

275

Very narrow & steep

Grid size - 1 mile

05

5

275

5

WEBSTER PASS Trail #77

NORTH FORK Trail #74

MIDDLE FORK Trail #74

© 2019 FunTreks, Inc.

Tippiness not exaggerated.

Rocky climb is easier for vehicles with good suspension travel.

Approaching Red Cone, 12,800 feet.

Even steeper than it looks here.

Four-door Jeep with 33-inch tires tackles first obstacle.

Overview: The thing you'll remember most about this trail is the extremely steep descent at the end. Although scenery is breathtaking at the top, you may be a bit preoccupied to enjoy it. Use your lowest gear and brake as little as possible. Do not lock up your brakes. If you feel your back end sliding sideways, you may have to apply a little gas to straighten yourself out. Seasonally closed April 1 to May 31.

Rating: Difficult. South end of trail winds steeply uphill through the forest with intermittent rocky and muddy sections. The climb continues above timberline to the very top of Red Cone. At that point, if you don't like what you see, you can turn around. Don't descend if BOTH sides of Webster Pass are blocked by snow. You'll be boxed in with no place to go. Vehicles with a moderate lift can do it when clear.

Stats: Length: 6 miles to Webster Pass. Time: About 3 hours plus exit time. High point: 12,800 ft. Best time of year: Late July-Sept.

Current Conditions: Pikes Peak N.F., South Platte R.D. Call (303) 275-5610.

Getting There: Take Hwy. 285 west from Denver. About 3.2 miles west of Grant, turn right on C.R. 60. Drive west about 5.1 miles avoiding roads that go left. Red Cone is marked F.S. 565, "Experienced Drivers Only."

MILEAGE LOG:

START

0.0 Zero trip odometer [Rev. Miles]
Head northeast uphill on rocky F.S. 565. [6.0]
01 N39 29.056 W105 48.178

0.4 First obstacle. [5.6]

1.9 Climb switchbacks through trees. [4.1]

3.0 Road gradually exits forest above timberline. [3.0]

3.4 Climb Little Rascal Hill. It's very steep with loose rock. [2.6]

5.3 Top of Red Cone where one-way descent begins. The first hill is not the steepest part. Check Webster Pass for snow conditions before descending. Turn around if you are not sure. [0.7]
02 N39 31.610 W105 49.330

6.0 Arrive at Webster Pass. [0.0]
03 N39 31.881 W105 49.966
Left at pass goes down Handcart Gulch and returns to where you started. (See Trail #77.) Right goes to Radical Hill, Trail #75, and Montezuma.

© 2019 FunTreks, Inc.

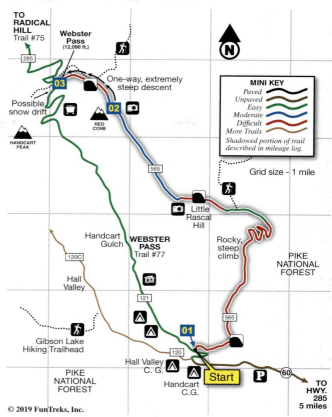

TO RADICAL HILL Trail #75

Webster Pass (12,096 ft.)

285

03

Possible snow drift

One-way, extremely steep descent

02

RED CONE

HANDCART PEAK

MINI KEY
Paved
Unpaved
Easy
Moderate
Difficult
More Trails

Shadowed portion of trail described in mileage log.

Grid size - 1 mile

565

Little Rascal Hill

Rocky, steep climb

PIKE NATIONAL FOREST

Handcart Gulch

WEBSTER PASS Trail #77

120C

Hall Valley

121

Gibson Lake Hiking Trailhead

565

01

120

Hall Valley C. G.

PIKE NATIONAL FOREST

Handcart C.G.

Start

P

60

TO HWY. 285 5 miles

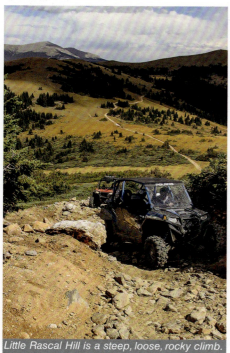

Little Rascal Hill is a steep, loose, rocky climb.

Don't come down Red Cone if Webster is blocked.

Lots of rocky terrain before switchbacks.

183

Narrow shelf road on Handcart Gulch is two-way traffic. Uphill traffic has right of way.

Creek crossing heading up Webster Pass.

Historical Highlight: In the late 1870s, the road up Handcart Gulch and over Webster Pass was an important mining road into Montezuma and Breckenridge. The road was built by William Emerson Webster and the Montezuma Silver Mining Company. The townsite of Webster and a cemetery are located northeast of the intersection of Highway 285 and Park County Road 60. Not much is left to see. Handcart Gulch got its name from handcarts used by miners to carry supplies up the valley. The road has remained open largely through the efforts of the state's 4-wheeling community.

Overview: Thrilling drive with outstanding scenery. It is easier to reach Webster Pass starting in Montezuma, since the south side of pass is often blocked by snow well into August. You will not be able to go down Handcart Gulch until the snow completely melts at the top. You can also reach Webster Pass by first driving Red Cone, Trail #76; however, you won't be able to return that way because Red Cone is one-way. Seasonally open 5/21 to 11/22.

Rating: Easy. The north side drive to the pass is relatively easy. However, as you descend into Handcart Gulch, the road is extremely narrow at the top. Closer to the bottom, Handcart Gulch is rocky. Here, stock SUVs will need to proceed slowly using careful tire placement. Skid plates are recommended.

Stats: Length: 10 miles as described here. Time: 2 to 3 hours. High point: 12,096 ft. Best time of year: Late July-early October.

Current Conditions: North side: White River N.F. Call (970) 468-5400. South side: Pike N.F. Call (303) 275-5610.

Getting There: **To drive south from Montezuma:** Get off Route 6 at east end of Keystone Ski Area following signs to Montezuma Road. (See map detail of exit.) Head south on Montezuma Road 5.2 miles where pavement ends. Continue into town of Montezuma. Unlicensed vehicles can stage south of Waypoint 02. **To drive north from Highway 285:** Follow directions to Waypoint 01 for Red Cone, Trail #76.

MILEAGE LOG:

0.0 Zero trip odometer [Rev. Miles]
Continue south through Montezuma on main road towards Deer Creek. [5.1]
01 N39 34.821 W105 52.057

1.1 Turn left for Webster. [4.0]
02 N39 34.083 W105 51.619

1.4 Go straight on 285. [3.7]

1.6 Continue straight after seasonal gate, trail swings right and crosses headwaters of Snake River. [3.5]

3.7 Stay left. Radical Hill, Trail #75, to right. [1.4]
03 N39 32.294 W105 50.504

5.1 Arrive at Webster Pass after climbing gentle switchbacks. Steep trail to left is one-way descent from Red Cone. Do not go up this way! [0.0]
04 N39 31.881 W105 49.966

0.0 Zero trip odometer
From Waypoint 04, stay right and descend other side of pass if clear of snow. [4.9]

1.0 Narrowest point of trail. Be careful. [3.9]

1.6 Water crossing. [3.3]

2.4 Pass through repaired bog area. [2.5]

2.8 Pass mine. [2.1]

3.1 Pass miner's cabin. [1.8]

4.9 Continue downhill through rocky section. Left is Red Cone, Trail #76. [0.0]
05 N39 29.056 W105 48.178

From Waypoint 05, you can return to pass via difficult Red Cone, or continue downhill past camping areas to County Road 60. This takes you to Highway 285 in about 5 miles.

Webster Pass as seen from Red Cone, Trail #76.

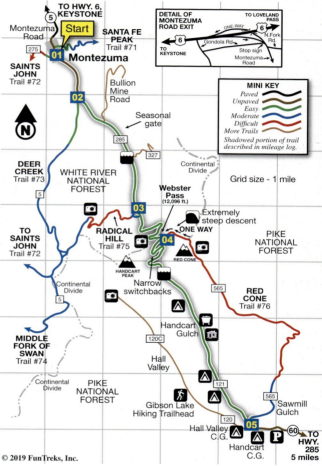

TO HWY. 6, KEYSTONE
Start
Montezuma Road
275
SANTA FE PEAK Trail #71
01 **Montezuma**
SAINTS JOHN Trail #72
Bullion Mine Road
02
Seasonal gate
285
327
DEER CREEK Trail #73
WHITE RIVER NATIONAL FOREST
Continental Divide
Grid size - 1 mile
5
Webster Pass (12,096 ft.)
03
Extremely steep descent
ONE WAY
TO SAINTS JOHN Trail #72
RADICAL HILL Trail #75
04
RED CONE
PIKE NATIONAL FOREST
HANDCART PEAK
Continental Divide
5
Narrow switchbacks
565
RED CONE Trail #76
Handcart Gulch
MIDDLE FORK OF SWAN Trail #74
120C
Hall Valley
121
PIKE NATIONAL FOREST
Continental Divide
Gibson Lake Hiking Trailhead
Sawmill Gulch
565
120
Hall Valley C.G.
05
Handcart C.G.
P
60 **TO HWY. 285** 5 miles

DETAIL OF MONTEZUMA ROAD EXIT
ONE-WAY
6 — 6
TO LOVELAND PASS
N.Fork Rd.
Gondola Rd.
TO KEYSTONE
Stop sign
Montezuma Road

MINI KEY
Paved
Unpaved
Easy
Moderate
Difficult
More Trails
Shadowed portion of trail described in mileage log.

© 2019 FunTreks, Inc.

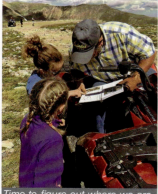

Time to figure out where we are.

UTVs squeeze by snowdrift on Handcart Gulch mid July.

185

Many people start at the pass because it's a shorter drive from the Front Range.

The main staging area at the bottom (Wpt. 01).

Historical Highlight: *Georgia Pass was the most popular way to reach Breckenridge from the south in the early 1860s. Thousands of eager miners brought their wagons over the pass and down through the Swan River Valley. Eventually Boreas Pass and Hoosier Pass became the more popular routes, and Georgia Pass was abandoned. Dredge mining continues on the west end of Tiger Road, but much of the larger dredged area has now been reclaimed.*

Overview: A short, but challenging climb to a relatively low pass. Dispersed camping is allowed south of Wpt. 03. You can make the trip more difficult by returning across Glacier Peak via F.S. 258. If you're heading back to Denver, head southeast from the pass on easy gravel roads to town of Jefferson. Open 5/21 to 11/22 or until it dries out.

Rating: Moderate. Very steep and chewed-up near the top, but not quite bad enough to be rated difficult yet. You'll need 4-wheel drive, low range gearing and high ground clearance. Novice drivers will find it challenging.

Stats: Length: 5.9 miles one way. Another 10 miles down to Jefferson if you go out that way. Time: 1 to 1½ hours to the pass. High point:11,585 ft. Best time: Late June through September.

Current Conditions: White River N.F., Dillon R.D. Call (970) 468-5400.

***Getting There:* From Breckenridge:** From Hwy. 9 about 3 miles north of Breckenridge, take Tiger Road east past Breckenridge Golf Course. Paved road changes to dirt after residential section. Watch for staging area on right after about 4.8 miles. **From Jefferson (to drive trail in reverse direction):** Head north on Michigan Creek Road, C.R. 35. It loops around and connects to C.R. 54 (see map). Continue north on C.R. 54 about 7 miles to Georgia Pass.

MILEAGE LOG:

0.0 Zero trip odometer [Rev. Miles] From staging area, head east on Tiger Road. [5.9]
01 N39 31.305 W105 57.607

0.9 Bear right and cross small bridge where F.S. 354 goes left. [5.0]

1.4 Go past tour business and turn hard right across dredge area. [4.5]
02 N39 30.392 W105 56.780

1.5 Turn left on other side of dredge area and head south. [4.4]

2.3 Bear left across bridge where American Gulch Road, GH-93 goes right into the Golden Horse-shoe Area. [3.6]
03 N39 29.686 W105 56.823

2.7 Forest gate. [3.2]

3.0 Stay left. Right crosses river to camp spot. [2.9]

4.2 Stay left. [1.7]

4.4 Continue uphill, staying left where trail splits. [1.5]

4.7 Stay left uphill. [1.2]

4.9 Another gate. [1.0]

5.0 Follow road as it curves left and serpentines uphill. This begins a challenging steep climb with various driver choices. [0.9]

5.9 Trail flattens out at a large parking area at Georgia Pass. [0.0]
04 N39 27.492 W105 54.990
Left at the pass climbs across Glacier Peak on

F.S. 258. This road has a very difficult hard-core challenge called Number 10 Hill just before it con-nects to Middle Fork of

the Swan River, Trail #74. Right at the pass takes you downhill on a series of gravel roads to the town of Jefferson on Hwy. 285.

This shot was taken driving downhill.

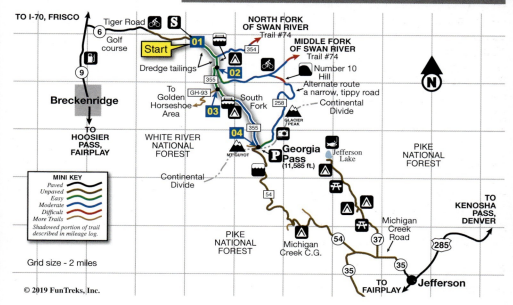

© 2019 FunTreks, Inc.

View from weather station at Waypoint 05 near top of Peak 10.

Popular hiking and biking area—take extra water and offer to others.

Historical Highlight:
Breckenridge Ski Area opened in December of 1961 with one double-chair lift and a T-bar. An adult lift ticket cost $4. Today Breckenridge has over 30 lifts and a daily undiscounted lift ticket costs more than $140. Breckenridge has about 3 million visitors a year, and half of that number is in the summer. Plan some time to walk around the town and down Main Street.

Overview: Climb Peak 9 through Breckenridge Ski Area and cross over to Peak 10 near the end. Absolutely stunning scenery, even if you don't go all the way to the top. A thrilling adventure. No unlicensed vehicles.

Rating: Moderate. Lower part through ski area is easy. At the top, trail narrows with tight switchbacks. Although the last mile has no real obstacles, it is very intimidating. Experienced drivers in aggressive stock SUVs can do it. Low-range gearing required at the top.

Stats: Length: 6.5 miles. Time: 2 to 3 hours. High point: 13,300 ft. Best time

of year: Mid July-Sept.

Current Conditions: Upper part is in White River N.F., Dillon R.D. They won't know about ski area. Best way to be sure trail is open is to drive there and see.

Getting There: From S. Park Avenue in Breckenridge, take Village Road west 0.3 mile. Turn left into parking lot for Beaver Run Resort, following signs to Breckenridge Stables. Go to back left corner of parking lot and exit to dirt road. Turn right and head uphill. This area is also used for overflow parking for big events and can be busy.

0.0 Zero trip odometer **[Rev. Miles]**
Head south on wide dirt road from parking lot. **[6.5]**
01 N39 28.463 W106 02.970

0.5 Road swings left past Peak 8 Super Connect ski lift. **[6.0]**

0.7 Bear right when you see stables on left. **[5.8]**
02 N39 28.131 W106 03.346

1.3 Left at switchback. **[5.2]**
1.4 Right at switchback. **[5.1]**
1.9 Left at switchback. **[4.6]**
3.0 Right at switchback. **[3.5]**
3.1 Right at switchback. **[3.4]**
3.2 Left past restaurant. **[3.3]**
3.7 Leave ski area. Road gets rougher. **[2.8]**
03 N39 27.481 W106 04.905

4.2 Climb above treeline. **[2.3]**
5.3 Wheeler Hiking Trail. **[1.2]**
5.4 Water crossing. **[1.1]**
5.5 Driver's choice. We went left. **[1.0]**
04 N39 26.919 W106 05.837

6.0 Cabin along steep switch-backs. **[0.5]**

6.5 Trail ends at weather monitoring station. **[0.0]**
05 N39 26.583 W106 05.965

Get FREE trail updates & GPS downloads at www.FunTreks.com

Looking north from Peak 10 at Peak 9 (center) and Peak 8 (right).

Leaving parking lot of Beaver Run Conference Center.

MINI KEY
Paved
Unpaved
Easy
Moderate
Difficult
More Trails
Shadowed portion of trail described in mileage log.

BRECKENRIDGE

TO **BOREAS PASS** Trail #80

Village Road

Start

Peak 9 Road C.R. 751

Peak 8 Lift

Boreas Pass Road

Stables

Large building

Overlook Restaurant

Leave ski area. Road gets rougher.

Ski lift

03

WHITE RIVER NATIONAL FOREST

Wheeler Hiking Trail

Breckenridge Ski Area Peak 9

DETAIL

Village Road

Beaver Run Resort

Conf. center parking lot

01

Follow signs to BRECKENRIDGE STABLES

PEAK 9

WHITE RIVER NATIONAL FOREST

04

PEAK 10

Weather monitoring station

05

Note: Ski areas are under special permit by National Forest Service. Trail usage is subject to change without notice. This route will likely not show on future MVUMs; however, this does not necessarily mean it is closed for public use. The best way to know if trail is open is to drive to it and see.

Grid size - 0.5 miles

© 2019 FunTreks, Inc.

Boreas Pass

View of Breckenridge Ski Area as you climb the north side on County Road 10.

Bakers Tank.

Restored Summit House at Boreas Pass.

Historical Highlight: A stagecoach route in the 1860s, Boreas Pass was converted to a railroad in the early 1880s and operated until 1937. Several key railroad features along the route have been preserved and restored, including Bakers Tank, the Summit House and the Roundhouse in Como. Kiosks along the route provide additional information.

Overview: Scenic drive with historic stops, seasonal wildflowers and fall color. Once a railroad, converted to auto traffic in 1952. See railroad exhibits at start, Boreas Pass and Como. No unlicensed vehicles are allowed on County Roads 10 and 33. Only place you can ride unlicensed vehicles is on Forest Roads 611, 593 and 537 between Hwy. 9 and C.R. 10 (see map).

Rating: Easy. Bumpy in places but suitable for passenger cars when dry.

Stats: Length: About 21 miles. Time: An hour one way. High point: 11,481 ft. Best time of year: June-October.

Current Conditions: North half: White River N.F., Dillon R.D. Call (970) 468-5400. South half: Pike N.F., South Park R.D. Call (719) 836-2031.

Getting There: From Highway 9, just south of downtown Breckenridge, turn east on paved Boreas Pass Road marked with normal street sign.

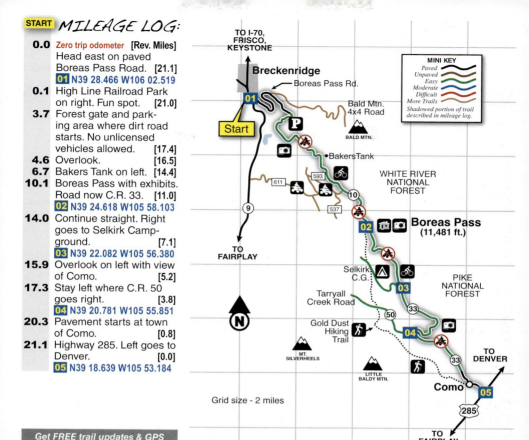

MILEAGE LOG:

0.0 Zero trip odometer [Rev. Miles]
Head east on paved
Boreas Pass Road. [21.1]
01 N39 28.466 W106 02.519

0.1 High Line Railroad Park
on right. Fun spot. [21.0]

3.7 Forest gate and parking area where dirt road
starts. No unlicensed
vehicles allowed. [17.4]

4.6 Overlook. [16.5]

6.7 Bakers Tank on left. [14.4]

10.1 Boreas Pass with exhibits.
Road now C.R. 33. [11.0]
02 N39 24.618 W105 58.103

14.0 Continue straight. Right
goes to Selkirk Camp-
ground. [7.1]
03 N39 22.082 W105 56.380

15.9 Overlook on left with view
of Como. [5.2]

17.3 Stay left where C.R. 50
goes right. [3.8]
04 N39 20.781 W105 55.851

20.3 Pavement starts at town
of Como. [0.8]

21.1 Highway 285. Left goes to
Denver. [0.0]
05 N39 18.639 W105 53.184

TO I-70,
FRISCO,
KEYSTONE

Breckenridge

Boreas Pass Rd.

01

Start

Bald Mtn.
4x4 Road

BALD MTN.

BakersTank

9

611

593

537

10

**WHITE RIVER
NATIONAL
FOREST**

02

Boreas Pass
(11,481 ft.)

Selkirk
C.G.

03

**PIKE
NATIONAL
FOREST**

Tarryall
Creek Road

50

33

Gold Dust
Hiking
Trail

04

33

**MT.
SILVERHEELS**

**LITTLE
BALDY MTN.**

Como

05

285

TO
DENVER

TO
FAIRPLAY

TO
FAIRPLAY

MINI KEY
Paved
Unpaved
Easy
Moderate
Difficult
More Trails
Shadowed portion of trail
described in mileage log.

N

Grid size - 2 miles

© 2019 FunTreks, Inc.

First view of town of Como (in distance) as you descend the south side of pass.

191

Trail ends here at large mine with cabin, collapsed structures and an abandoned truck.

Old truck at mine at Waypoint 04.

First 4 miles is very easy.

Historical Highlight: Several small cabins mark the general location of Geneva City, built in the 1870s. A smelter, built later at the bottom of Smelter Gulch, allowed the town to process its own ore. The silver crash in 1893 crippled the town, which ceased all operations by the turn of the century.

Overview: Beautiful valley offers a wide range of easily accessible activities, including hiking, mountain biking, horseback riding, fishing and hunting. You can camp in a forest campground for a fee, or select from many great designated free camp spots along the route. (We counted more than 40 numbered spots.) Interesting cabins and mines in various stages of decline at Geneva City and surrounding area. MVUM showed no seasonal closures, but Hwy. 62, Guanella Pass Road, is closed in winter.

Rating: Moderate. First 4.6 miles is bumpy but doable in most cars. We saw large camping trailers within the first few miles. After Wpt. 02, the road gets rockier, narrower and steeper. Creek crossings may be deep during spring runoff. Muddy spots.

Stats: Length: 6.8 miles one way. Time: Allow 3-4 hours for round trip. High point: 11,800 ft. Best time of year: July-September.

Current Conditions: Pike N.F., South Platte R.D. Call (303) 275-5610.

Getting There: From Georgetown: Take paved Hwy. 62 south. After going over Guanella Pass, continue another 6.1 miles downhill to F.S. 119 on right (near mile marker 7). **From Grant:** Take Hwy. 62 north about 7 miles.

0.0 Zero trip odometer [Rev. Miles]
Head northwest on F.S. 119 from Duck Creek Picnic Ground. **[6.8]**
01 N39 31.773 W105 43.934

0.1 Continue straight on 119. F.S. 119B on left goes to fee campground. **[6.7]**

0.8 Dispersed camping begins. **[6.0]**

3.2 Small creek crossing. **[3.6]**

4.0 Seasonal gate. Road fenced on sides through private property. **[2.8]**

4.6 Creek crossing with steep banks. Moderate rating starts here. **[2.2]**
02 N39 34.359 W105 47.458

4.9 Stay right uphill. Left is gated. Narrow shelf road climbs up valley and gets rougher. **[1.9]**

6.0 Continue straight at intersection where steep illegal shortcut goes uphill to left. **[0.8]**

6.1 Turn hard left uphill before lake. Follow best-traveled road uphill. **[0.7]**
03 N39 34.431 W105 48.824

6.3 Stay left downhill. **[0.5]**

6.5 Cross creek. Cabin on right. **[0.3]**

6.6 Continue straight. Road on left goes to cabins. **[0.2]**

6.7 Cross muddy, rutted meadow. **[0.1]**

6.8 End of trail at interesting mine. Walk uphill to see fallen cabin and old truck. Valley is location of historic Geneva City. **[0.0]**
04 N39 34.452 W105 49.567

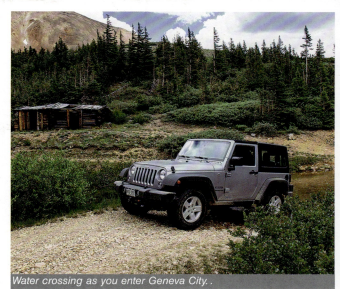

Water crossing as you enter Geneva City. .

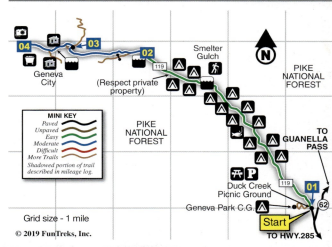

MINI KEY
Paved
Unpaved
Easy
Moderate
Difficult
More Trails
Shadowed portion of trail described in mileage log.

Grid size - 1 mile

© 2019 FunTreks, Inc.

Smelter Gulch

PIKE NATIONAL FOREST

PIKE NATIONAL FOREST

Geneva City

(Respect private property)

TO GUANELLA PASS

Duck Creek Picnic Ground

Geneva Park C.G.

Start

TO HWY. 285

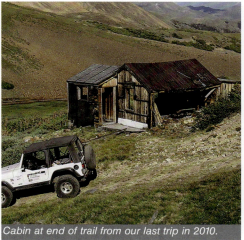

Cabin at end of trail from our last trip in 2010.

Eight years later, cabin at left looked like this.

Optional obstacle is steeper than it looks.

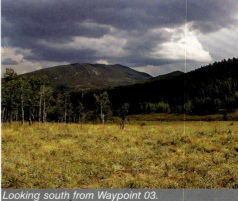
Looking south from Waypoint 03.

Cross open area, then descend towards gulch.

Overview: A fun loop close to Denver. Most of the trail is in the trees and not very scenic but that doesn't hurt the experience. Watch for horseback riders and hikers. Can be closed in spring if too muddy. Call ahead before making the trip out to the trail. Popular area for unlicensed vehicles; always anticipate possible oncoming traffic.

Rating: Difficult. Narrow, tippy and rutted with washouts, small rock obstacles, tree roots and steep sections. Not overwhelmingly difficult for a well-equipped vehicle, but enough challenge to make it interesting. Roof damage possible due to tippy section through tight trees. Trail conditions can change drastically without notice throughout the year.

Stats: Length: Entire loop returning to start is 11.5 miles. Time: 2 to 3 hours. High point: 9,500 ft. Best time of year: June-October.

Current Conditions: Pike N.F., South Platte R.D (Front). Call (303) 275-5610.

Getting There: Take Hwy. 285 southwest from Denver. At a point 25 miles from C470, turn right on C.R. 43A at traffic light by large gas station. C.R. 43A becomes 43. At 6.5 miles from 285, turn left on Saddlestring Road.

MILEAGE LOG:

0.0 Zero trip odometer [Rev. Miles]
Head southwest on
Saddlestring Road. [8.6]
01 N39 29.862 W105 31.737

0.3 Bear right after parking
area at yellow sign. [8.3]
02 N39 29.741 W105 31.937

2.9 Bear right on F.S. 105 to
start loop. [5.7]
03 N39 28.635 W105 32.822

3.8 Fence marks high point.
Begin descending. At bot-
tom of hill, trail swings left
in gulch. [4.8]

*Get FREE trail updates & GPS
downloads at www.FunTreks.com*

4.4 Road narrows and gets
more difficult. [4.2]

4.5 Driver's choice at stream
crossing. [4.1]

5.1 Tippy spot through tight
trees. [3.5]

5.5 Turn left uphill at driver's
choice. Rough road
climbs over ridge. [3.1]
04 N39 27.573 W105 33.528

7.3 Reconnect with F.S. 101
and turn left. Right is
locked gate. [1.3]
05 N39 28.302 W105 32.060

8.6 Return to start of loop at
Waypoint 03. Turn right to
exit the way you came in. [0.0]

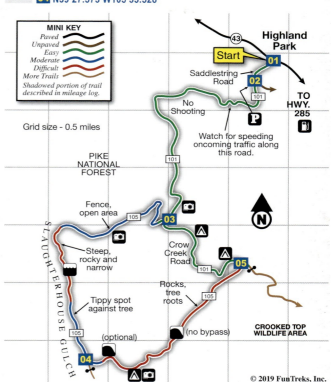

MINI KEY
Paved
Unpaved
Easy
Moderate
Difficult
More Trails
*Shadowed portion of trail
described in mileage log.*

Grid size - 0.5 miles

Highland Park

Start

Saddlestring Road

No Shooting

Watch for speeding oncoming traffic along this road.

TO HWY. 285

PIKE NATIONAL FOREST

Fence, open area

Steep, rocky and narrow

Tippy spot against tree

(optional)

SLAUGHTERHOUSE GULCH

Crow Creek Road

Rocks, tree roots

(no bypass)

CROOKED TOP WILDLIFE AREA

N

© 2019 FunTreks, Inc.

Good signage on the trail.

Dispersed camp spot along route.

Tippy spot, when wet, can slide you into trees.

195

Colorado Springs, Pueblo, Pikes Peak Region

Many people are surprised to learn that we don't include the Pikes Peak Highway in this book. The reason is simple: it's not a backroad or a 4-wheel-drive trail. That's not to say we don't think you should drive it. To the contrary, it's a great paved toll road that we highly recommend. It's also very easy to find.

The importance of Pike's Peak to us, however, is that it acts a beacon to draw people to Pike National Forest, in which are located many easily accessible backroads and camp spots. Once here, you'll learn it's hard to take a picture without Pikes Peak in the background.

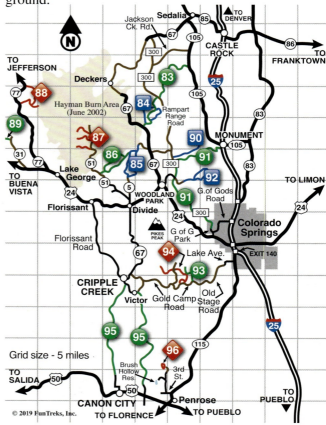

View of Pikes Peak from Schubarth Loop, Trail #92, rated moderate.

Start here on left at western end of Dakan Road.

Cross this rock slab at 4.4 miles.

Road is wide most of the way, but fun to drive.

Overview: A handy, fun way for licensed and unlicensed vehicles to traverse Rampart Range diagonally from northeast to southwest (or reverse direction). Departs south of Sedalia from the western end of Dakan Road and ends up at Rainbow Falls OHV Area off Hwy. 67 north of Woodland Park. Camping restricted to designated sites only on north end. Closed in winter from Dec.1 to May 1 or until road dries out in the spring. Many OHV side roads to explore especially on the south end (see Rainbow Falls, Trail #84).

Rating: Easy. Fun mix of twisting, undulating, banked dirt roads. Prone to washouts and ruts, but typically suitable for stock, high-clearance 4x4 SUVs and pickup trucks. Side roads vary from easy to very difficult.

Stats: Length: 17.8 miles as described here. Time: 2 to 4 hours. High point: About 9,000 ft. Best time to go: June-October.

Current Conditions: Pike National Forest. North half South Platte R.D., (303) 275-5610; south half Pikes Peak R.D., (719) 636-1602.

Getting There: **From Sedalia:** Head southwest 0.6 mile on Highway 67 and turn left on Highway 105. Go south 9.2 miles to Dakan Road, C.R. 22, on right. Follow wide Dakan Road west 4.9 miles to start. **To drive trail from south end:** See directions to Rainbow Falls, Trail #84.

0.0 Zero trip odometer [Rev. Miles]
Bear left at T, and follow
F.S. 563 south. **[8.3]**
01 N39 18.550 W105 01.869

0.2 Driver's choice. Best to
stay right. **[8.1]**

0.5 When roads rejoin,
continue south through
seasonal gate. **[7.8]**

1.6 Continue straight. Large
parking/staging area on
right. **[6.7]**

4.4 Cross interesting rock
slabs and ledges. **[3.9]**

4.5 Stay left uphill where F.S.
503 goes right. **[3.8]**
02 N39 15.758 W105 03.469

7.6 Great camp spot with rock
overhang on left. **[0.7]**

8.3 First half of trail ends at
Rampart Range Road
300. Turn right and go
800 ft. to F.S. 348 on left.
(Unlicensed vehicles see
comment on map.) **[0.0]**
03 N39 13.195 W105 03.710

0.0 Zero trip odometer **[9.5]**
04 N39 13.149 W105 03.874

4.0 Stay left. F.S. 650 multiuse
trail on right. **[5.5]**

5.1 Pass through seasonal
forest gate. **[4.4]**

5.5 Curve left through open
area, then follow 348
south (right). Don't follow
F.S. 351 east. **[4.0]**
05 N39 09.706 W105 05.058

6.2 Stay left on 348. **[3.3]**

6.7 Stay on wider 348 as
it curves left then right
downhill. Ignore lesser
side roads. **[2.8]**

7.4 Turn right where 348B
goes straight. **[2.1]**

9.1 Continue straight downhill. Exit point of Rainbow
Falls, Trail #84, on left.
Nice camp spots in this
area. **[0.4]**

9.5 Arrive at OHV parking
area on left with vault
toilet (no overnight camping). After parking area,
turn left on Rainbow
Falls Road to reach Hwy.
67. Left on 67 goes to
Woodland Park in about
10 miles. **[0.0]**
06 N39 08.140 W105 06.335

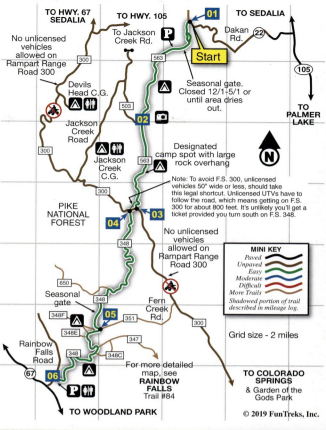

TO HWY. 67
SEDALIA

TO HWY. 105

TO SEDALIA

01

Dakan
Rd. 22

To Jackson
Creek Rd.

No unlicensed
vehicles
allowed on
Rampart Range
Road 300

300

P

563

Start

105

Seasonal gate.
Closed 12/1-5/1 or
until area dries
out.

TO
PALMER
LAKE

Devils
Head C.G.

503

02

Jackson
Creek Road

Designated
camp spot with large
rock overhang

300

Jackson
Creek
C.G.

563

N

Note: To avoid F.S. 300, unlicensed
vehicles 50" wide or less, should take
this legal shortcut. Unlicensed UTVs have to
follow the road, which means getting on F.S.
300 for about 800 feet. It's unlikely you'll get a
ticket provided you turn south on F.S. 348.

PIKE
NATIONAL
FOREST

300

04

03

No unlicensed
vehicles
allowed on
Rampart Range
Road 300

348

650

Seasonal
gate

348

Fern
Creek
Rd.

300

MINI KEY
Paved
Unpaved
Easy
Moderate
Difficult
More Trails
*Shadowed portion of trail
described in mileage log.*

348F

05

351

347

Grid size - 2 miles

348E

Rainbow
Falls
Road

348

348C

For more detailed
map, see
**RAINBOW
FALLS**
Trail #84

TO COLORADO
SPRINGS
& Garden of the
Gods Park

67

06

TO WOODLAND PARK

© 2019 FunTreks, Inc.

Camp in designated sites only, like this one on left at 7.6 miles.

199

One of several large, gorgeous camp spots around Waypoint 07. Pikes Peak seen in the distance.

Heading up F.S. 350A after Waypoint 02.

F.S. 344 descends steeply from Waypoint 06.

Overview: Popular OHV area. Route selected here is just one way to go and is wide enough for Jeeps; many more connecting 50" trails to explore. A fun area with twisting high banks, narrow sections and scenic overlooks. Lots of dispersed camping for weekend outings. Large staging area with toilet at start; no camping here. Follow posted rules and use marked routes only. The 2018 MVUM showed no seasonal closures on main route shown here; however, F.S. 348, just north of this map, is closed Dec. 1 to May 1.

Rating: Moderate. Some easy stretches, but mostly moderate. Steep and narrow with unexpected washouts possible. Not recommended for large SUVs. Side trails can be quite difficult.

Stats: Length: Selected route is 7.7 miles. Time: 1 to 2 hours. High point: 8,600 ft. Best time: Late June-October.

Current Conditions: Pike N.F., Pikes Peak R.D. Call (719) 636-1602.

Getting There: From Woodland Park, head north on Highway 67 about 10 miles. One-half mile after mile marker 87, turn right on Rainbow Falls Road, County Road 49. Drive in ¼ mile to signed parking area on right.

MILEAGE LOG:

0.0 Zero trip odometer [Rev. Miles]
From parking lot, head
north on F.S. 350. [4.5]
01 N39 08.114 W105 06.314
1.1 Turn right on 350A. [3.4]
02 N39 09.000 W105 06.644
1.6 Stay left over hump where
918 joins. [2.9]
1.9 Stay right. [2.6]
2.3 Stay right where 350B
joins on left. [2.2]
2.7 Turn right on larger
F.S. 348. [1.8]
03 N39 09.462 W105 05.478
3.3 Turn left on F.S. 347. [1.2]
04 N39 09.198 W105 05.136
3.6 Continue straight past
camp spot on right. [0.9]
4.5 Turn hard right, reversing
direction on F.S. 344. [0.0]
05 N39 09.225 W105 03.969
0.0 Zero trip odometer at Wpt. 05
From Waypoint 05, head
west on F.S. 344. [3.2]
0.5 Stay left. Right ends. [2.7]
0.7 Climb very steep hill, then
stay left where 348B joins
on right. [2.5]
06 N39 08.941 W105 04.600
1.6 Stay right. Optional Moab
Hill on left. [1.6]
2.0 Big mud hole. More to
come. [1.2]
2.7 Stay right. [0.5]
2.8 Turn left on F.S. 348.
Good camping here. [0.4]
07 N39 08.238 W105 06.245
3.2 Return to start. [0.0]

Some side trails are restricted to 50"-wide vehicles.

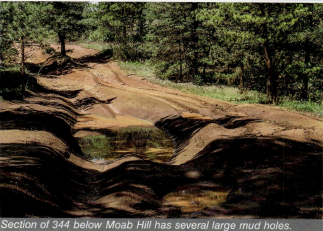

Section of 344 below Moab Hill has several large mud holes.

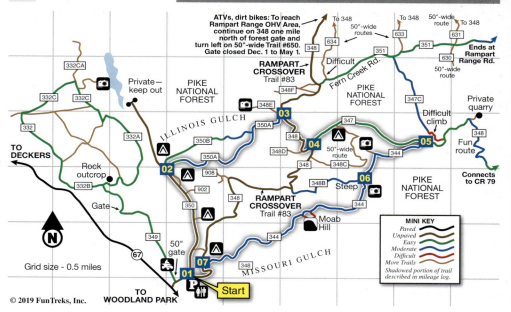

ATVs, dirt bikes: To reach
Rampart Range OHV Area,
continue on 348 one mile
north of forest gate and
turn left on 50"-wide Trail #650.
Gate closed Dec. 1 to May 1.

© 2019 FunTreks, Inc.

TO WOODLAND PARK

201

F.S. 357 is easy but fun to drive in a full-size vehicle.

50"side-by-side perfect for area.

Many large, flat dispersed camp spots suitable for camping trailers.

Descending 358 from Wpt. 04.

Overview: Great area for weekend and vacation getaways. Many fun trails to explore beyond what is shown on our map. Lots of large dispersed camp spots for big RVs and camping trailers at both ends of the trail. Very popular area for ATVs and dirt bikes because of the 50"-wide 717 Trail System, which criss-crosses everywhere. We've selected a mostly easy route wide enough for full-size vehicles. Side roads can be more difficult. No seasonal closures shown on MVUM, but expect snow in winter.

Rating: Moderate. Most of this route is easy except for a short downhill section on F.S. 358 between Waypoints 04 and 06. This section is steep and rough in spots. An optional side loop, starting at Wpt. 03 and going around 357A and 357B, is quite narrow and steep. When we attempted to drive it in our stock Wrangler, we encountered some badly washed-out sections. The area is better suited for ATVs and dirt bikes.

Stats: Length: 15.1 miles as described here. Time: 2-3 hours. High point: 9,168 ft. Best time of year: Late June-early October.

Current Conditions: Pike N.F., Pikes Peak R.D. Call (719) 636-1602.

Getting There: From traffic light in center of Divide, head north on C.R. 5. Continue straight at 0.5 mile where C.R. 51 curves left. Go another 3.8 miles north. Road changes to dirt just before start of trail at Wpt. 01. To start at north end at Wpt. 05, take Hwy. 67 north 7 miles from Woodland Park. Turn left on Painted Rocks Road and go 2.6 miles to staging area on left.

MILEAGE LOG:

0.0 Zero trip odometer [Rev. Miles]
From end of pavement at C.R. 5, continue north into forest on wide gravel road F.S. 357. **[9.0]**
01 N39 00.015 W105 09.604

0.3 Large staging area on left with vault toilet. **[8.7]**

0.9 Continue straight where F.S. 355 goes left. **[8.1]**

1.0 Stay right where F.S. 364 goes left. **[8.0]**
02 N39 00.677 W105 09.919

2.6 Stay left. Right is optional side loop on F.S. 357A and 357B. Very narrow with washouts at bottom. Jeeps can do it, but it's best suited for ATVs. **[6.4]**
03 N39 01.318 W105 08.652

2.9 Stay left. Right is exit from side loop on 357B. **[6.1]**

2.9+ F.S. 357F goes right 1.5 miles. **[6.1]**

4.5 Continue straight. 357G goes right 1.3 miles. **[4.5]**

4.7 Trail 717A crosses. **[4.3]**

6.6 Continue straight where F.S. 358 goes left. **[2.4]**
04 N39 04.315 W105 08.708

7.2 Stay right where 357J goes left 1.0 mile. **[1.8]**

7.9 Stay left where 341A goes right to Painted Rocks Road (shortcut). **[1.1]**

9.0 Staging area at end of F.S. 357 at Painted Rocks Road. Right takes you to Hwy. 67 in 2.6 miles. **[0.0]**
05 N39 06.094 W105 07.960
To return to start via valley route 364, go back to Wpt. 04.

0.0 Zero trip odometer at Wpt. 04
Head west downhill on steeper F.S. 358. **[6.1]**

0.6 At bottom, turn left on 364 and cross private land. Go slowly. Leave gates as you find them. **[5.5]**
06 N39 04.084 W105 09.216

2.3 Stay left. **[3.8]**

2.4 Trail 717A crosses. **[3.7]**

3.6 Continue straight where 966 goes right. **[2.5]**

3.7 Stay left where 365 goes right. **[2.4]**

5.2 Back to Wpt. 02. Turn right to return to staging area and Wpt. 01. **[0.9]**

6.1 Back to start. **[0.0]**

Get FREE trail updates & GPS downloads at www.FunTreks.com

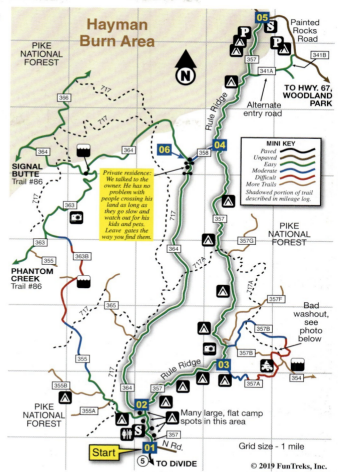

Hayman Burn Area

PIKE NATIONAL FOREST

TO HWY. 67, WOODLAND PARK

Painted Rocks Road

Alternate entry road

Rule Ridge

SIGNAL BUTTE Trail #86

Private residence: We talked to the owner. He has no problem with people crossing his land as long as they go slow and watch out for his kids and pets. Leave gates the way you find them.

PHANTOM CREEK Trail #86

PIKE NATIONAL FOREST

MINI KEY
Paved
Unpaved
Easy
Moderate
Difficult
More Trails
Shadowed portion of trail described in mileage log.

PIKE NATIONAL FOREST

Many large, flat camp spots in this area

Bad washout, see photo below

Rule Ridge

Start **01** N Rd.
5 TO DIVIDE

Grid size - 1 mile

© 2019 FunTreks, Inc.

Riders turn around at washout on Trail 717A (see map).

203

Roads are often washed out and rutted like this, but we encountered nothing significant.

Great dispersed camping along the route.

Historical Highlight: *The Hayman Fire burned 138,000 acres and, as of this writing, remains the largest fire by area in Colorado. The fire destroyed 133 homes and caused $40 million in damages. It started on June 8, 2002, as the result of carelessness on the part of a federal forestry officer, who was later convicted of arson and sent to prison. Some areas were just lightly grazed, but many more areas were completely scorched, leaving no seed for regrowth. The fire shut down many 4x4 roads, including the very popular Gulches, Trail #87. Most of the roads have now reopened, and many new OHV roads have been added. The area remains one of the most popular OHV destinations in southern Colorado.*

Overview: A convenient loop that meanders through forest with views of Pikes Peak and Signal Butte. Northern portion of trail passes through Hayman Burn Area, providing a close-up look at the destruction and Mother Nature's way of repairing the damage. Lots of dispersed camping along the route. Large parking area at Waypoint 02 provides convenient access to the popular 50"-wide 717 Trail System for unlicensed vehicles. No seasonal closures except for winter snow.

Rating: Easy. Rutted dirt road. Fairly wide except on north end where switchbacks wind tightly downhill. Creek crossing at Waypoint 03 can be deep during spring runoff.

Stats: Length: Loop is almost 14 miles. Time: About 2 hours. High point: 9,187 ft. Best time of year: June-October.

Current Conditions: Pike N.F., Pikes Peak R.D. Call (719) 636-1602.

Getting There: From Highway 24 in Divide, head north on C.R. 5. Swing left at 0.5 mile onto C.R. 51. Go another 2.9 miles and bear right, staying on C.R. 51. After another 5.9 miles, turn right on Phantom Creek Road, F.S. 363.

MILEAGE LOG:

START

0.0 Zero trip odometer **[Rev. Miles]**
Head north on wide dirt
road 363. **[6.7]**
01 N39 01.274 W105 15.177

0.5 Large kiosk with detailed
map of the area. **[6.2]**

0.6 Bear right following signs
for F.S. 363 through large
parking area. OHV Trail
#717 crosses just before
parking area. **[6.1]**
02 N39 01.576 W105 14.719

4.7 Stay left where 363B goes
right to Trail 85. **[2.0]**

5.1 Rock outcrop on right with
view of Pikes Peak. **[1.6]**

6.7 After twisty downhill
switchbacks, trail inter-
sects with F.S. 364 after
creek crossing. Turn left
on 364 to continue. **[0.0]**
03 N39 04.001 W105 10.932
Zero trip odometer
Head west on 364 about
200 feet, then bear right
uphill. **[7.1]**

1.3 Continue straight where
366 goes right. **[5.8]**

1.4 Bear left and follow 362
back to parking area. **[5.7]**
04 N39 04.386 W105 11.960

6.5 Turn right at parking area
on 363. **[0.6]**

7.1 Return to Waypoint 01 at
C.R. 51. Left goes back to
Divide. **[0.0]**

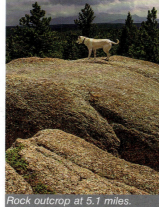

Rock outcrop at 5.1 miles.

Creek crossing at Wpt. 03.

We found the burn area starkly beautiful on this stormy day.

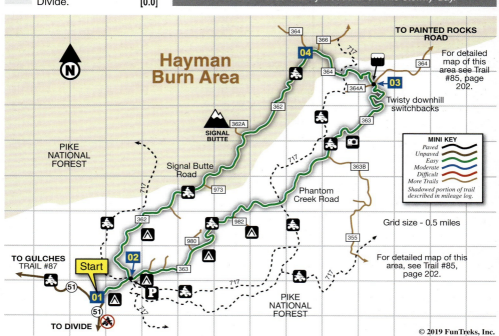

The Gulches

Longwater Gulch drops dramatically into Wildcat Canyon through the Hayman Burn Area.

Hackett Gulch has several large rock obstacles.

IMPORTANT NOTICE: *After the Hayman Fire in 2002, Hackett Gulch, Longwater Gulch and Metberry Gulch were closed by the Forest Service. The closures were considered permanent unless another public entity volunteered to take them over. Almost immediately, Predator 4 Wheel Drive, which has worked hard for years to keep these trails open, began working with Teller County. In the end, Teller County accepted responsibility for the roads and that's why the trails are open today. Extreme environmental groups have been trying for years to permanently close this area to motorized recreation. Do your part by following the rules. Don't cross the river.*

Overview: Hackett Gulch, Longwater Gulch and Metberry Gulch are three of the most popular hard-core trails in the Pikes Peak region. Each section of trail offers something fun and different. The area is extremely popular on weekends. Trails are closed in the spring until things dry out. Cedar Mountain Road allows unlicensed vehicles north of Trail #86. Trails officially end at the Teller County line before the Platte River. Do not cross river. We'll try to post updates at www.funtreks.com. Better yet, call Predator 4-Wheel Drive for the latest.

Rating: Difficult. Steep, loose descents and climbs with interspersed rock obstacles and muddy spots. Lots of fun twists and turns. A winch might come in handy. You'll need lockers, good articulation and a confident driver.

Stats: Length: Hackett and Longwater each measure 3.9 miles one-way. Metberry is 4.5 miles. Time: 3 to 5 hours for all three trails combined. High point: 9,000 ft. Best time: July-Sept.

Current Conditions: Pike N.F., South Park R.D. (719) 836-2031. See Motor Vehicle Travel Map (not MVUM). Or, call Predator 4WD at (719) 528-5790.

Getting There: From Hwy. 24 in Divide, head north on C.R. 5. Swing left at 0.5 mile on C.R. 51. Turn right at 3.5 miles, staying on C.R. 51. At 10 miles stay left following C.R. 51/Cedar Mountain Road. Go another 0.8 mile to large staging and parking area. Continuing north from parking area, Hackett Gulch is 4.5 miles, Longwater Gulch is 6.4 miles and Metberry Gulch is 6.8 miles.

MILEAGE LOG:

0.0 Zero trip odometer [Rev. Miles]
HACKETT GULCH:
Head west downhill. [3.9]
01 N39 04.701 W105 16.318
2.0 Hackett Rock. [1.9]
2.3 Stay right. Scenic overlook on left. [1.6]
3.7 Stay left. Closed road on
right is original route to
Longwater Gulch. [0.2]
3.9 Reach county line. Return
to Wpt. 01 and head north
1.9 miles to Wpt. 02. [0.0]
0.0 Zero trip odometer
LONGWATER GULCH:
Head west uphill. [3.9]
02 N39 05.888 W105 16.503
2.9 Longwater Rock, no
bypass. [1.0]
3.9 Reach county line. Return
to Wpt. 02 and head north
0.4 mile to Wpt. 03. [0.0]
0.0 Zero trip odometer
METBERRY GULCH:
Stay left where main road
goes right. [4.5]
03 N39 06.158 W105 16.627
2.7 Driver's choice. [1.8]
3.0 Driver's choice. [1.5]
3.5 Stay left downhill. [1.0]
3.8 Descend steep hill. [0.7]
4.5 Trail ends at camp spots
along river. [0.0]
04 N39 07.441 W105 19.612

Longwater Rock is a popular spot to take pictures.

Metberry, like all the other trails, has lots of steep twists and turns.

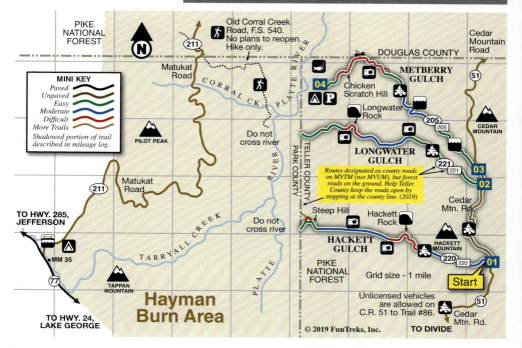

PIKE NATIONAL FOREST

Old Corral Creek Road, F.S. 540. No plans to reopen. Hike only.

DOUGLAS COUNTY

Cedar Mountain Road

211

Matukat Road

CORRAL CK.

PLATTE RIVER

MINI KEY
Paved
Unpaved
Easy
Moderate
Difficult
More Trails
Shadowed portion of trail
described in mileage log.

PILOT PEAK

Do not cross river

04

P

Chicken Scratch Hill

Longwater Rock

METBERRY GULCH

51

205

CEDAR MOUNTAIN

211

Matukat Road

TELLER COUNTY / PARK COUNTY

LONGWATER GULCH

Routes designated as county roads on MVTM (not MVUM), but forest roads on the ground. Help Teller County keep the roads open by stopping at the county line. (2019)

221

03

02

TO HWY. 285, JEFFERSON

MM 35

77

TAPPAN MOUNTAIN

Steep Hill

Do not cross river

Hackett Rock

Cedar Mtn. Rd.

HACKETT GULCH

HACKETT MOUNTAIN

220

01

PIKE NATIONAL FOREST

Grid size - 1 mile

Start

TARRYALL CREEK

PLATTE

Hayman Burn Area

TO HWY. 24, LAKE GEORGE

Unlicensed vehicles are allowed on C.R. 51 to Trail #86.

51

Cedar Mtn. Rd.

TO DIVIDE

© 2019 FunTreks, Inc.

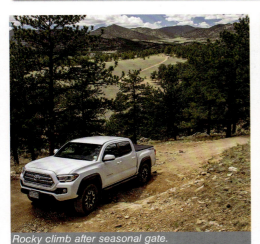
Rocky climb after seasonal gate.

Going down optional China Wall obstacle.

Trail crosses wide flat valley after Waypoint 02.

Stay The Trail promotes safe riding at trailhead.

Overview: Trail ends at great picnic and camp spots along Tarryall Creek. If you like to fish, take a pole. Popular trail for groups and 4-wheel-drive clubs on weekends. Good winter snow run before January. Unlicensed vehicles can access Round Mountain trails via F.S. 212A. Closed seasonally Jan. 1 to June 15.

Rating: Difficult. This rating applies to just one rocky section on F.S. 212. China Wall obstacle is optional. High-clearance stock SUVs with a skilled driver in dry conditions can do it.

Stats: Length: Almost 7 miles. Time: About 3 hours. High point: 9,100 ft. Best time: June-October.

Current Conditions: Pike N.F., South Park R.D. Call (719) 836-2031.

Getting There: From Highway 24 just west of Lake George, head north on County Road 77. Go 11 miles and turn right on F.S. 212.

MILEAGE LOG:

0.0 Zero trip odometer [Rev. Miles]
Head east on 212. Dispersed camping on left. [3.5]
01 N39 06.658 W105 28.406

0.6 At intersection, continue straight uphill on rougher F.S. 212. [2.9]
02 N39 06.818 W105 27.795

2.5 Bear right on 212. Left is exit route F.S. 204. Immediately after intersection, there is an optional obstacle you can try. [1.0]
03 N39 06.732 W105 26.875

3.0 Stock vehicles use careful tire placement here. [0.5]

3.1 Driver's choice. Right is easier. [0.4]

3.3 Continue straight. Large rock on right is China Wall, from which trail gets its name. [0.2]

3.4 Steep, rocky downhill section. Left is easier. Choose line carefully. [0.1]

3.5 Arrive at camping spots along Tarryall Creek. Go left or right. [0.0]
04 N39 06.870 W105 26.375
Turn around and return to Waypoint 03.

0.0 Zero trip odometer
From Waypoint 03, head north on 204. [1.8]

0.3 Stay left between two trees up rock face. [1.5]

0.5 Start narrow switchbacks. [1.3]

1.0 Stay right following fence. [0.8]

1.8 Proceed through gate to County Road 77. [0.0]
05 N39 07.750 W105 27.720

Tarryall Creek at Waypoint 04.

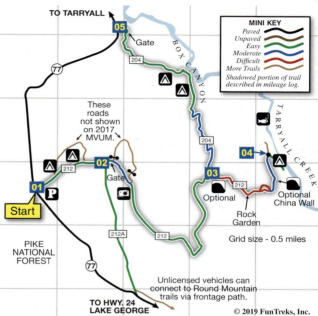

TO TARRYALL

05 Gate
204
MINI KEY
Paved
Unpaved
Easy
Moderate
Difficult
More Trails
Shadowed portion of trail described in mileage log.

77

These roads not shown on 2017 MVUM.

204

204

03
212

02 Gate
212

04

Optional

Rock Garden

Optional China Wall

01
P

Start

212A
212

Grid size - 0.5 miles

TARRYALL CREEK

BOX CANYON

PIKE NATIONAL FOREST

77

TO HWY. 24 LAKE GEORGE

Unlicensed vehicles can connect to Round Mountain trails via frontage path.

© 2019 FunTreks, Inc.

Classic older FJ Cruiser carefully navigates through the Rock Garden.

Trees obscure view at La Salle Pass.

Popular area for OHVs around the pass.

After pass, trail gets easier heading down into South Park.

Overview: Beautiful drive in September when aspens are changing color. Great backcountry option to paved Wilkerson Pass. Trail twists and turns through meadows and aspen groves on the way to La Salle Pass. The pass is located where Badger Mountain Road 228 goes left. This route is part of the Round Mountain trail system with many side trails to explore. Follow all posted signs. Close to China Wall, Trail #88. Closed seasonally January 1 to June 15.

Rating: Easy. Smooth dirt road with a few muddy spots and mild rocky patches. West side is slightly rougher than east side. Badger Mountain Road 228 is rockier than F.S. 44.

Stats: Length: La Salle 9.3 miles. Time: About 2 hours. High point: 11,300 ft. Best time: Mid June-Early October.

Current Conditions: Pike N.F., South Park R.D. Call (719) 836-2031.

Getting There: Head west on Highway 24 from Woodland Park about 26 miles. Turn right on well-marked C.R. 31 just west of mile marker 259. Head north 5 miles to sign for LaSalle Pass, F.S. 44, on left.

MILEAGE LOG:

0.0 Zero trip odometer [Rev. Miles]
LA SALLE PASS:
Head west on F.S. 44. [4.1]
01 N39 05.367 W105 29.438

1.0 Bear left continuing on 44. F.S. 227 goes right. [3.1]
02 N39 05.512 W105 30.468

1.7 Continue straight. [2.4]

2.2 Log building on left. [1.9]

4.1 Continue straight at La Salle Pass. Left goes towards Badger Mtn., described at right. [0.0]
03 N39 05.097 W105 32.813

0.0 Zero trip odometer
From Waypoint 03, continue west on 44. [5.2]

0.4 Bear right where F.S. 226 goes left. [4.8]

0.8 Bear left where 229 goes right. [4.4]

1.1 Continue straight where 44.2A crosses. [4.1]

1.5 Continue on F.S. 44. [3.7]

1.7 Turn hard left on 44. [3.5]

1.9 Bear left where 44.2B goes right. [3.3]

2.5 Continue straight. F.S. 44.2A on left. [2.7]

2.8 Turn right on Clear Creek Rd. at T intersection. [2.4]

3.2 Turn hard left on Turner Gulch Road. [2.0]
04 N39 04.066 W105 35.117

5.2 Highway 24. Left returns to Colorado Springs. [0.0]
05 N39 02.887 W105 33.683

0.0 Zero trip odometer [Rev. Miles]
BADGER MOUNTAIN:
Head south from Waypoint 03 on F.S. 228. No unlicensed vehicles allowed. [1.3]

1.2 Good view of South Park on right. [0.1]

1.3 Good place to turn around before road becomes private. No signs indicate where private begins. Not much to see beyond this point, even at top. [0.0]

© 2019 FunTreks, Inc.

Lower part of Badger Mountain Road has good views of South Park. Upper part is private.

View of Pikes Peak from high point.

Ruts and undulations will test articulation.

Balanced Rock can be seen from road.

Overview: Fun, undulating road that descends through thick aspen groves and pine forest to upper Palmer Lake Reservoir. Good camping along route, but not allowed at bottom near the reservoir. Obey all posted regulations. Entrance to trail from Rampart Range Road is convenient to vehicles coming up Mt. Herman Road, Trail #91, from Monument. Balanced Rock Road is fun for ATVs, UTVs and dirt bikes, but it's a long way to drive for such a short trail. Also, the MVUM shows no legal side roads to explore. Open all year weather permitting. Unlicensed vehicles are not allowed on Rampart Range Road or Mt. Herman Road.

Rating: Moderate. Upper part is easy, but lower end is steeper with large ruts and undulations. Suitable for aggressive high-clearance SUVs with good articulation and/or lockers. Keep in mind it will be harder driving back up.

Stats: Length: Almost 8 miles one way. Time: 2-3 hours. High point: 9,300 ft. Best time of year: Mid June-October.

Current Conditions: Pike N.F., Pikes Peak R.D. Call (719) 636-1602.

Getting There: Follow directions for Mt. Herman Road, Trail #91. Turn right when you reach Rampart Range Road 300 at end of Mt. Herman Road. Head north (right) 1 mile to Balanced Rock Road 322 on right.

MILEAGE LOG:

0.0 Zero trip odometer [Rev. Miles]
Head east on F.S. 322 from Rampart Range Road 300. [7.6]
01 N39 04.000 W105 01.400

0.2 Campspot on left. [7.4]

0.6 Continue straight. Steep road downhill on right.[7.0]

0.7 Stay left, then left again just ahead. [6.9]

0.8 Curve to right. [6.8]

1.7 Campspot on left. [5.9]

2.1 Stay left. Closed F.S. 322A is on right. [5.5]
02 N39 04.483 W104 59.506

2.5 Continue straight. Balanced Rock on left. (Not to be confused with Balanced Rock in Garden of the Gods Park.) [5.1]

2.6 Stay right. [5.0]

3.2 Stay right downhill. [4.4]

4.5 Stay left downhill. Closed road on right. [3.1]
03 N39 04.971 W104 57.503

5.0 Stay right. Small road goes left uphill to camp spot with views. [2.6]

6.5 Stay right. [1.1]

7.0 Tight switchback. [0.6]

7.2 Moderate. Bigger ruts and undulations. [0.4]

7.6 Turnaround area. Road on left goes to west side of reservoir. Straight is gated road to east side of reservoir. [0.0]
04 N39 06.424 W104 56.475

Trail descends its entire length. Harder coming back up.

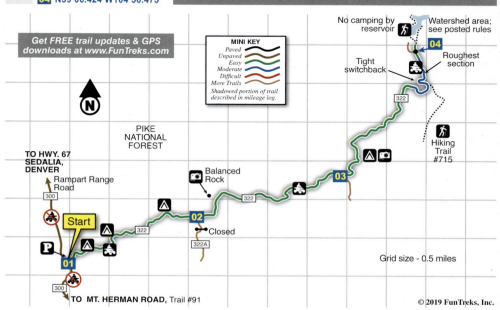

Short hike to the reservoir from end of road.

Get FREE trail updates & GPS downloads at www.FunTreks.com

MINI KEY
Paved
Unpaved
Easy
Moderate
Difficult
More Trails
Shadowed portion of trail described in mileage log.

No camping by reservoir

Watershed area; see posted rules

04

Tight switchback

Roughest section

322

N

PIKE NATIONAL FOREST

TO HWY. 67 SEDALIA, DENVER

Rampart Range Road
300

Balanced Rock

322

03

Hiking Trail #715

Start

322

02

Closed

322A

P

01

300

Grid size - 0.5 miles

TO MT. HERMAN ROAD, Trail #91

Unique rock outcrops along the route.

Mt. Herman Road as it climbs out of Monument.

Wide, easy drive most of the way.

Overview: We've combined Mt. Herman Road, an easy 4x4 drive, with the best part of Rampart Range Road. The southern end of Rampart Range Road is maintained and offers stunning views as it descends to famous Garden of the Gods Park. No unlicensed vehicles are allowed on the main route described here. Most of the side roads are short and are used mostly for camping, except for F.S. 315 and 318 off Mt. Herman Road. These two side roads are open to unlicensed ATVs, UTVs and dirt bikes, but don't take long to ride. For unlicensed vehicles, we recommend nearby Schubarth Loop, Trail #92. MVUM shows no seasonal closures.

Rating: Easy. You'll see cars on the upper parts of Rampart Range Road near Woodland Park and Rampart Reservoir. Fewer cars go all the way to Garden of the Gods Park because the road gets increasingly rougher as it descends. The condition of Mt. Herman Road varies depending on recency of maintenance. It is narrow and steep in places and ruts are possible at times.

Stats: Length: About 36 miles. Time: 4 to 5 hours. High point: 9,300 ft. Best time of year: Mid June-early October.

Current Conditions: Pike N.F., Pikes Peak R.D. Call (719) 636-1602.

Getting There: From I-25 in Monument, use exit 161. Head west on Hwy. 105 and continue west on 2nd St. through town. Cross R.R. tracks and turn left on Mitchell Ave. Head south 0.6 mile and turn right on Mt. Herman Road. Follow Mt. Herman Road west 2.4 miles to well-marked F.S. 320 on left.

MILEAGE LOG:

START

0.0 Zero trip odometer [Rev. Miles]
Head south on well-marked F.S. 320. [14.6]
01 N39 05.306 W104 54.666

2.6 Curve left past Mt. Herman hiking trail on right. [12.0]

5.4 Continue straight past 320A on right. First of several short side roads, mainly for camping. [9.2]

7.8 F.S. 318 on left is short side trip that allows unlicensed vehicles. [6.8]

8.3 F.S. 315 leads to small network of roads open to unlicensed vehicles. [6.3]

10.5 Turn left on Rampart Range Road 300. [4.1]
02 N39 03.357 W105 01.098

13.1 Stay left. Paved road on right goes to Woodland Park. [1.5]

14.6 Continue straight. Paved Loy Creek Road goes right to Woodland Park. Left goes to Schubarth Loop, Trail #92. [0.0]
03 N39 00.274 W105 00.937

0.0 Zero trip odometer
From Waypoint 03, continue south on Rampart Range Road 300. [21.5]

3.7 Continue straight. Paved road on left goes to Rampart Reservoir. [17.8]
04 N38 57.689 W104 59.731

9.0 Hiking trail goes to point pictured at right. [12.5]

9.4 Observation deck on right. See Pikes Peak and Waldo Canyon Fire. [12.1]

21.5 Trail ends at Garden of the Gods Park near Balanced Rock. Left goes to visitor center. [0.0]
05 N38 51.952 W104 53.787

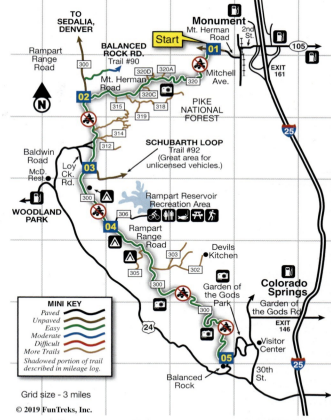

MINI KEY
Paved
Unpaved
Easy
Moderate
Difficult
More Trails
Shadowed portion of trail described in mileage log.

Grid size - 3 miles

© 2019 FunTreks, Inc.

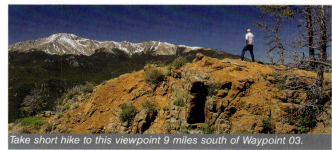

Take short hike to this viewpoint 9 miles south of Waypoint 03.

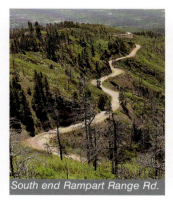

South end Rampart Range Rd.

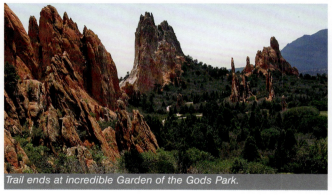

Trail ends at incredible Garden of the Gods Park.

F.S. 307 crosses private land and has great views of Pikes Peak.

Tippy spot on F.S. 311A. Not exaggerated.

View of Colorado Springs at end of F.S. 311A.

Overview: Popular area close to Woodland Park and an easy drive from Colorado Springs. Trail is loop with network of legal side roads to explore. Narrow, twisty and fun. Lunch at fantastic overlook above Air Force Academy. Great area for a weekend campout with lots of dispersed camping once inside forest boundary. First 2.5 miles crosses sensitive private land and USAF property. Pass through quietly and courteously to avoid conflicts with property owners. Staging for unlicensed vehicles available at forest boundary. MVUM shows no seasonal closures.

Rating: Moderate. Roads undulate with banked turns and narrow spots. Marked side roads are steep in places with occasional rocky challenges. Tippy spot on F.S. 311A gets your attention.

Stats: Length: 19 miles to do entire trail. Time: 4 to 5 hours. High point: 9,300 ft. Best time: Mid June-early Oct.

Current Conditions: Pike National Forest, Pikes Peak Ranger District. Call (719) 636-1602.

Getting There: Take Highway 24 to Woodland Park and turn north on Baldwin Street at traffic light by McDonald's. Continue north on Baldwin 3 miles and bear right on Loy Creek Road. Climb uphill 1.4 miles to Rampart Range Road at Wpt. 01 and continue straight on Schubarth Road.

MILEAGE LOG:

START

0.0 Zero trip odometer [Rev. Miles]
Head southeast on 307. Ignore private roads. [8.8]
01 N39 00.257 W105 00.947

0.3 Road narrows at bottom of hill. Follow signs for Schubarth Road. Avoid private side roads. [8.5]

1.7 Bear left uphill. Private road goes right. [7.1]

2.5 Forest boundary. Parking on left. [6.3]

2.9 Stay left on main road past large boulder. [5.9]

3.3 Bear right. Great camp spot with view on left. [5.5]
02 N39 00.095 W104 58.839

4.0 Bear right where 307A goes left. [4.8]

5.1 Turn left on 311. [3.7]
03 N39 00.402 W104 57.383

7.5 Continue straight where 311A goes right. [1.3]
04 N39 01.916 W104 56.347

8.8 Turn around here after visiting overlook on right. Left downhill is narrow, difficult trail. [0.0]
05 N39 02.529 W104 55.517
Return to Wpt. 04.

0.0 Zero trip odometer
From Wpt. 04 head southeast on F.S. 311A. [3.6]

0.7 Turn right on F.S. 313. [2.9]

1.5 Rock outcrop to right. [2.1]

2.5 Turn right on 307. [1.1]
06 N39 00.521 W104 56.435

3.6 Complete loop at Waypoint 03. Left goes out the way you entered. [0.0]

Huge rock outcrop on F.S. 313. Note person on ledge.

These folks are set up for camping at Wpt. 02. What a view!

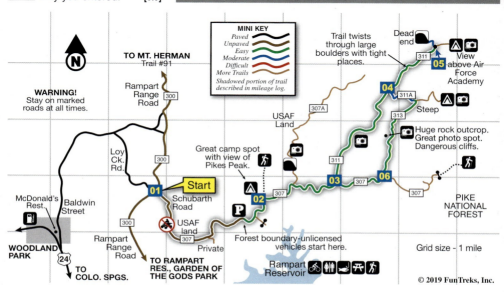

© 2019 FunTreks, Inc.

217

Mount Baldy

Great views of Colorado Springs below as you approach Waypoint 03.

SUVs come back down after visiting Mt. Baldy.

Water crossing before Frosty Park.

Overview: Trail ends at a large gate below Mt. Baldy and south of Almagre Mountain. You can hike to both peaks. On a clear day, enjoy views of south Colorado Springs below. Great camp spots along first half of trail where it passes through Frosty Park. After you reach the top, return the way you came or drive west on F.S. 379 through scenic Elk Park. Difficult Eagle Rock, Trail #94, connects to Mt. Baldy as it passes through Deer Park. No seasonal closures at time of this writing.

Rating: Easy. This road is used to service communication towers at the top of Mt. Baldy. It is usually maintained, but frequent rock slides along narrow ledge road 379A can make the road more difficult. If you run into a rock slide, you may have to back up a considerable distance to find a wide spot to turn around.

Stats: Length: 6.1 miles. Time: About an hour one way. High point: 11,800 ft. Best time of year: Mid July-Sept.

Current Conditions: Pike N.F., Pikes Peak R.D. Call (719) 636-1602.

Getting There: Take Nevada Avenue south from Colorado Springs and turn west on Lake Avenue towards the Broadmoor Hotel. Bear right before going into the hotel, then at the next roundabout, bear left and circle around the back of the hotel. When you reach Penrose Blvd., stay left and go south about a half mile. Turn right uphill on Old Stage Road through upscale residential area. Road soon changes to dirt as it winds steeply uphill. After 7 miles, it runs into Gold Camp Road. Continue another 5.6 miles to well-marked F.S. 379 on right.

MILEAGE LOG:

0.0 **Zero trip odometer** **[Rev. Miles]** Head north on F.S. 379. Private property on both sides of road. **[6.1]**
01 N38 44.439 W104 57.375

1.4 Stay left as you pass through Frosty Park ignoring roads to right. Good camping through this area. **[4.7]**

2.4 Road begins climbing switchbacks. **[3.7]**

3.7 Stay right. Road on left connects to Eagle Rock, Trail #94. **[2.4]**

4.5 Turn hard right, almost reversing direction, uphill on 379A. Road winds around front of mountain and begins climbing narrow shelf road. Watch for possible fallen rock along this stretch of road. **[1.6]**
02 N38 45.664 W104 58.981

6.1 Trail ends at gate with views of south Colorado Springs below. Lots of room to turn around. Hike to top of Mt. Baldy or north to Almagre Mountain. **[0.0]**
03 N38 46.607 W104 59.110

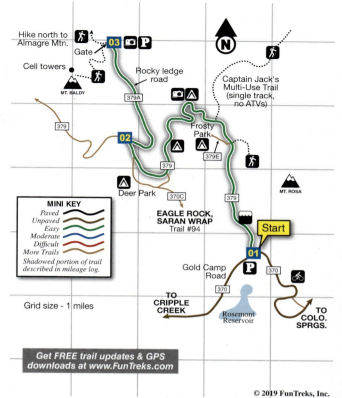

Hike north to Almagre Mtn.
Gate
Cell towers
MT. BALDY
Rocky ledge road
379A
Captain Jack's Multi-Use Trail (single track, no ATVs)
N
Frosty Park
379
379E
Deer Park
379
MT. ROSA
370C
EAGLE ROCK, SARAN WRAP Trail #94
379
Start
01
Gold Camp Road
370
370
TO CRIPPLE CREEK
Rosemont Reservoir
TO COLO. SPRGS.

MINI KEY
Paved
Unpaved
Easy
Moderate
Difficult
More Trails
Shadowed portion of trail described in mileage log.

Grid size - 1 miles

Get FREE trail updates & GPS downloads at www.FunTreks.com

© 2019 FunTreks, Inc.

Trail is open to all vehicles.

Rock slides are common on F.S. 379A and can increase difficulty.

Several large flat campsites along trail.

219

Tight spots—a spotter really helps on this trail.

UTVs will find this trail extra challenging.

Big ruts with constantly shifting loose boulders.

Overview: Eagle Rock is a very popular hard-core trail, and with heavy use has gotten more difficult in recent years. The challenges are changing every year. Extend the difficulty by first driving Saran Wrap, which connects to the lower part of Eagle Rock. Travel with other vehicles and plan for a long day, but if you need more to drive, add Mt. Baldy, Trail #93, or Bull Park, located at the end of the trail. No seasonal closures make this a challenging snow run.

Rating: Difficult. Very steep with huge ruts and large boulders that move around in loose soil. Extreme articulation needed. Without lockers or a winch, you'll quickly become a bottleneck for faster moving vehicles that are likely to be behind you.

Stats: Length: Eagle Rock is about 2.1

miles to F.S. 379. Add another 4 miles to exit west on 379. A faster way out is to head east on 379 via Mt. Baldy, Trail #93. The basic loop for Saran Wrap is about a mile, but you can add another 2 miles by going all the way to the end of 370DA. Time: 4 to 6 hours depending on number of vehicles. High point: 11,300 ft. Best time of year: July-September.

Current Conditions: Pike N.F., Pikes Peak R.D. Call (719) 636-1602.

Getting There: From the west side (back side) of the Broadmoor Hotel, head south to intersection with Penrose Blvd. and Old Stage Road. Follow Old Stage Road uphill (start mileage here) about 15 miles to F.S. 370C on right. To drive Saran Wrap first, continue another 0.3 mile to F.S. 370D on right.

MILEAGE LOG:

0.0 Zero trip odometer [Rev. Miles]
EAGLE ROCK:
Cross water and head uphill on marked 370C. (See below to enter via Saran Wrap.) [3.0]
01 N38 44.110 W104 59.274

0.3 Stay right through open area on 370C. Saran Wrap joins on left. [2.7]
02 N38 44.240 W104 59.116

0.8 First of many steep, rocky climbs. [2.2]

2.2 Stay left at meadow. Right is shortcut to Mt. Baldy, Trail #93, the quickest way back to Colorado Springs. [0.8]
03 N38 45.243 W104 58.457

2.5 Continue straight as you connect with 379 to head west. [0.5]

3.0 Continue straight. F.S. 379A on right goes to Mt. Baldy, Trail #93. [0.0]
04 N38 45.654 W104 58.977

0.0 Zero trip odometer
From Wpt. 04 head north on F.S. 379. [2.8]

0.5 Bear right where lesser road goes left uphill. Stay on the trail; do not drive through meadow. [2.3]

1.7 Climb rocky hill. [1.1]

2.8 After long steep descent, intersect with wider 376 and turn left downhill to return to start. Directly across road is water crossing, then fun, short side road Bull Park. [0.0]
05 N38 46.226 W105 01.099

0.0 Zero trip odometer
SARAN WRAP:
Continue on Gold Camp Road another 0.3 mile past Eagle Rock entrance. Turn right on 370D and head uphill. [0.6]
06 N38 44.177 W104 59.538

0.1 Bear right. [0.5]

0.6 Driver's choice. Right takes you on a wild ride to Waypoint 02 in another 0.4 mile. Left takes you up 370DA. This way starts with a difficult driver's choice obstacle, after which most people turn around, but the trail continues another mile before it fades at a steep hill in the trees. [0.0]
07 N38 44.404 W104 59.337

Group rests at end of optional Bull Park trail.

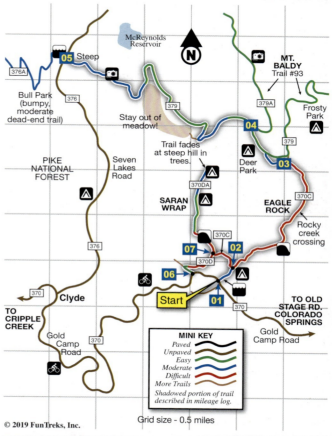

McReynolds Reservoir

N

Steep

MT. BALDY Trail #93

Bull Park (bumpy, moderate dead-end trail)

Stay out of meadow!

Frosty Park

Trail fades at steep hill in trees.

Deer Park

PIKE NATIONAL FOREST

Seven Lakes Road

SARAN WRAP

EAGLE ROCK

Rocky creek crossing

Clyde

Start

TO OLD STAGE RD. COLORADO SPRINGS

TO CRIPPLE CREEK

Gold Camp Road

Gold Camp Road

MINI KEY
Paved
Unpaved
Easy
Moderate
Difficult
More Trails
Shadowed portion of trail described in mileage log.

Grid size - 0.5 miles

© 2019 FunTreks, Inc.

Rocky creek crossing during a snowy winter run.
Photo by Mitch Rush

Curved steel bridge on Phantom Canyon Road.

Second tunnel on Phantom Canyon Road.

Historical Highlight: *Phantom Canyon follows an old train route that once connected Cripple Creek and Florence. At its peak in the late 1890s, the train transported over 230,000 passengers. The curved bridge you cross was originally a wooden railroad trestle, which was destroyed by fire in 1896. It was hastily rebuilt as a steel trestle and later converted to automotive use. The modern bridge pictured above was completely rebuilt in recent years. Kiosks along the route explain much of the history.*

Watch for Window Rock on Shelf Road.

Overview: We start this route just south of historic Cripple Creek, where you can gamble in Colorado-style casinos. Many historic mining attractions can be seen along the route and along paved Highways 67 and 81, which circle through Victor and Goldfield. The loop described here is part of a well-known BLM Gold Belt Tour and sees comparatively heavy traffic on summer weekends. A network of 4x4 roads departs from Shelf Road west of Sand Gulch Campground and south of The Banks Campground, a popular climbing area (see map). Unlicensed vehicles can ride on these side roads but not on the main loop. Red Canyon Park has picnic area in dramatic red rock formations.

Rating: Easy. Phantom Canyon is a car road but has a few narrow, high spots. Shelf Road is rougher, steeper and nar-rower but can be done in a high-clear-ance, two-wheel-drive SUV when road is dry. Check status before you go as roads sometimes close due to washouts.

Stats: Length: 60.3 miles as described. Time: About 4-5 hours. High point: 9,734 ft. Best time: Mid-May thru Oct.

Current Conditions: BLM Royal Gorge Field Office. Call (719) 269-8500.

Getting There: From Highway 24 in Divide, head south on Highway 67 to Cripple Creek. Pass through center of town on Bennett Avenue to bottom of the hill. Turn left on Second Street. Go 0.2 mile and turn right on C.R. 88. If you prefer to drive Phantom Canyon first, continue following Hwy. 67 (2nd St.) through Victor, then follow signs south to Phantom Canyon.

MILEAGE LOG:

0.0 Zero trip odometer **[Rev. Miles]**
SHELF ROAD:
Head south on dirt road marked C.R. 88. **[30.8]**
01 N38 44.563 W105 10.582

1.3 Mound City site with kiosk on left. **[29.5]**

5.1 Pass gated tunnel (look left), then watch for Window Rock. **[25.7]**

12.8 Road curves left and becomes paved. Right goes to The Banks Campground. **[18.0]**
02 N38 36.882 W105 13.498

12.9 Continue straight. Sand Gulch C.G., right, leads to 4x4 roads. **[17.9]**

15.6 Continue straight. F24 goes right into Red Canyon Park. **[15.2]**
03 N38 34.748 W105 14.127

19.2 Garden Park Fossil Area on right. **[11.6]**

19.4 Cleveland Quarry on left. Kiosks, toilet. **[11.4]**

19.6 OHV road on right goes to Dinosaur Flat Recreation Area, camping and shooting range. **[11.2]**

22.5 Bear left on Field Ave.**[8.3]**
04 N38 29.510 W105 12.540

24.8 Turn left on Pear St., then immediately jog right onto Raynolds Ave. **[6.0]**

25.6 Turn left on Hwy. 50. **[5.2]**
05 N38 26.900 W105 12.412

30.8 Turn left onto Hwy. 67 at major intersection. **[0.0]**
06 N38 26.243 W105 06.840

0.0 Zero trip odometer
PHANTOM CANYON:
Continue north from Waypoint 06 on Hwy. 67. **[29.5]**

4.9 Pavement ends. **[24.6]**

7.1 First tunnel. **[22.4]**

7.8 Picnic area with toilet on left. **[21.7]**

10.8 Second tunnel. **[18.7]**

13.5 Curved bridge. **[16.0]**

18.5 Rest area on left. **[11.0]**

28.7 Stay left as C.R. 861 joins on right. **[0.8]**

29.5 Arrive on east side of Victor. Parking area with mine display on right. **[0.0]**
07 N38 42.630 W105 07.990
Straight takes you through town of Victor on Hwy. 67 and returns to Cripple Creek in about 6 miles. Right on C.R. 81 goes to Goldfield and back to Colorado Springs.

TO DIVIDE & COLORADO SPRINGS
67

CONNECTS TO HWY. 67. SHORTEST WAY BACK TO COLORADO SPRINGS

Cripple Creek
01 Start
88
Molly Katheen Mine Tour
67
81
Goldfield
Mound City site
07 Victor
861
Window Rock
86

MINI KEY
Paved
Unpaved
Easy
Moderate
Difficult
More Trails
Shadowed portion of trail described in mileage log.

Shelf Road
Gold Belt Tour sign

The Banks Campground & Climbing Area
9
67
Phantom Canyon Road

4x4 Rd.
Sand Gulch CG
No unlicensed vehicles allowed on this road.
02
Curved steel bridge

Red Canyon Park
F24
03
Adelaide site

Garden Park Fossil Area
Tunnel
McCourt

Dinosaur Flat Rec.Area (OHV roads, shooting range)
Cleveland Quarry
Gold Belt Tour sign

9
Tunnel

Phelps Avenue
04
Field Avenue

Cañon City

Grid size - 2 miles

Raynolds Avenue

67
Phantom Canyon Road

TO SALIDA
50 **05**
BLM/FS Ranger Station
50
06
TO PUEBLO (32 miles)

© 2019 FunTreks, Inc.

N

Phantom Canyon Road narrows to one lane in several places.

Independence

96

AREA 7 map on page 196

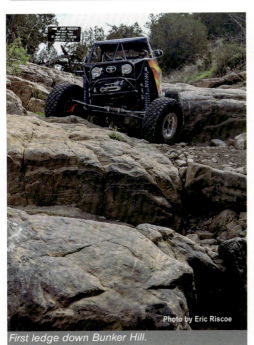

First ledge down Bunker Hill.

Exiting Patriot Trail usually requires a winch.

Historical Highlight: The name "Independence" came from the fact that construction of this trail system began on July 4th, a very hot time in this part of Colorado. With approval of the BLM, the canyons were made passable through the persistent efforts of Predator 4 Wheel Drive and the Rock Hoppers Four Wheel Drive Club, both of Colorado Springs. Work to clear the first trail, which opened in the spring of 1999, took about a year. Other trails followed in succession.

Overview: The Independence Trail System is composed of four extreme trails: Independence, Freedom, Patriot and Liberty. The trails wind through interconnected rocky canyons with winch points. Rock stacking is discouraged, but if required, rocks must be removed after use. Bring fuel-spill cleanup kit. Hot in summer. Watch for rattlesnakes. Camp at existing fire rings. Bring your own firewood. Pack out all trash. Violation of rules could result in closure of area.

Rating: Extremely difficult. Rock ledges and giant boulders 4 to 5 feet high. Expect roll-overs and vehicle damage. Lockers, roll cage and giant tires are a must. Scout trail first. Canyons are too difficult for ATVs and UTVs, but there are other trails to explore in the surrounding area.

Stats: Length: Total of all trails about 1.2 miles. Time: 1 to 4 hours or more. High point: 6,000 ft. Open all year except after periods of rain and snow, which occur infrequently in this semi-arid part of Colorado.

Current Conditions: BLM Royal Gorge Field Office. Call (719) 269-8500.

Getting There: Just north of Penrose, between mile markers 16 and 17 on Highway 115, turn west on 3rd Street following signs to Brush Hollow Reservoir. At 0.2 mile, turn right on E Street (C.R. 127). Continue north about 3 miles. Don't turn for boat ramp or anywhere else. After weaving through trees, cross cattle guard at BLM gate. Turn left 0.1 mile after gate and proceed to metal sign at parking area. Park and camp on Road 6100.

MILEAGE LOG:

0.0 **Zero trip odometer** **[Rev. Miles]**
Enter canyon at one of three points. Independence Trail heads west from parking area. **[0.9]**
01 **N38 29.630 W105 01.900**

0.2 To enter via Freedom Trail, head north from parking area and follow trail around to left, then turn south. You'll see the exit point of Patriot immediately on right. **[0.7]**
02 **N38 29.680 W105 02.010**

0.9 Easiest entrance is at north end of Liberty. Continue past Wpt. 02 and follow road north along edge of canyon. **[0.0]**
03 **N38 30.160 W105 02.030**

0.0 **Zero trip odometer**
ALTERNATE WAY TO REACH NORTH END OF LIBERTY TRAIL:
Go back to Road 6100 where you first turned into parking area. Follow good road north. **[1.0]**

0.4 Bear left at fork. **[0.6]**
0.8 Turn left. **[0.2]**
1.0 Entrance to Liberty is slightly to right. Once in canyon, head south. **[0.0]**

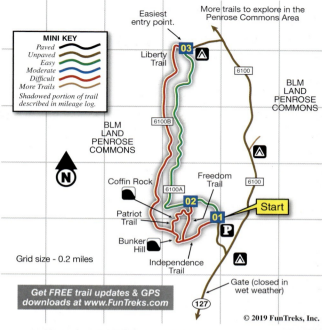

MINI KEY
Paved
Unpaved
Easy
Moderate
Difficult
More Trails
Shadowed portion of trail described in mileage log.

Easiest entry point.

More trails to explore in the Penrose Commons Area

Liberty Trail

BLM LAND PENROSE COMMONS

BLM LAND PENROSE COMMONS

Coffin Rock

Freedom Trail

Patriot Trail

Bunker Hill

Independence Trail

Start

Gate (closed in wet weather)

Grid size - 0.2 miles

Get FREE trail updates & GPS downloads at www.FunTreks.com

© 2019 FunTreks, Inc.

Trail closed when area is wet.

Coffin Rock, Patriot Trail.

Photo by Eric Riscoe

Having a good spotter is critical and a basic necessity.

Photo by Eric Riscoe

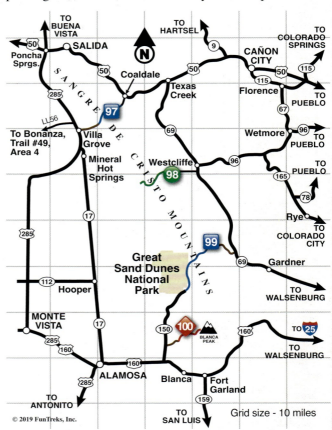

Sangre De Cristo Mountains, Great Sand Dunes N.P.

The jagged Sangre De Cristo Mountain Range forms an 80-mile-long barrier between the Front Range and the San Luis Valley. There are no major roads that cross this barrier and very few 4-wheel-drive roads. A popular weekend trip combines two trails. If you leave early, you can cross Medano Pass through Great Sand Dunes National Park in the morning and ascend Blanca Peak in the afternoon. That leaves the next day to get down Blanca Peak and return home. If you return via Medano Pass, you'll go through the national park again, so remember to save your receipt.

© 2019 FunTreks, Inc.

Grid size - 10 miles

From the top near Blue Lakes on Blanca Peak, Trail #100, rated difficult.

The steep, rutted road going up the north side follows the right side of a scenic valley.

The main burn area is near the top, and the drive through it is brief.

Historical Highlight: In the 1870s, long before Highway 50 was built, a very different road system existed in Colorado. At that time Villa Grove was a major mining supply center linked to a network of roads created by Otto Mears. (Trail #49 in this book is also known as the Otto Mears Toll Road.) Hayden Pass was the main route to Villa Grove from the east. In 1938, one alternative for construction of Highway 50 included going over Hayden Pass. This plan was killed because the road would bypass Salida. (Source: www.route50.com/history.htm, "A Brief History of America's Backbone," by Alvin Edlund Jr.)

Overview: A gorgeous drive on a clear day with enough challenge to make it fun. Forest Service fee campground at Waypoint 02 before you start the climb up the north face. Burn area is growing back quickly with new seasonal wildflowers. Small picnic area on left when you reach Villa Grove. We saw no operating gas station in town. A long drive back to Coaldale. We circled north through Poncha Springs and Salida rather that go back over the trail.

Rating: Moderate. Steep with ruts and embedded rock. Best done when trail is dry in the summer. In the fall, water pools on the road near the pass and can freeze at night, creating dangerous patches of ice on a narrow shelf road. High-clearance 4-wheel drive with low range recommended.

Stats: Length: 15.9 miles from Coaldale to Villa Grove. Time: About 2 hours one way. High point: 10,709 ft. Best time of year: Late June-early September.

Current Conditions: San Isabel N.F., Salida R.D. Call (719) 539-3591.

Getting There: Take Route 50 west from Pueblo or south from Salida. Turn south at Coaldale 0.7 mile west of mile marker 242.

MILEAGE LOG:

0.0 Zero trip odometer [Rev. Miles]
Head southwest from
Coaldale on C.R. 6. [15.9]
01 N38 22.060 W105 45.154

4.6 Rainbow Trail crosses.
(For ATVs, dirt bikes, mtn.
bikes & hiking.) [11.3]

5.0 At Hayden C.G., turn left
uphill on F.S. 6. Road is
steep and rutted in places
with embedded rock.[10.9]
02 N38 19.776 W105 49.399

6.6 Camp spots at ridgetop
with views on both sides
of the ridge. [9.3]

8.0 Enter the main part of the
burn area. It doesn't last
long. [7.9]

8.3 Road narrows across
shelf. In the fall, ice
patches may form on the
road. [7.6]

9.0 Hayden Pass. Enter Rio
Grande N.F., where road
becomes F.S. 970. Con-
tinue straight down other
side of pass. [6.9]
03 N38 17.582 W105 50.997

10.9 Exit trees at wide spot.
Road swings right and
continues downhill. Follow
main road. [5.0]
04 N38 16.748 W105 52.147

15.9 Arrive at Villa Grove on
Highway 285. Small picnic
area on left with primitive
public toilet. [0.0]
05 N38 14.944 W105 56.951
Return the way you came
or head north to Salida on
285. To reach south end
of Trail #49, take LL56
west from 285 starting
just north of Villa Grove.

ATVs come up the easier south side from Villa Grove.

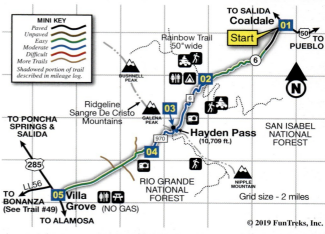

MINI KEY
Paved
Unpaved
Easy
Moderate
Difficult
More Trails
Shadowed portion of trail
described in mileage log.

TO SALIDA
Coaldale
Start
TO PUEBLO
Rainbow Trail
50" wide
01
50
6
02
6
BUSHNELL PEAK
Ridgeline
Sangre De Cristo
Mountains
GALENA PEAK
03
970
Hayden Pass
(10,709 ft.)
SAN ISABEL
NATIONAL
FOREST
TO PONCHA
SPRINGS &
SALIDA
04
285
LL 56
RIO GRANDE
NATIONAL
FOREST
NIPPLE
MOUNTAIN
Grid size - 2 miles
TO
BONANZA
(See Trail #49)
05 Villa
Grove
(NO GAS)
TO ALAMOSA

© 2019 FunTreks, Inc.

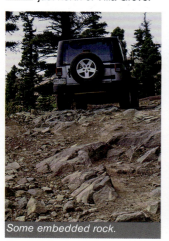
Some embedded rock.

Small picnic area on left at Highway 285 in Villa Grove.

Hermit Pass

West view from near the top on an overcast, stormy day. Horseshoe Lake lower right.

Trail is rocky and slow, but wide most of the way.

Historical Highlight: As you start up the trail, you'll see intermittent views of the old Conquistador Ski Area on the left. The area first opened in 1978 with minimal equipment. Two chairlifts were installed in 1982, but the area continued to struggle with poor snow conditions. After financial failure, the government took over, but the area finally shut down in 1988. A new owner opened the area for one disastrous season in 1992 under the name of Mountain Cliffe. The chairlifts were removed and sold in 1996.

Overview: Long climb with many switchbacks to extremely high pass. Lower portion is mainly in the trees, but once above timberline, views are outstanding. Great hiking trails and high fishing lakes. Accesses the 100-mile-long Rainbow Multiuse Trail System, which is very popular with ATVs and dirt bikes. Take short hike from Middle Taylor Creek Campground to photogenic waterfall. No seasonal closures.

Rating: Easy. Rocky and rough but no major obstacles. Road is one lane wide in some spots. Stock SUVs with low-range gearing and high ground clearance should be okay. Trail conditions could worsen over time.

Stats: Length: 9 miles one way. Time: About 2 hours to the top. High point: 13,000 ft. Best time of year: Mid July-September.

Current Conditions: San Isabel N.F., San Carlos R.D. Call (719) 269-8500.

Getting There: From the intersection of Hwys. 69 and 96 in Westcliffe, head south on 69 just 0.3 mile. Across from gas station, turn right on paved road following signs to Hermit Lake. Continue straight at 3.1 miles when paved road goes left. Go another 3.3 miles on dirt road to start of F.S. 160 on left. You can park here, along roadside, to unload unlicensed vehicles.

MILEAGE LOG:

0.0 Zero trip odometer **[Rev. Miles]**
Follow F.S. 160 southwest past old Conquistador Ski Area. **[9.0]**
01 N38 07.993 W105 34.498

2.0 Stay right past camp spots before passing Rainbow Multiuse Trail. **[7.0]**

2.7 Enter State Wildlife Area. Read and follow posted regulations. **[6.3]**

3.0 Stay right past Middle Taylor Creek Campground and Picnic Area. Waterfall shown below, right, is short hike from south end of campground. **[6.0]**
02 N38 06.327 W105 36.235

3.5 Stay right. **[5.5]**
5.1 Stay right. **[3.9]**
5.8 Road curves sharply right where Hermit Lake Hiking Trail goes left. **[3.2]**
03 N38 05.598 W105 37.905

7.3 Climb above timberline past Horseshoe Lake.**[1.7]**

9.0 Arrive at Hermit Pass. Road starts down other side but soon ends. Turn around and return the way you came. **[0.0]**
04 N38 05.667 W105 39.293

To see up close, Hermit Lake requires a hike.

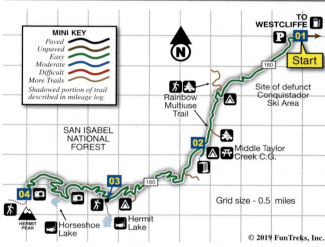

MINI KEY
Paved
Unpaved
Easy
Moderate
Difficult
More Trails
Shadowed portion of trail described in mileage log.

N

TO WESTCLIFFE
P
01
Start
160
Site of defunct Conquistador Ski Area

Rainbow Multiuse Trail

SAN ISABEL NATIONAL FOREST

02
Middle Taylor Creek C.G.

160
03

Grid size - 0.5 miles

04

HERMIT PEAK
Horseshoe Lake
Hermit Lake

© 2019 FunTreks, Inc.

Bumpy trip all the way up.

Slopes of old Conquistador Ski Area in distance.

Short hike to waterfall from Mid. Taylor Creek. C.G.

About a dozen water crossings. In the spring, some may get deeper than this.

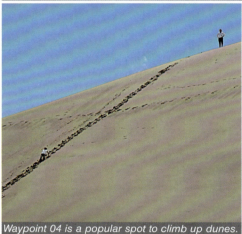

Waypoint 04 is a popular spot to climb up dunes.

Dirt bikers chat with Jeepers.

Historical Highlight: The Great Sand Dunes National Monument was designated a national park in 2004. Medano Pass, in its early history, was not used by wagons because of the challenging sand on the south side. Since then, it has continued to be ignored for development. To the delight of backcountry travelers, the route, with the exception of signs and gates, remains much the same today as it was a century ago. "Médano" means "dune" in Spanish. In English, there is no accent mark on the "e," but emphasis in pronunciation is still put on the first syllable.

Overview: This trail is the back entrance to Great Sand Dunes National Park. Camp in numbered designated sites only along route inside park or at Pinon Flats Campground. Picnic next to stream at base of giant sand dunes. Great fall color. Fee required entering or leaving park at main gate on south side. **Unlicensed vehicles are not allowed inside the national park**, but you can access the 100-mile-long Rainbow Multiuse Trail via F.S. 412. Latest MVUM shows this trail open to 50"-wide vehicles all the way to Hermit Pass, Trail #98, and beyond. No seasonal closures.

Rating: Moderate. Mostly easy with a few steep, rocky spots. Soft sand inside the park may require airing down tires. Narrow in spots. Numerous water crossings can be deep in the spring during peak flow.

Stats: Length: 20 miles. Time: 2 to 3 hours. High point: 9,950 ft. Best time of year: June-October.

Current Conditions: Call Great Sand Dunes National Park Visitor Center at (719) 378-6395. North side: San Isabel N.F., San Carlos R.D at (719) 269-8500.

Getting There: From Westcliffe, take Highway 69 west 23.7 miles. Turn left on well-marked County Road 559. You can also drive trail in reverse direction starting in the park.

MILEAGE LOG:

START

0.0 Zero trip odometer [Rev. Miles]
Head west on C.R. 559, muddy at times. **[20.0]**
01 N37 50.191 W105 18.457

0.9 Bear left. **[19.1]**

6.9 Enter San Isabel National Forest. **[13.1]**
02 N37 51.646 W105 24.141

7.4 Continue straight as roads go to camp spots. F.S. 412 to right connects to 100-mile-long Rainbow Multiuse Trail open to less than 50"-wide vehicles. **[12.6]**

9.3 Arrive at Medano Pass. Continue straight down other side. (Call in advance to make sure gate is open.) No unlicensed vehicles beyond this point. **[10.7]**
03 N37 51.356 W105 25.935

9.9 Stay left. Right is hiking trail to Medano Lake. **[10.1]**

10.8 First of many creek crossings. **[9.2]**

17.8 Fun picnic area next to stream and dunes. Soft sandy road continues. Air down tires to avoid getting stuck. **[2.2]**
04 N37 46.299 W105 30.433

18.5 Parking on left. **[1.5]**

20.0 Continue straight to paved road to visitor center and park exit. **[0.0]**
05 N37 44.658 W105 30.431

Get FREE trail updates & GPS downloads at www.FunTreks.com

Keep momentum to avoid getting stuck in sand.

F.S. 412 connects to 100-mile-long Rainbow Multiuse Trail

Ridgeline Sangre De Cristo Mountains

TO WESTCLIFFE

Enter N.F.

RIO GRANDE NATIONAL FOREST

MOUNT HERARD

Medano Pass (9,950 ft.)

Start

TO WALSENBURG

SAN ISABEL NATIONAL FOREST

Sandy 4x4 road

Great Sand Dunes National Park

Visitor Center

Pinon Flats Campground

Mosca Pass (9,713 ft.)

Entrance (Pay fee.)

TO BLANCA PEAK (Trail #100)

Grid size - 2 miles

MINI KEY
Paved
Unpaved
Easy
Moderate
Difficult
More Trails
Shadowed portion of trail described in mileage log.

© 2019 FunTreks, Inc.

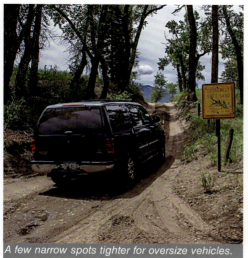

A few narrow spots tighter for oversize vehicles.

Starting descent into park from Medano Pass.

233

Blanca Peak

Talus shelf road overlooks valley. Stop and let hikers pass.

Beautiful Lake Como at 11,000 ft.

Muddy section before Jaws 4 is challenging with wet tires.

Trail is best done with small group.

Overview: Also known as Lake Como Road, this is one of the best hard-core trails in Colorado. A mix of dangerous obstacles and incredible beauty. Popular weekend outing includes an overnight campout at invigorating Lake Como. Take a fishing pole. At 14,335 feet, Blanca Peak is the highest mountain in the Sangre De Cristo Range and the 7th highest in the contiguous United States. A very popular "fourteener" hiking trail. Be courteous to hikers. Insanely difficult for short wheel-based unlicensed vehicles. Seasonally open 5/16 to 3/14.

Rating: Difficult. Four named obstacles; only one has a bypass. Jaws 2 is the most dangerous with a history of rollovers down a steep embankment. Many drivers stop at Lake Como to avoid Jaws 4. Minimum 33" tires and at least one locker. Breakdowns and use of winch are common. Passing is very difficult much of the way. Expect backups and long waits on busy summer weekends.

Stats: Length: 5 miles one way. Time: 4 to 6 hours. High point: 12,200 ft. Best time of year: Mid July-September.

Current Conditions: Rio Grande N.F., Conejos Peak R.D. (East). Call (719) 274-8971.

Getting There: Take Interstate 25 to Walsenburg and Hwy. 160 west. Just after small town of Blanca, turn north on Hwy. 150 and go 3.2 miles to County Road 975 on right. Head west on bumpy flat road past several open areas to camp, park and unload. Tight switchback and sign at 3.5 miles marks start of trail. Alternate way to reach trail is via Medano Pass, Trail #99.

START MILEAGE LOG:

0.0 Zero trip odometer [Rev. Miles]
Road climbs steeply up tight switchbacks. Engine overheating common. [5.0]
`01` N37 33.088 W105 33.398

1.8 Mud holes with possible deep standing water. [3.2]

2.3 Jaws 1. Avoid left. [2.7]
`02` N37 34.104 W105 32.393

2.8 Jaws 2. Keep tires against rock wall on right. Rollovers occur when vehicles slide on loose rock to left. Use winch if necessary. [2.2]
`03` N37 34.195 W105 31.873

3.1 Some call this spot Jaws 2½. [1.9]

3.2 Driver's choice. Right bypasses V-notch at Jaws 3. [1.8]
`04` N37 34.179 W105 31.560

4.0 Road forks after talus ledge. Camping to right at Lake Como. Trail continues to left. [1.0]
`05` N37 34.197 W105 30.943

4.3 Cross muddy section and climb into trees to go up Jaws 4. [0.7]
`06` N37 34.106 W105 30.723

5.0 Trail ends at Blue Lakes. Turn around. Hardy souls can hike to peak from here. Watch for bighorn sheep. [0.0]
`07` N37 34.317 W105 30.143

Get FREE trail updates & GPS downloads at www.FunTreks.com

Jaws 2 is more dangerous than it first appears. Be very careful.

Fish at the largest of the Blue Lake at 12,200 ft.

Upper part of trail winds through rocks and alpine tundra.

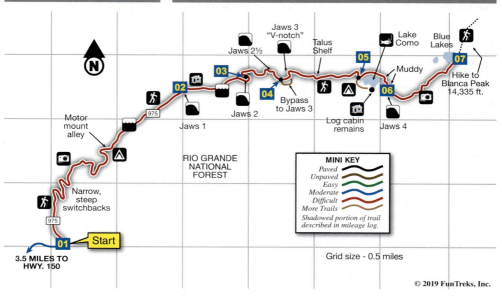

Jaws 3 "V-notch"

Jaws 2½

Talus Shelf

Lake Como

Blue Lakes

Jaws 2½

`03`

`05`

`07`

`02`

975

`04`

Bypass to Japs 3

Muddy

`06`

Hike to Blanca Peak 14,335 ft.

Motor mount alley

Jaws 1

Jaws 2

Log cabin remains

Jaws 4

RIO GRANDE NATIONAL FOREST

MINI KEY
Paved
Unpaved
Easy
Moderate
Difficult
More Trails
Shadowed portion of trail described in mileage log.

Narrow, steep switchbacks

975

`01` **Start**

3.5 MILES TO HWY. 150

Grid size - 0.5 miles

© 2019 FunTreks, Inc.

Charles (Chuck) Wells bought his first 4-wheel-drive SUV in 1993, and he had no idea how it would change his life. Like most SUV owners in Colorado, he bought the vehicle primarily for winter driving. But one summer day, he saw an intriguing dirt road that headed into the mountains. Off he went on his first real trip beyond the pavement. It was so much fun, he searched for other roads to duplicate the experience. Many more trips followed.

As his confidence grew, he ventured farther and farther into the backcountry. He realized he needed some guidance, so he bought every guidebook and map he could find. Unfortunately, most of the information was vague, incomplete or inaccurate. He continued to get lost, run into places too difficult for his vehicle and waste time on boring roads. This frustration led him to write his first book, *Guide to Colorado Backroads & 4-Wheel Drive Trails*, in 1998. Sales took off immediately. Within a year, he quit his job and started FunTreks Publishing.

Many years later, Wells has 10 books in print (many in second, third and now fourth editions). His books include easy and moderate routes for stock SUVs, difficult trails for serious 4-wheelers and trails for unlicensed vehicles (ATVs, UTVs and dirt bikes). Today his books are standard equipment for thousands of motorized adventurers. He strongly promotes responsible use of public lands.

In his 70s, Wells has slowed down a bit, but still continues to direct his company, scout trails and work on new books.

Wells graduated from Ohio State University in 1969 with a degree in graphic design. After practicing design in Ohio, he moved to Colorado Springs in 1980 and worked 18 years in the printing business. He and his wife, Beverly, have two adult children and four grandchildren. They live in Monument, Colorado, close to their business.

Matt (PT) Peterson got into 4-wheeling in 2000 after graduating from college. He built several off-road 4x4s starting with bolt parts, and later progressed to custom-built off-road buggies. Wanting to share his new pastime, he and a few friends started their own 4-wheel-drive club in Michigan, and the club is still going strong today. He has always had an interest in exploring less-traveled roads, which is why he picked up and moved to Colorado in 2003.

He worked as a graphic designer after college, chose a new path for his career and joined FunTreks in 2008. Today he manages the tech side of the company, scouts trails and works on new books.

Peterson graduated from Bethel College in 2000 with a degree in graphic design. He met his wife, Cassie, soon after moving to Colorado. Together, they enjoy exploring and sharing with others Colorado's enormous backyard.